Acknowledgements

Photoshop Studio Skills
A Design Graphics publication

Concept and Art Direction
Colin Wood

Project Editor
Colleen Bate

Contributors
Ben Wilmore
Bill Flemng
Brian P, Lawler
Carl Stevens
Colin Wood
Daniel Brown
Daniel Wade
Julieanne Kost
Katrin Eismann
Michael Ninness
Rita Amladi
Russell Preston Brown

Proofreading
Daniel Wade

Designers
Shannon Nation
Stuart Colafella

Pre-production
Stuart Colafella

Cover design
Colin Wood
Lauren Stevens

DESIGNGRAPHICS

PHOTOSHOP®
Studio Skills

Photoshop Studio Skills

A Design Graphics publication

Conceived and produced by DG Books Pty Ltd
2 Sherbrooke Road
Sherbrooke VIC 3789
Australia

DG Books is a member of the Xandia group of companies.

From the Xandia Group, Design Graphics publishes:
Design Graphics magazine (monthly)
Art & Design Education Resource Guide (annual)
Oz Graphix (annual)

Photoshop Studio Skills

A Design Graphics publication

Published by
Wiley Publishing, Inc.
909 Third Avenue
New York, NY 10022
www.wiley.com

ISBN: 0-7645-4176-5
Manufactured in the United States of America
10 9 8 7 6 5 4 3 2 1
1K/RX/RS/QT/IN
Published by Wiley Publishing, Inc., Indianapolis, Indiana
Published simultaneously in Canada

For general information on our other products and services or to obtain technical support, please contact our Customer Care Department
within the U.S. at 800-762-2974, outside the U.S. at 317-572-3993 or fax 317-572-4002.
Wiley also publishes its books in a variety of electronic formats. Some content that appears in print may not be available in electronic books.
Library of Congress Cataloging-in-Publication Data

Library of Congress Cataloging-in-Publication data is available from the publisher.

DESIGNGRAPHICS

PHOTOSHOP®
Studio Skills

Contents

Chapter 1
Palettes and Tools

Contents

Chapter 2
Paths, Selections, Channels and Masks

Chapter 3
Layers

 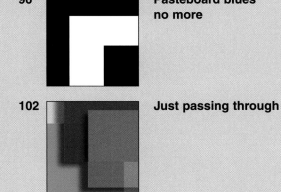

Chapter 4
Colour Effects and Correction

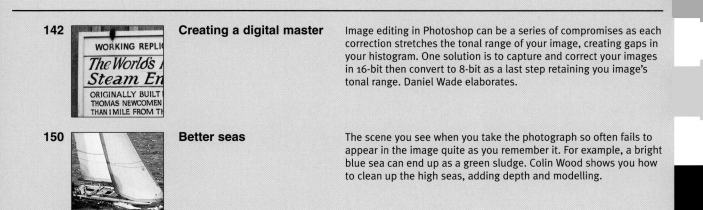

Contents

Chapter 5
Light and shadow effects

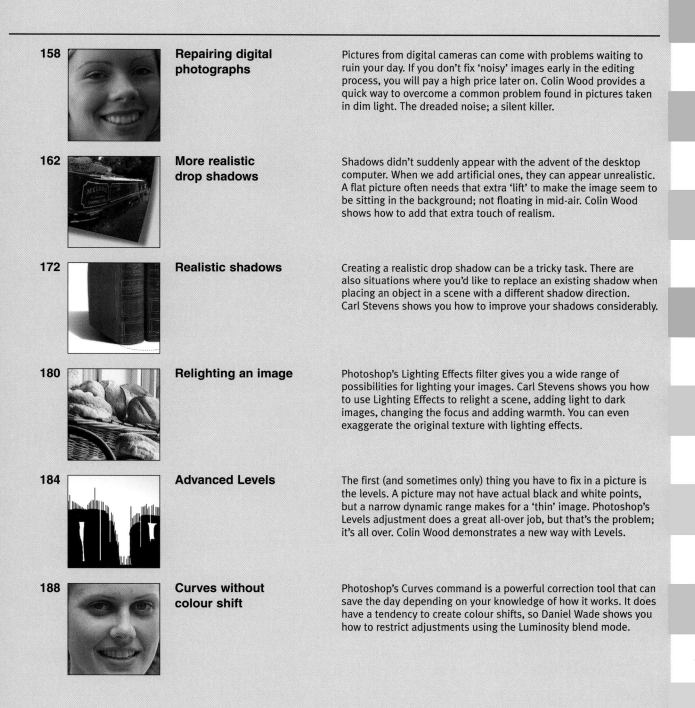

Chapter 6
Palettes & Tools

Chapter 7
Special F/X

Contributors

Contributors

Rita Amladi

Rita Amladi is owner of Orion Arts & Communications, a digital imaging training and consulting company in San Francisco. She has a BFA in Graphic Design and is a Certified Technical Trainer (CTT) and an Adobe Certified Trainer for Adobe Photoshop (ACE). A staff member at Adobe Systems for six years, Rita is now author of training CDs, published by Virtual Training Company, Inc. (www.vtc.com) – her latest offering is "ICC Color Management in Photoshop 7".

Daniel Brown

Daniel joined Adobe systems in 1998. Taking on the role of "Evangelist" and lending a hand in product development, marketing, interface design, and customer education. He currently focuses on Adobe's Digital Video Products, and is a frequent speaker at industry events world-wide. (For more information, visit http://www.adobeevangelists.com.)

Russell Preston Brown

A graduate of the University of Washington with a BFA in graphic design and an M.A. from the Art Center College of Pasadena, California, Russell (www.russellbrown.com) has been a creative force at Adobe Systems Incorporated for the last 15 years – he is currently Senior Creative Director there. The prolific creator of Photoshop, Illustrator, and GoLive tips and tricks, Russell has mesmerised audiences at conferences and seminars worldwide.

Contributors

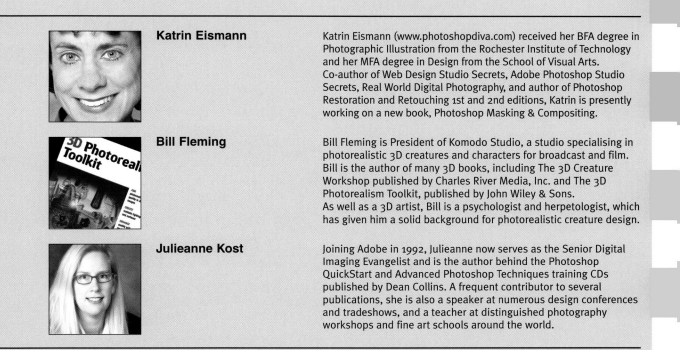

Katrin Eismann

Katrin Eismann (www.photoshopdiva.com) received her BFA degree in Photographic Illustration from the Rochester Institute of Technology and her MFA degree in Design from the School of Visual Arts. Co-author of Web Design Studio Secrets, Adobe Photoshop Studio Secrets, Real World Digital Photography, and author of Photoshop Restoration and Retouching 1st and 2nd editions, Katrin is presently working on a new book, Photoshop Masking & Compositing.

Bill Fleming

Bill Fleming is President of Komodo Studio, a studio specialising in photorealistic 3D creatures and characters for broadcast and film. Bill is the author of many 3D books, including The 3D Creature Workshop published by Charles River Media, Inc. and The 3D Photorealism Toolkit, published by John Wiley & Sons. As well as a 3D artist, Bill is a psychologist and herpetologist, which has given him a solid background for photorealistic creature design.

Julieanne Kost

Joining Adobe in 1992, Julieanne now serves as the Senior Digital Imaging Evangelist and is the author behind the Photoshop QuickStart and Advanced Photoshop Techniques training CDs published by Dean Collins. A frequent contributor to several publications, she is also a speaker at numerous design conferences and tradeshows, and a teacher at distinguished photography workshops and fine art schools around the world.

Contributors

Contributors

Brian P Lawler

Brian Lawler is a graphic arts and prepress consultant and author. A contributor to Pre, MacUSER, MacWEEK and other publications, he is based in San Luis Obispo, California.
More information on his books, articles and expertise can be found at www.thelawlers.com.

Michael Ninness

Studying for a BFA in Graphic Design at the University of Washington unleashed a passion in Michael for design and teaching. He combines these interests by creating software for design professionals and detailing his experience. Lead Product Manager in the Advanced Technology group at Microsoft, he is also the Conference chair for the Professional Photoshop Conference at Macworld and author of Photoshop Power Shortcuts.

Carl Stevens

Born in Farsley, Yorkshire, Carl Stevens started his career as an apprentice retoucher in 1972. The graphics industry gave him access to live in various cities in Australia, New Zealand and South Africa. He and his wife have settled in Sydney, Australia which he quotes is 'the best place in the world to live'.
He believes that graphics 'continually stretches, challenges and gives our imagination a good workout!'

Contributors

Daniel Wade

Daniel Wade was the Editor of Design Graphics magazine for nine years, and during that time focused on digital technology as it relates to graphic design. His term as editor exposed him to many of the industry's heros and he has written several tips in the Studio Skills series.

Ben Willmore

Ben Willmore is Founder of Digital Mastery (www.digitalmastery.com.), a training and consulting firm based in Colorado. He has personally trained over 20,000 Photoshop users and is a featured speaker at worldwide events. Author of the best-selling book, Official Adobe Photoshop Studio Techniques (5.0, 6.0 and 7.0 versions), Ben is also certified as an Adobe Certified Expert, a recognised worldwide standard for excellence in Adobe software.

Colin Wood

Colin Wood is Founder and Publisher of Design Graphics. His original training was in industrial design – this provided the perfect grounding to combine design, technology and communication in publishing. Publisher of various international design publications over two decades, Colin developed the Studio Skills concept and style. He continues to take up the challenge of writing tips and techniques that are easily understood at all levels, yet useful to power users too.

1
Palettes & Tools

01 - Palettes & Tools

Difficulty: Easy	**Daniel Wade**

Painting straight lines

Photoshop's controls over straight lines and angles are not as obvious as they may initially seem to be. In this article we show you how to make better layer masks and channels using some of Photoshop's built-in features.

Brush Tool B
Pencil Tool B

Painting straight lines
Question: If your hand is not steady enough (whose is?) to paint a perfectly straight line with either a cursor or a stylus , how do you do it in Photoshop?
Answer: with a little help from the Shift key.

Where to use the technique?
This technique is particularly useful when painting on layer masks and tidying up channels to mask objects that have straight edges.

The technique
1. Using any of the painting tools, click once anywhere to start painting and then release the mouse or stylus. At this stage it is not necessary to hold down the Shift key.

2. Your image will look like this; a simple dot.

3. Here is our simple dot as the starting point of a sequence.

4. Now hold down the Shift key and click anywhere else. The two points will be joined by the brush tool. You do not have to hold down the Shift key between clicks.

5. When you are ready, hold down the Shift key and click again at a new point. All you have to remember is not to click without the Shift key held down as this discontinues the sequence.

The steps ...

1. Here is the original image showing a section the sky we wish to isolate from the edges of the buildings. We'll use Photoshop's Quick Mask and the straight line technique to build our mask.

2. Using the Brush tool at a Hardness of 85%, we paint around the edges of the building using Shift-clicking to follow the edges. The 85% Hardness avoids the problem of the edges looking too sharp against the sky.

3. When the Quick Mask is complete, we are left with a selection that we can use to adjust the sky with a Hue/Saturation adjustment layer.

Quick Mask
Quick Mask mode lets you add or subtract areas of your mask by painting with black or white respectively. To create an edge around the buildings, we paint with a black brush.

Making a mask
The sky behind the buildings is a bit dull. To liven up just the sky, we'll need to mask out the buildings. The easy way to do this is to use Quick Mask mode. Select Quick Mask from the Tool box, then select the Brush tool. In the Brushes palette, set the Hardness to 85%, then use the Shift-click technique to follow the edges of the building. Paint manually around difficult edges.

Fill it in
When you've completed the outline of the buildings, select a larger brush, and paint in the rest of the buildings
Be careful to avoid leaving gaps between your original outline. When the buildings are completely painted, you're ready to turn them into a selection.

Standard mode
Clicking the Standard mode button turns the area outside your Quick Mask into a selection. In this case, the sky is completely selected.

Sky selection
With our selection of the sky we have several options.
We can save the selection (Select > Save Selection) which will create a channel for later use, or we can create an adjustment layer which will create a mask using our selection.

Hue/Saturation
Add a Hue/Saturation adjustment layer by selecting it from the bottom of the Layers palette.

Masks for free
A layer mask is automatically added to the Hue/Saturation adjustment. To make the sky a little more lively, we push the Saturation to 50 and shift the Hue further into the blues. Double-click on the adjustment layer to change the effect.

	Difficulty: Easy	Design Graphics
Freeform and straight lines	The Lasso tool has been familiar to us since Photoshop's inception. Its sibling, the Polygon Lasso, was introduced in Photoshop 4 and, in Photoshop 5, another family member, the Magnetic Lasso Tool, joined the clan. Here we show how to combine freeform and straight line selections.	

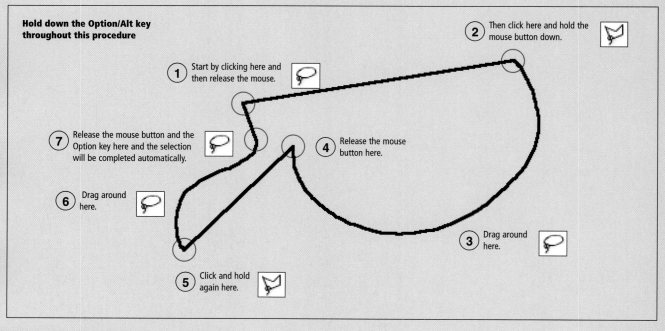

Hold down the Option/Alt key throughout this procedure

2 Then click here and hold the mouse button down.

1 Start by clicking here and then release the mouse.

7 Release the mouse button and the Option key here and the selection will be completed automatically.

4 Release the mouse button here.

6 Drag around here.

3 Drag around here.

5 Click and hold again here.

Path described by the Lasso tool

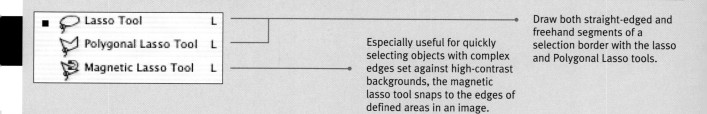

■ Lasso Tool	L	
Polygonal Lasso Tool	L	
Magnetic Lasso Tool	L	

Especially useful for quickly selecting objects with complex edges set against high-contrast backgrounds, the magnetic lasso tool snaps to the edges of defined areas in an image.

Draw both straight-edged and freehand segments of a selection border with the lasso and Polygonal Lasso tools.

Freeform to straight lines
While the Lasso is essentially a freeform tool, it can also be constrained to straight lines.

This is how it's done:
With the Lasso Tool selected, hold and keep down the Option/Alt key while clicking around your image to produce a series of straight lines.

Note: You will notice that the Lasso tool icon changes to the Polygonal Lasso tool icon when the Option/Alt key is selected. It will revert to the Lasso tool icon when you drag around a shape (as in 3). To draw freeform as part of the complete selection: Using the Lasso tool, click and hold the mouse button down and drag.

Tip 1:
If you want a quick straight line on an angle, draw a curved line (an arc is good) between two points. Release the mouse and the Lasso selection will return to the starting point directly.

Tip 2:
You can release the mouse for the selection to be completed with a straight line back to the starting point.

Tip 3:
Individual Lasso tools can be accessed by pressing 'Shift L' on your keyboard.

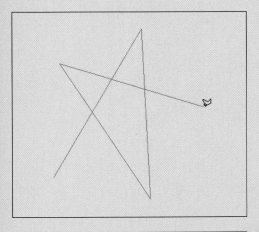

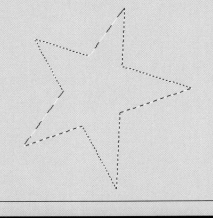

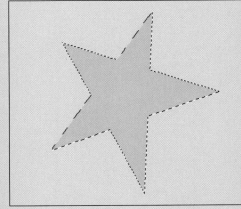

Tip: You can add to an existing lasso or marquee selection by holding down the Shift key, and subtract from the selection by holding down the Option/Alt key.

Straight lines to freeform

Another way to make straight line selections is to use the Polygonal Lasso tool.

Here we have used the Polygonal Lasso to draw a five-cornered star. Simply place the cursor where you want to begin and click once to anchor the lasso.

You can now proceed to click once at the position of each of the star points, and then back to the starting point to close the lasso (the cursor will change to a closed loop to indicate that you are over the starting point).

Just as you combine straight line drawing with the Lasso tool, you can combine freehand drawing with the Polygonal Lasso by holding down the Option key as you drag the mouse.
Note: You will notice that the Polygonal Lasso tool icon changes to the Lasso tool icon when the Option/Alt key is selected. It will revert to the Polygonal Lasso tool icon when the Option/Alt key is released.

Automation with Actions

Difficulty: Intermediate

Michael Ninness

Ever needed to quickly find the centre of an image and/or create horizontal and vertical guides that marked the centre of an image? Here's how to construct an Action in Adobe Photoshop that will instantly create the guides for you and align them in one easy step.

Ready for Actions
Create a new document. Turn on the Rulers if they are not already on (Command/Ctrl-R) and open the Info palette (Window > Info or F8.)

Get set ... go!
Bring up the Actions palette (Window > Actions) and select the New Action button to bring up the New Action dialogue. Give the Action a name like 'Find Centre' and assign a function key to it if you wish. When you click Record, the action will start recording.

Stop playing/recording

Create new action

Measuring up
Choose Edit>Preferences>Units & Rulers (or Command/Ctrl-K) to open General Preferences, then select Units & Rulers from the pop-up menu). Choose Percent from the Units pop-up.

Find your centre
Drag a vertical guide out from the vertical ruler and let go when the Info palette reads 50% for the X value. Drag a horizontal guide out from the horizontal ruler and let go when the Info palette reads 50% for the Y value.Change the measurement system for the Units & Rulers preference back to your previous setting. That's it—click the Stop Recording button to stop recording the action.

Align both ways

One of the greatest things about Photoshop Actions is that they can be used to create shortcuts for commands that don't already have keyboard equivalents for them. For instance, I find that when I want to align objects on linked layers, I may not necessarily want to align them both vertically and horizontally at the same time. Currently, the only way to do this in Photoshop is to use the mouse and the pull down guides twice, once for vertically and then again for horizontally. It is much better to just press F15 (or whatever shortcut you assign to it) and have the alignment just happen automatically.

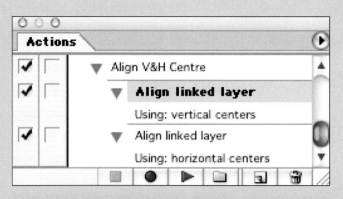

Record the action

Here are the steps to record the action.
• Select the layer that you want to align the other layers to. (In this case, layer 0.)
• Link the other layers you want aligned to the selected layer using the link icon in the Layers palette.
• Click the New Action button to start recording the action.
• Choose Layer > Align Linked > Vertical Centre, then choose Layer > Align Linked > Horizontal Centre.
• That's it—click the Stop Recording button to stop recording the action.

Using the action

When you want to use the action, ensure you select the layer that you want to align the other layers to, and then link the other layers you want aligned to the selected layer before playing the action.
If not, a warning dialog box will appear informing you that the 'Align' command is not currently available.

Difficulty: Easy	Julieanne Kost

Painterly effects with the Art History Brush

Photoshop's Art History Brush lets you paint with stylised strokes using source data from a History State or Snapshot. By experimenting with different options, you can simulate the textures of painting with different artistic styles. Julieanne Kost shows how to achieve these painterly effects.

Open the file
Images with bold, easy to recognise subjects typically work the best.

Note: There are many different ways to use the Art History brush. The easiest way is to paint directly on a layer. However, painting on a copy of the source layer or a new layer gives the added flexibility of blending the stylised image with the original.

Create a new Snapshot
Open the History palette (Window > History) and select the New Snapshot button. In the New Snapshot dialogue box, name the snapshot Merged and choose Merged Layers from the pop-up menu. Click OK.

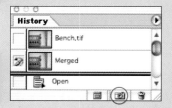

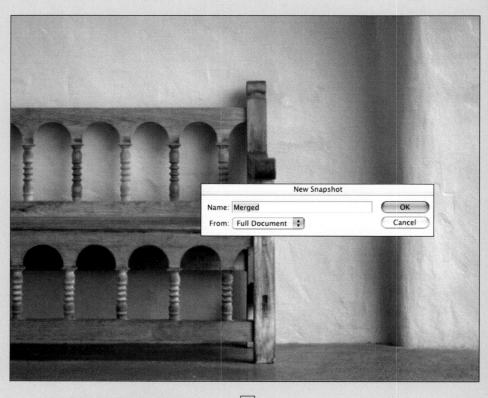

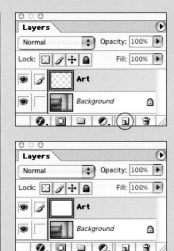

New layer
From the Layers palette, select the New Layer button. In the New Layer dialogue box, name the layer Art. Click OK.

Fill the layer
Select Edit > Fill. Use white as the foreground colour with 100% Opacity and Normal Mode. Click OK.

History Brush Tool   Y
Art History Brush   Y

Selecting the Art History Brush in the Tools palette brings up the **Art History Brush Options** in the Options Bar.

Set the options for painting
From the Tools palette, click and hold on the History Brush to select the Art History Brush. In the History palette, set the Art History Brush to sample from the merged snapshot by clicking in the well to the left of the snapshot thumbnail.

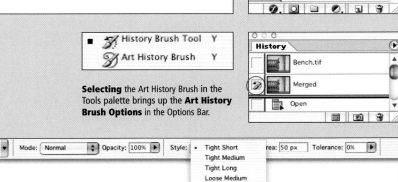

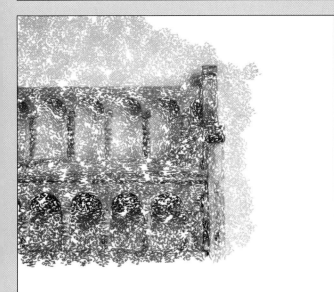

Select a style
Select a paint style for the Art History Brush tool in the Options Bar. The paint styles including 'Tight' and 'Loose' refer to how closely the paint strokes will follow the contours of the original image.

Begin painting
From the Brushes palette, choose a small brush and begin painting in the image area. The Art History brush samples from the data in the snapshot and applies the painterly style to it. To get a feel for how the tool works, start by using a small number for the Area setting as well as a small brush size.

Note: The resolution of an image determines the size of the brush and the area setting you will use.

Art History Brush options
Once you're familiar with how the basic settings work, try adjusting the following options for the Art History Brush tool in the Options Bar.

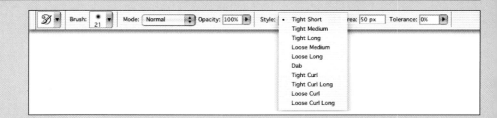

Paint with colours
To paint with colours that deviate from the snapshot, select Colour Dynamics from the Brushes palette and adjust the Hue Jitter, Saturation Jitter or Brightness Jitter. This allows Photoshop to introduce colours that were not in the original image, adding a variety of colour.

Note: To paint with colours in **Photoshop 6,** you can use the Fidelity slider in the Options Bar. 0% Fidelity will introduce colours into the image while 100% will not introduce colours.

Limit the regions
To limit the regions where Photoshop applies paint, adjust the Tolerance slider. A low tolerance lets you paint unlimited strokes anywhere in the image. A high tolerance limits paint strokes to areas that differ considerably from the colour in the source state or snapshot.

(left) **Settings**
Brush: Dab; Opacity 100%;
Tolerance 0%

(right) **Settings**
Brush: Dab; Opacity 100%;
Tolerance 100%

Lessen the opacity
To lessen the opacity of the Art History Brush, lower the opacity of the tool.
To fade a single stroke made with the Art History Brush, select Filter > Fade Art History Brush.
Note: the more you paint, the more detailed the image appears.

(left) **Settings**
Brush: Dab; Opacity 100%;
Tolerance 0%

(right) **Settings**
Brush: Tight Short; Opacity 30%;
Tolerance 0%

Variation one
Not all areas have to be painted with the Art History Brush. Leaving some areas of the canvas blank can create an antique or weathered look.

Variation two
The entire image doesn't have to have the paint style applied, nor does it have to be the same paint style. Experiment with painting only the background or foreground subject of an image to enhance it or set it apart from the other elements. Use multiple paint styles, different brush sizes and a variety of settings for opacity and tolerance, to create some unique effects.

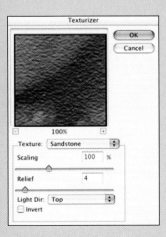

Variation three
Make the image appear to be painted on a textured surface. After creating a painterly effect with the Art History Brush, try adding a texture over the resulting artwork.
There are several options for textures in Photoshop available by selecting Filter > Texture > Texturizer.
Here we have used the Canvas and Sandstone options.

Difficulty: Intermediate	Daniel Brown

Let Photoshop Do The Work

Hands up all the lazy Photoshop users who'd prefer that it did a little more of the work? The truly lazy Photoshop users wouldn't raise their hands, they'd just nod and say 'Yeah. I'm lazy'. Daniel Brown shows you how to do more with less effort using Photoshop's automation features.

There are those that strive to know every keyboard shortcut, every magic workaround, every sub-menu within sub-menus. There are books on top of books on top of web sites to tell you a thousand different ways to do most any task in Photoshop. This will only get you so far. As anyone in a real production environment can tell you, the real idea isn't to memorise. The idea is to finish before you told the client you would but bill them for the time anyway. This is called 'Going home at the end of the day' or 'Getting to know your family'. The beauty of a computer is that it can do the same thing (or similar things) over and over, for hours, days, even months, and it never gets bored (as far as we know). Even if you haven't quite mastered all 300+ keyboard shortcuts in Photoshop, there are still ways to get things done faster and smarter. Let the computer (and, in this case, other software) work for you.

Adobe Evangelists
For more Photoshop tips, with a side order of Illustrator, LiveMotion, ImageReady and GoLive, visit: www.adobeevangelists.com

Actions
An action can be applied to multiple documents (via the File > Automate menu option) or it may be assigned to a keyboard stroke for use on an as-needed basis. The 'seed' for the Automation menu and for

'Droplets' (introduced in Photoshop 6.0) is the Actions palette. Here is where you define the processes you wish to be performed. The Actions palette is fairly simple so only few things need to be known to use it.

An action is simply a series of steps recorded by Photoshop as you perform them. Hitting the red record button will prompt you for a name, and then start the recording process. (Note that some items, such as brush strokes, cannot be recorded.)

To prompt or not to prompt?
The small square to the right of the checkmarks is a VERY important ingredient in Photoshop. This option decides whether the dialogue box for a command is displayed for input, or if the settings recorded with the Action are used. With the symbol turned on, the application will stop and prompt the user to specify the settings, and then resume the other actions.

Groups
Actions in a group can be triggered sequentially. So, if you have several steps that you use on a regular basis and you want them ALL to be applied to a group of files, place them all in one group, select the group, and hit play.

Selectively apply actions
Note that steps in a group can be activated or deactivated with the checkmark. This allows you to apply actions selectively.

Actions submenu
The Action palette submenu lists options for simplifying the Actions palette. The 'Button Mode' can be activated and the individual steps are hidden, the F-Key is displayed in the command, and the buttons can even be colour-coded. In this mode, selecting a step and pressing 'Play' is no longer necessary. Simply tapping a button will trigger the action to play. At the very bottom of the Actions palette are 'Action Presets'. Choosing one of these will load that set.

Record, Play and Stop
The buttons for recording, stopping and playing an action can all be found at the bottom of the Actions palette. When recording or playing the icons will be red.

New Action/New Group
The new page icon at the bottom of the Actions palette creates a new action. The folder icon creates a new group that can hold multiple actions.

Assigning Function Key shortcuts
Also worthy of note is that you can double-click any action and assign a Function Key to it. This allows you to trigger one or more steps with a single keystroke. You can also augment this with modifier keys (Shift, Option/Alt, etc.)

At present, one of the more difficult processes to automate is the opening
of images in the correct colour space with the right colour profile.
Here, we'll show you a technique for automating this task
using Conditional Mode Change.

Action creation

Creating an action is as simple
as pressing the record button
in the Actions palette, then
performing a number of steps
or commands. Each step will
appear in the Actions palette as
you execute it and at the end of
the process, you'll have a series
of steps that can be applied to
any image with a single click.

Open a typical image

Start with an image that
you would generally want
to apply your new action to.

Missing profile

The first problem that normally
arises is an image without a
colour profile. If your Colour
Management Policies in the
Color Settings are set to
Preserve Embedded Profile, this
will stop your action in its tracks
when you try to open the file.

Action!

The beauty of actions is that
you can automate almost every
command or setting. So, let's
do this with our Color Settings.
Choose the record button in the
Actions palette, and name your
action (in this case, Open
Colour Managed). Click Record.
Now, select Color Settings
(Edit > Color Settings) and
change the Color Management
Policy to Convert to Working
RGB, Convert to Working CMYK,
and Convert to Working Gray.
Now, your images will be
opened in your default colour
space defined in the Working
Spaces (in the Color Settings
dialogue). Click OK.

Colour Management Policies

By converting images to the working
space, you solve the problem of knowing
what colour profile you are using. If you
use your action as a Batch Action, you can
elect to suppress Color Profile Warnings.

Missing Profile

The RGB document does not have an embedded color profile.

How do you want to proceed?
- ○ Leave as is (don't color manage)
- ● Assign working RGB: Adobe RGB (1998)
- ○ Assign profile: Adobe RGB (1998)
  - ☐ and then convert document to working RGB

Cancel   OK

Color Settings

Settings: Custom

☐ Advanced Mode

Working Spaces
- RGB: Adobe RGB (1998)
- CMYK: U.S. Web Coated (SWOP) v2
- Gray: Gray Gamma 1.8
- Spot: Dot Gain 20%

Color Management Policies
- RGB: Preserve Embedded Profiles
- CMYK: Preserve Embedded Profiles
- Gray: Preserve Embedded Profiles
- Profile Mismatches: ☑ Ask When Opening ☑ Ask When Pasting
- Missing Profiles: ☑ Ask When Opening

Description

OK
Cancel
Load...
Save...
☑ Preview

Color Management Policies
- RGB: Convert to Working RGB
- CMYK: Convert to Working CMYK
- Gray: Convert to Working Gray
- Profile Mismatches: ☑ Ask When Opening ☑ Ask When Pasting
- Missing Profiles: ☑ Ask When Opening

Conditional Mode Change

Conditional Mode Change is a powerful command that allows you to take many images from one of several colour spaces and convert them into any other colour space (as part of a Batch Action or Droplet). This allows you to use images from several colour spaces and convert them to one colour space within the one action.

A small hiccup with this command if you want to run the action unsupervised is that if the image is in the same colour space you are converting other images to, a dialogue will pop up to tell you so. Not ideal, if you're already home eating dinner.

Conditional Mode Change

Source Mode
- ☑ Bitmap
- ☑ Grayscale
- ☑ Duotone
- ☑ Indexed Color
- ☑ RGB Color
- ☑ CMYK Color
- ☐ Lab Color
- ☑ Multichannel

[All] [None]

OK
Cancel

Target Mode
Mode: [Lab Color ▼]

Changing spaces (LAB)

Our next step is to perform a colour mode change. Select Conditional Mode Change (File > Automate > Conditional Mode Change). We don't want to convert an image that is already in the preferred colour space, so we need to convert into a colour space that our original images are not likely to be in (Lab Color). Choose All in Source Mode and uncheck Lab Color, then select Lab Color as the target mode. Click OK.

Conditional Mode Change

Source Mode
- ☐ Bitmap
- ☐ Grayscale
- ☐ Duotone
- ☐ Indexed Color
- ☐ RGB Color
- ☐ CMYK Color
- ☑ Lab Color
- ☐ Multichannel

[All] [None]

OK
Cancel

Target Mode
Mode: [RGB Color ▼]

Changing spaces (RGB)

We'll now convert into our final target space which is RGB. Select Conditional Mode Change (File > Automate > Conditional Mode Change). We know that the colour space of the images will be in Lab Color, because the previous Action has converted them to LAB. Select the None button and then check Lab Color. Next change the Target Mode to RGB and click OK. All of our images at this point will now be RGB.

Note

Any time you change from one colour space to another, you risk a colour shift due to different colour gamuts. Make sure you test your images thoroughly to ensure that you don't create extra problems for yourself.

Save As

[📁 Processed ▼]   [🖴] [🔖] [🕐]

Name	Date Modified

Name: [Ferris wheel.tif]   [New 📁]
Format: [TIFF ▼]

Save: ☐ As a Copy   ☐ Annotations
      ☐ Alpha Channels   ☐ Spot Colors
      ☐ Layers
Color: ☐ Use Proof Setup: Working CMYK
       ☑ Embed Color Profile: Adobe RGB (1998)

[?]   [Cancel] [Save]

Save

Our next step is to save the result of our mode changes and in the process attach a colour profile to each image. Select File > Save As, name the file, and select the format. In this case we want to save as a TIFF.

Now is also a good time to create a destination folder that you want your processed images to be put in.

Finally, ensure that Embed Color Profile is checked and that it is the correct profile (your RGB working space) which in this case is Adobe RGB (1998). Click Save.

Important!

Whenever you create an action, it is important that you test it thoroughly before you put it in the production workflow.

Test your actions with several types of image in various colour modes. When you're satisfied your action is working, it's time to create a Droplet that will perform our action when images are dragged onto it.

Color Management Policies

RGB: [Preserve Embedded Profiles ▼]
CMYK: [Preserve Embedded Profiles ▼]
Gray: [Preserve Embedded Profiles ▼]
Profile Mismatches: ☑ Ask When Opening ☑ Ask When Pasting
Missing Profiles: ☑ Ask When Opening

Back to normal

We now want to return our Color Settings to the state they were in before the Action started. Select Color Settings (Edit > Color Settings) and change the Color Management Policy back to Preserve Embedded Profiles and click OK. In the Actions palette, click the stop button. The Action is now complete.

Droplets allow you to drag-and-drop images or folders of images onto them which then launch Photoshop to execute the action commands they contain. Their beauty is that they're convenient and are easily shared.

The Create Droplet dialogue looks complicated with its many options, but not everything is relevant to your needs.

1. Create Droplet
To bring up the Create Droplet dialogue, choose File > Automate > Create Droplet.

2. Save Droplet In
First up, select Choose and name and save your droplet. Make the file name meaningful or you may forget what it's for.

4. Destination
Destination lets you choose where your images will be saved. You'll want to save your images to a new folder rather than save over the originals, so choose Folder as Destination and select the folder you created earlier for Processed images.
Leave Override Action "Save In" unchecked because the Save in our Action ensures the correct colour profile is added.
You can also append numbers or dates to the filenames of your processed images and add file extensions for compatibility.

3. Play
Select the Set that contains your action, then the action itself. The next three options are for specific circumstances. If your action needs to load other images for things like a displacement map, then don't check this option. Check Include All Subfolders if you want to apply folders (and folders in folders) of images to your droplet. If you are not concerned with Color Profiles, you can elect to ignore warnings.

5. Log Errors To File
Choose to Log Errors To File and select a name and location for the text file. This means your Action won't stop if it finds an error and your remaining images will be processed. Finally, click OK to save your Droplet.

A tiny Droplet
The droplet of your action will appear where you specified in Save Droplet In. To use the droplet, simply drag your image files onto it. The droplet will then open Photoshop automatically and start running the action.

Cross-platform compatibility
If your Action was created under Windows, simply drag your droplet onto the Photoshop application icon on a Mac to launch and update the droplet. To use a droplet created under Mac OS in Windows add .EXE after the filename and it will then work.

Before you go to the trouble of creating your own actions, take a look at Photoshop's Action sets (via the Actions palette menu) which feature several categories including: Production Actions; Command Sets; Frames; Image Effects; Text Effects; and Textures.

To see examples of each of these actions, take a look in the Photoshop Actions Folder inside the Presets folder in the Photoshop application folder.

Button mode
When you are using multiple sets of actions, it helps to use the Actions Button Mode (via the Actions palette menu) and to

also colour-code sets of actions by double-clicking on an action while not in Button mode and using the Color pull-down menu in the Action Options dialogue.

Command shortcuts

Command shortcuts
This action is best used when the Action palette is set to button mode.

Action	F-Key	Description
Cut (selection)	F2	Cuts a selection and stores it on the clipboard
Copy (selection)	F3	Copies a selection and stores it on the clipboard
Paste	F4	Pastes the contents of the clipboard
Show Color	F6	Displays the Color palette
Show Layers	F7	Displays the Layers palette
Show Info	F8	Displays the Info palette
Show Actions	F9	Displays the Actions palette
Show Navigator	F10	Displays the Navigator palette
Image Size	F11	Shortcut to Image Size menu item
Revert	F12	Shortcut to Revert menu item
Crop (selection)		Shortcut to Crop menu item
Flatten Image	Shift F2	Shortcut to Flatten Image (Layers palette menu)
Purge All	Shift F3	Shortcut to Purge All (Edit menu item)
Select Similar (selection)	Shift F4	Shortcut to Select Similar menu item
Grow (selection)	Shift F5	Shortcut to Grow Selection menu item
Flip Horizontal	Shift F6	Shortcut to Flip Horizontal menu item
Flip Vertical	Shift F7	Shortcut to Flip Vertical menu item
Rotate 90 CW	Shift F8	Shortcut to Rotate 90 CW menu item
Rotate 90 CCW	Shift F9	Shortcut to Rotate 90 CCW menu item
Rotate 180	Shift F10	Shortcut to Rotate 180 menu item
New Snapshot	Shift F11	Shortcut to New Snapshot (History palette menu)
New Snapshot/Clear History	Shift F12	Creates new snapshot, then clears History

Production Actions

Production Actions
Use this action for tasks that you'd frequently perform in a production setting such as creating standard-sized documents, custom mode changes and saving files.

Action	Description
Letter Canvas 150	Creates a 150ppi file measuring 8-1/2" x 11"
Letter R Canvas 150	Creates a 150ppi file measuring 11" x 8-1/2"
Tabloid Canvas 150	Creates a 150ppi file measuring 11" x 17"
Tabloid R Canvas 150	Creates a 150ppi file measuring 17" x 11"
Legal Canvas 150	Creates a 150ppi file measuring 8-1/2" x 14"
Legal R Canvas 150	Creates a 150ppi file measuring 14" x 8-1/2"
640 x 480	Creates a 72ppi file measuring 640 pixels by 480 pixels
Save as GIF89a	Saves the image as a GIF file
Conditional Mode Change	Shortcut to the Conditional Mode Change menu dialogue
Batch Processing	Shortcut to the Batch menu dialogue
Reduced Color Palette	Reduces Color Palette and exports as a GIF file
Fit Image	Shortcut to the Fit Image menu dialogue
Custom RGB to Grayscale	Allows you to control the amounts of the Red, Green and Blue channels used to make a grayscale.
Custom CMYK to Grayscale	Allows you to control the amounts of the Cyan, Magenta, Yellow and Black channels used to make a grayscale.
Make Clip Path	Make a selection and run the action. When saved, the clipping path will be saved as well and will act as a mask for the image when placed in a page layout program.
Save As JPEG Medium	Saves the image as a JPEG (quality level 5) file
Save As Photoshop PDF	Saves the image as a Photoshop PDF, including layers, transparency, and font embedding
Make Button	Constrains image to 75 pixels and adds a 2 pixel stroke/bevel

A Bumper Crop	**Difficulty: Easy**	**Julieanne Kost**
	Photoshop 6 saw the Crop tool promoted to its own spot on the toolbar with a host of productive features such as Shielding, Perspective, Hide or Delete and cropping, based on the foremost image's dimensions. Julieanne Kost demonstrates.	

Since Photoshop 6 there have been several very useful features for the Crop tool. Aside from being given its own spot on the tool palette (instead of being hidden under the Rectangular Marquee tool), it also has the ability to shield out the area that you are cropping in the image from view.

Shields up
While you select the area in the image that you want to keep, Photoshop temporarily masks over the surrounding areas with a colour and level of opacity that you define (the default is 75% black).
After making a selection, you can move the selection by clicking within the selection and dragging. While dragging, the Shift key will constrain to horizontal and vertical movement.

The edge handles can be modified with the Shift key (to constrain the aspect ratio) and the Option/Alt key (to fix the rotation point).
The edges of the selection will snap to the edges of the image.

Tip
Hold down the Option/Alt key to expand or contract keeping the rotation point fixed. Note that the rotation point can be moved. If the rotated selection is moved, the corners will snap to the edges of the image.

Adjusting a selection
Holding down the Shift key once you have a selection will preserve the aspect ratio of the selection, when resizing.

Guides
An undo or going back in History after a crop doesn't retain the selection. Guides speed up the remaking of a selection.

Rotating the selection
The selection can be rotated around the (movable) rotation point. Take care not to overstep the bounds of your image.

Rotated and cropped
By committing the crop, the image will be cropped and rotated according to the dimensions of your selection.

Delete vs. Hide

It used to be that if you cropped an image, anything that was outside of the image area that you cropped was gone for good. However, now you can choose to merely hide the cropped area in case you want to change your mind at a later time and bring those image areas back.

Hidden and revealed

Though the image appears to be cropped, the original information can be returned at any time using the Reveal All command (Image > Reveal All) which reveals all of those hidden areas that you can't see by making the canvas size of the image large enough to encompass them.

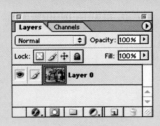

Important

You do have to be on a layer to hide information. If you're on the background, Photoshop will automatically delete the cropped information.

Trim

Related to cropping, is the Trim command found under the Image menu (Image > Trim). This feature gives you the ability to trim a file based on transparency or colour, from any side of the image.

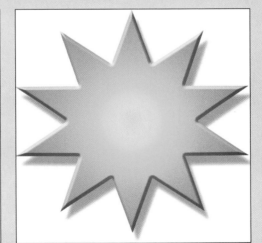

More than you'd expect

Using the Trim command with Transparent Pixels selected will trim the transparent areas around your image. Though the surrounding areas of your object may still appear transparent, there is pixel information still there. If you cropped this sort of image by eye, you might inadvertently lose image information.

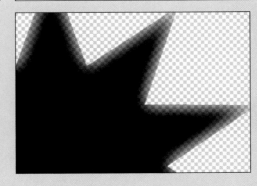

01 - Palettes & Tools

For this Crop Tool tip, make sure that you have the Perspective box checked in the Options Bar.

With the Perspective checkbox checked in the Options Bar we can drag individual handles of the selection to match the distorted perspective of the barn door. Drag each of the four corner handles to match the corners of the barn doors.

Perspective corrections
The Crop tool can now do perspective corrections. If you've ever taken a photo of an object that wasn't quite straight, then you'll get a lot of use out of this tool. Keep in mind, you have to be trying to fix a natural perspective since this option takes the area that you define and puts it on the face of a cube and rotates it through space. If you don't chose a real-life scenario Photoshop may not be able to correct it.

Barn work
Here we start with an image of a barn with a reasonable amount of perspective distortion. Choose the face of the object which is obviously distorted. In this case, the barn doors are the best reference point. Select the Crop tool from the Toolbar and draw a rough selection around the barn doors (see above). Don't worry too much about the accuracy of the selection as we'll be adjusting it in the next step.

Expand the area

Hit it!

Drawing out the side handles will specify the area of the image that will crop to a square picture.

Capturing the surroundings

Once your selection fits the barn doors, we want to extend the crop area to take in the rest of the object.

We do this by extending each of the centre handles until the object and its surrounds are in the crop area *(left)*. Finally, hit Enter or double-click the selection to commit the crop.

Cropped and in perspective

Above, our barn is now looking much better thanks to the perspective correction.

The addition of Perspective to the Crop tool reduces the amount of time this correction would take and can also be used to change the perspective of your images for more dramatic effects.

Note

The Delete/Hide options are not available when using Perspective. The image within the crop will be all that remains of your image. The rest is deleted.

Automatic masking tools	Difficulty: Intermediate	**Julieanne Kost**

There are a variety of ways to isolate a foreground object from its background and delete it so you can replace it with another background. Julieanne Kost shows you how to use Photoshop's masking tools for quick results.

Eraser tool

Magic Eraser (automated)

Background Eraser (automated)

Masking a background

There are a variety of ways to isolate a foreground object from the background and delete it so you can replace it with another. Here we'll look at Photoshop's Eraser tool, and the automated Magic Eraser and Background Eraser tools.

All of these tools can be found in Photoshop's Tool palette.

A Master Class in Advanced Photoshop

The Automatic Masking tools tip is based on the Advanced Selection lesson from the Software Cinema Advanced Techniques CD-ROM presented by Julieanne Kost.

Visit: www.deancollins.com

Eraser

The Eraser tool can be found in the Photoshop Tool palette.

Eraser tool
The Eraser tool can remove a background, but instead of erasing to transparency, it erases to the background colour. If we erase the sky, it fills the painted area with white (the background colour).

Thanks to the Photoshop 6 Options Bar, you can easily set the brush attributes for the Eraser to get soft-edged brushes for erasing.

Magic Eraser

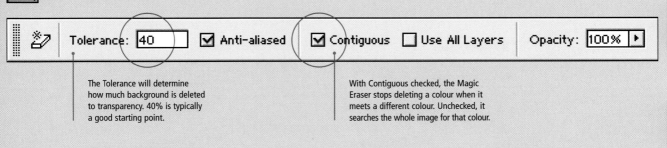

The Tolerance will determine how much background is deleted to transparency. 40% is typically a good starting point.

With Contiguous checked, the Magic Eraser stops deleting a colour when it meets a different colour. Unchecked, it searches the whole image for that colour.

Magic Eraser tool
The Magic Eraser selects based on colour, just like the Magic Wand, but also deletes to transparency. The Magic Eraser settings are in the Options Bar. With the Magic Eraser tool active, select Contiguous in the Options Bar with a Tolerance of 40% before clicking on the blue sky. You'll notice the Magic Eraser selected most of the blue sky pixels to delete. If we had not selected Contiguous, instead of stopping at the edges of the cathedral, it would have searched the entire image for that same shade of blue and deleted it.
Uncheck Contiguous and click on the remaining sky above the arch to remove the shades of blue from the areas behind the cathedral.

No more blue skies
There's a little sky information behind the windows on the left hand side of the cathedral. By clicking in this area, the remaining sky disappears. So using the Magic Eraser works well where your background is made up of similar colours.

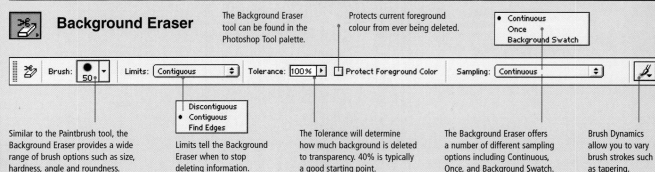

Background Eraser

The Background Eraser tool can be found in the Photoshop Tool palette.

Protects current foreground colour from ever being deleted.

- Continuous
- Once
- Background Swatch

Brush: 50

Limits: Contiguous

- Discontiguous
- Contiguous
- Find Edges

Tolerance: 100%

Protect Foreground Color

Sampling: Continuous

Similar to the Paintbrush tool, the Background Eraser provides a wide range of brush options such as size, hardness, angle and roundness.

Limits tell the Background Eraser when to stop deleting information.

The Tolerance will determine how much background is deleted to transparency. 40% is typically a good starting point.

The Background Eraser offers a number of different sampling options including Continuous, Once, and Background Swatch.

Brush Dynamics allow you to vary brush strokes such as tapering.

Background Eraser

Instead of the Magic Eraser, we'll use the Background Eraser tool. You'll notice that the Background Eraser tool has a crosshair inside of the brush icon. The Background Eraser uses the crosshair to determine where it is sampling from. Note: circle size will change depending on brush size.

Crosshair
The Background Eraser uses the crosshair to determine where it is sampling from.

Sampling Options

To begin, we select Continuous sampling and increase our brush size to 100 pixels. By clicking in a red stripe area, you'll notice that just the red is deleted, but if we move into the white area, it too will be deleted because it is sampling continuously.

Sampling
Continuous

Limits
Contiguous

Sampling: Once

To restrict the sampling to one colour, we'll set sampling to Once. Now when we click on an area and paint, it will only delete the colour that was first selected. Dragging over the white area has no effect, but the next red stripe is deleted to transparency.

Sampling
Once

Limits
Contiguous

Limits: Contiguous

You can set Limits on the Background Eraser to sample Contiguously or Discontiguously. To illustrate Contiguous, we'll choose a very large brush and set the Limits to Contiguous. When the Background Eraser hits the edge of the white borders, it stops deleting the red.

Sampling
Once

Limits
Contiguous

Limits: Discontiguous

Setting Limits to Discontiguous, will delete all of the red stripes within the brush area.

Sampling
Once

Sampling
Discontiguous

So, the Background Eraser provides more flexibility than the Magic Eraser and also gets rid of the colour that bleeds or is in the anti-aliased area.

Background Eraser: part 2

The task is to place the model against the leafy lane. To do this we will need to remove the model's studio background. This time we will use the Background Eraser.
Start by putting both images in the same file.

The Background Eraser tool can be found in the Photoshop Tool palette.

Tip

When compositing two images it is better to have them in the same file so that you see how the contouring works against the background. Sometimes, small flaws will not show up against detailed grounds.

Move into position

Position the model using the Move tool so she looks like she's standing in the shot. We're now ready to use the Background Eraser to erase the model's studio background. A potential problem is that there are beige colours in her sweater and in the background. Fortunately, the Background Eraser has a Find Edges setting in the Limits menu which will restrict the Background Eraser from deleting the beige colours inside the sweater area.

Brush: 100 | Limits: Find Edges | Tolerance: 30% | ☐ Protect Foreground Color | Sampling: Continuous

Limits
Discontiguous
To erase the sampled colour wherever it occurs under the brush.
Contiguous
To erase areas that contain the sampled colour and are connected to one another.
Find Edges
To erase connected areas containing the sampled colour while better preserving the sharpness of shape edges.

Tolerance
Enter a value or drag the slider. A low tolerance limits erasure to areas that are very similar to the sampled colour. A high tolerance erases a broader range of colours.

Protect Foreground Colour
Prevents the erasure of areas that match the foreground colour in the toolbox.

Sampling options
'Continuous' samples colours continuously as you drag.
'Once' erases only areas containing the colour that you first click.
'Background Swatch' erases only areas containing the current background colour.
Drag through the area you want to erase. The background eraser tool pointer appears as a brush shape with a cross hair indicating the tool's hot spot.

Removing the background

With the Background Eraser selected, set the Limits to Find Edges and the Tolerance to 30% (a higher Tolerance will delete into the model's sweater). Making sure you're on the Model layer, paint around her sweater with a medium-sized brush. Now you'll see that we're deleting the background of the model, showing the trees behind it, but we're not going into the sweater area even though it contains the same colours as the background. Continue painting around the model, up to her hair which will require some different treatment.

Brush: 50 | Limits: Discontiguous | Tolerance: 30% | ☐ Protect Foreground Color

Working with hair

When we get to the model's hair, there are gaps between her hair, so we need to take off the Limit of Find Edges and set it to Discontiguous so that it will jump over the strands of hair. Choose a smaller brush, then paint closely around the hair. The strands of hair won't be deleted and stroke by stroke the background will show through.

Lasso

To remove the remaining studio background area, use the Lasso tool to select the rest of the background.
Hit the Delete key to delete the unwanted background and then deselect (Command/Ctrl-D).
If there are any remaining background artifacts, select them with the Lasso tool and delete them, then be sure to Deselect (Command/Ctrl-D).

Whoops, too much

It seems we've deleted too much detail in the cuff of the sweater. To repair this, select the History Brush and show the History palette (Window > Show History).
Set the History Brush to paint from a state before we used the Background Eraser (Move in this case) by clicking in its well. Choose a small paintbrush and paint over the affected area to return the information.

Blurring for realism

Our image isn't looking very realistic yet because both the model and the background are in focus. There's also a discrepancy between the colour of the light on the model and the ambient light.
First we'll throw the background out of focus using Gaussian Blur (Filter > Blur > Gaussian Blur). Here we set a radius of 4.2 pixels to blur the background.

Model colouring

As is often the case with photographs taken in different places at different times, the ambient light is different.
A very good way to fix this is to sample a typical colour in the background, create a new layer and fill the layer with the sampled colour. Use Color mode. Group the colour layer with (in this case) the model.

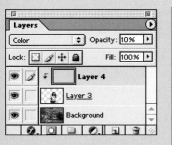

Same time, same place

Reduce the opacity of the Color layer to about 10%.
Because it is grouped with the model layer, it will affect only that layer. So a little reflected light splashes across our model and the scene looks complete and convincing.

Difficulty: Easy	Design Graphics

Photoshop blend modes

Blending modes are one of the most powerful features of Photoshop allowing you to alter the behaviour of a tool or layer to interact with the underlying image. With help from the Adobe Photoshop 7 manual, we explain and show you what each blending mode does.

Sample images
Our sample images are designed to show the effects of the blend modes. We have included black, white, 50% grey (in RGB mode), a spectrum of color and some transparency.

Blend modes
There are five new blend modes and the entire list has been regrouped in Photoshop 7.

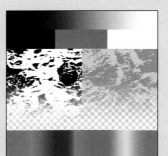

- Normal
  Dissolve
  Behind

  Darken
  Multiply
  Color Burn
  Linear Burn

  Lighten
  Screen
  Color Dodge
  Linear Dodge

  Overlay
  Soft Light
  Hard Light
  Vivid Light
  Linear Light
  Pin Light

  Difference
  Exclusion

  Hue
  Saturation
  Color
  Luminosity

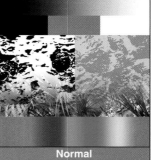

Normal

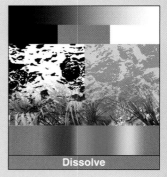

Dissolve

Blending modes are one of the most powerful features of Photoshop allowing you to alter the behaviour of a tool or layer to interact with the underlying image.

Selecting a blending mode
The blending mode specified in the options bar controls how pixels in the image are affected by a painting or editing tool. It's helpful to think in terms of the following colors when visualising a blending mode's effect:
- The base color is the original color in the image.
- The blend color is the color being applied with the painting or editing tool.
- The result color is the color resulting from the blend.

Normal
Edits or paints each pixel to make it the result color. This is the default mode. (Normal mode is called Threshold when you're working with a bitmapped or indexed-color image.)

Dissolve
Edits or paints each pixel to make it the result color. However, the result color is a random replacement of the pixels with the base color or the blend color, depending on the opacity at any pixel location.

Group 2		Group 3	

Darken

Color Burn

Lighten

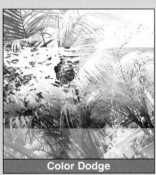
Color Dodge

Multiply

Linear Burn

Screen

Linear Dodge

Darken
Looks at the color information in each channel and selects the base or blend color–whichever is darker–as the result color. Pixels lighter than the blend color are replaced, and pixels darker than the blend color do not change.

Multiply
Looks at the color information in each channel and multiplies the base color by the blend color. The result color is always a darker color. Multiplying any color with black produces black. Multiplying any color with white leaves the color unchanged. When you're painting with a color other than black or white, successive strokes with a painting tool produce progressively darker colors. The effect is similar to drawing on the image with multiple magic markers.

Color Burn
Looks at the color information in each channel and darkens the base color to reflect the blend color by increasing the contrast. Blending with white produces no change.

Linear Burn
Looks at the color information in each channel and darkens the base color to reflect the blend color by decreasing the brightness. Blending with white produces no change.

Lighten
Looks at the color information in each channel and selects the base or blend color–whichever is lighter–as the result color. Pixels darker than the blend color are replaced, and pixels lighter than the blend color do not change.

Screen
Looks at each channel's color information and multiplies the inverse of the blend and base colors. The result color is always a lighter color. Screening with black leaves the color unchanged. Screening with white produces white. The effect is similar to projecting multiple photographic slides on top of each other.

Color Dodge
Looks at the color information in each channel and brightens the base color to reflect the blend color by decreasing the contrast. Blending with black produces no change.

Linear Dodge
Looks at the color information in each channel and brightens the base color to reflect the blend color by increasing the brightness. Blending with black produces no change.

Group 4

Overlay

Hard Light

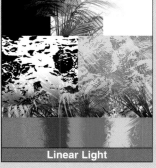

Linear Light

Soft Light

Vivid Light

Pin Light

Overlay

Multiplies or screens the colors, depending on the base color. Patterns or colors overlay the existing pixels while preserving the highlights and shadows of the base color. The base color is not replaced but is mixed with the blend color to reflect the lightness or darkness of the original color.

Soft Light

Darkens or lightens the colors, depending on the blend color. The effect is similar to shining a diffused spotlight on the image. If the blend color (light source) is lighter than 50% gray, the image is lightened as if it were dodged. If the blend color is darker than 50% gray, the image is darkened as if it were burned in. Painting with pure black or white produces a distinctly darker or lighter area but does not result in pure black or white.

Hard Light

Multiplies or screens the colors, depending on the blend color. The effect is similar to shining a harsh spotlight on the image. If the blend color (light source) is lighter than 50% gray, the image is lightened, as if it were screened. This is useful for adding highlights to an image. If the blend color is darker than 50% gray, the image is darkened, as if it were multiplied. This is useful for adding shadows to an image. Painting with pure black or white results in pure black or white.

Vivid Light

Burns or dodges the colors by increasing or decreasing the contrast, depending on the blend color. If the blend color (light source) is lighter than 50% gray, the image is lightened by decreasing the contrast. If the blend color is darker than 50% gray, the image is darkened by increasing the contrast.

Linear Light

Burns or dodges the colors by decreasing or increasing the brightness, depending on the blend color. If the blend color (light source) is lighter than 50% gray, the image is lightened by increasing the brightness. If the blend color is darker than 50% gray, the image is darkened by decreasing the brightness.

Pin Light

Replaces the colors, depending on the blend color. If the blend color (light source) is lighter than 50% gray, pixels darker than the blend color are replaced, and pixels lighter than the blend color do not change. If the blend color is darker than 50% gray, pixels lighter than the blend color are replaced, and pixels darker than the blend color do not change. This is useful for adding special effects to an image.

Group 5	Group 6	

Difference

Hue

Color

Saturation

Exclusion

Luminosity

Difference
Looks at the color information in each channel and subtracts either the blend color from the base color or the base color from the blend color, depending on which has the greater brightness value. Blending with white inverts the base color values; blending with black produces no change.

Exclusion
Creates an effect similar to but lower in contrast than the Difference mode. Blending with white inverts the base color values. Blending with black produces no change.

Hue
Creates a result color with the luminance and saturation of the base color and the hue of the blend color.

Saturation
Creates a result color with the luminance and hue of the base color and the saturation of the blend color. Painting with this mode in an area with no (o) saturation (gray) causes no change.

Color
Creates a result color with the luminance of the base color and the hue and saturation of the blend color. This preserves the gray levels in the image and is useful for coloring monochrome images and for tinting color images.

Luminosity
Creates a result color with the hue and saturation of the base color and the luminance of the blend color. This mode creates an inverse effect from that of the Color mode.

Difficulty: Intermediate	Russell Brown

Custom Picture Packages

Photoshop's Picture Package feature is a great way to print the same image at several sizes on a page. But what if you want to print different images? Russell Brown shows you how to take advantage of Photoshop's Actions to create your own custom picture packages.

Standard Picture Package

Personalised Picture Package

Picture Package
This is what a typical Picture Package looks like. A single photo is laid out multiple times on a grid based on the Picture Package (File > Automate > Picture Package) default page size and configuration.

Promo pages with different images
Need a quick way to present your images for clients or potential clients? Photoshop's Picture Package is ok if you want to show the same image several times, but that's no fun; you want to be able to customise and add your company logo to each package.

www.russellbrown.com
For more tips on Adobe's products, visit Russell Brown's web site at: www.russellbrown.com

Let Photoshop do the work
For more tips on automating Photoshop using actions, refer to p.34.

Opening images in order

Our action relies on the images being loaded in the correct order. Here we have four images: picture 1; picture 2; picture 3; and picture 4. So, we load the picture 4 image first, then picture 3, picture 2 and picture 1.

Select your images

Open the images you'd like to appear on your page in reverse order from how you will place them on the page. So first open the image that you will place last on the page, and move towards the image you place first.

This order is very important when we start recording the action. Changing the order using the window menu will not work.

Resolution

When selecting a resolution, keep in mind that you might print the page or save it as a PDF, so a higher resolution might be needed.

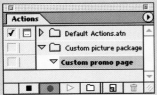

Words of advice for recording actions

You want to move very slowly and deliberately when creating an action. Certain things cannot be recorded, but as we go through the process, you will learn some of the tricks that make recording an action easy.

Recording your action

Let's begin recording our action. Show the Actions palette. Create a new set by clicking the new set icon at the bottom of the Actions palette. Name the set (Custom picture package). Within this set, we can create actions. Again, at the bottom of the Actions palette, click the new action icon. Name the action (Custom promo package) and click Record. Now everything we do—well almost everything—will be recorded, and we will see it listed in the Actions palette. Let's begin recording our action.

Custom page

To start, we will create a custom page. Choose File > New and enter an exact page size and resolution. You do not have to use predefined defaults. You can also name the page so each time you play the action, it will give the page that name. In this case we named the document 'Promo package'. We'll also keep our page white, but you could change the colour. Click OK.

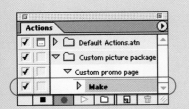

Create your guides

Now let's create some guides for laying out the page.
Go to View > Show Rulers and from within the rulers, click and drag out a guide. Hold down the Shift key to snap the guide to the ruler increments.
Let's place a guide for each side, for the top and bottom, and just below centre.
If you look at the Actions palette, you can see that what you have done so far has been recorded.

Guides

You can drag guides out from the top ruler or the left ruler. Holding down the Option/Alt key while positioning a guide allows you to toggle between vertical and horizontal.

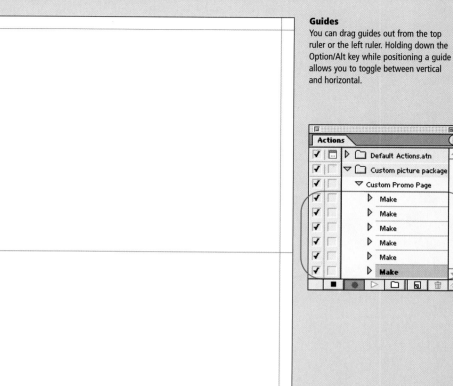

Copying in order

Next, very carefully, we're going to click on the first image (picture 1), just behind the 'Promo Package' page and bring that image forward. Now, select the image (Select > Select All) and Copy.

Tip number 1

Through extensive testing, I've found that clicking on the photo to bring it forward while recording an action is more reliable than using the Window menu and choosing the image.

Tip number 2

You cannot drag and drop when recording an action to copy and paste an image. You must do it via the Edit menu or via the keyboard shortcuts.

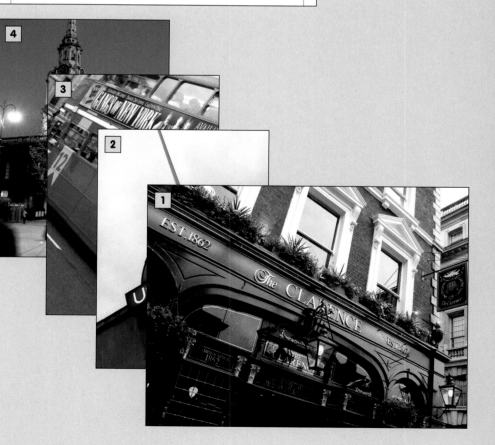

Tip number 3

In order to move something and record that movement, you must transform it. Doing so allows you to not only move an object to a new position and record that action, but also to rotate, scale and skew and record doing those actions too.

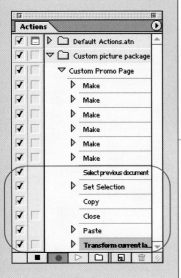

Pasting and placing

Close the image you just copied and then paste it onto your 'Promo package' page. It will automatically be placed in the centre of the page.
Don't get your Move tool out too quickly to reposition this image though. We must use the transformation option in order to record the new position. Choose Edit > Free Transform. In this case we want to scale and move the image to the top. First we reduce the image to 60% of its original size in the Options Bar. Then we drag the image towards the guides until it snaps in place.
To record the movements, you must press the Return/Enter key. Notice how the movements show in your Actions palette.

Scale Options Bar quick tips

While using Free Transform, in the Options Bar, click on the letters to highlight the field where you'll enter a value. You can press the Tab key to cycle through the fields.

Next image

Let's place the next image, just as we did the last one. Click the next image to bring it forward. Select All. Copy. Then close the image and Paste into the 'Promo package' page. Again, we need to use Edit > Free Transform to move and scale the image.
Type the percentage of the scaling into the Options bar (here we use 25%). Click the lock button to constrain the width and height percentages. Lastly, move the image into position on the centre guide and press the Return/Enter key to set and record the movements.

Paste and place again

Continue the process of selecting, copying, pasting and positioning until you have all of your photos in position. Once you're done, you'll have learned everything you need to know to create a standard picture package with multiple images at different sizes. Now let's move beyond the basics to enhance this 'Promo package' page with additional graphics.

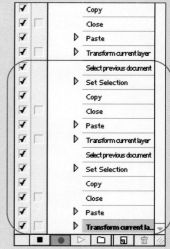

Add a gradient

First, let's put a gradient in the background. While still recording, show the Layers palette. Select the background layer. Set the swatches to their defaults by pressing the D key. Then, from the Tool palette, select the Gradient tool.
In the Options Bar, we select a foreground to background linear gradient.
Starting at the bottom of the image and holding down the Shift key to constrain the angle, click and drag part way up the image. And in comes the gradient.

Cleaning up guides and rulers

Let's clean up some by turning off the rulers (Command/Ctrl-R) and clearing the guides (View > Clear Guides). Those actions are recorded, which is just fine.

Reset swatches

Whenever swatches are used within an action, it's always a good idea to reset them to their defaults (black foreground/ white background) because you never know when you go to play the action what state they will be in.

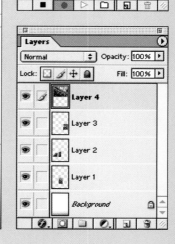

Get your logo

If you have a logo in Photoshop you'd like to add to your page, then use the File > Open and locate the image. Select All and copy the logo. Here we choose a simple logo with transparency.

Paste your logo

Paste your logo into the 'Promo package' page. To scale and position your file, remember to use Free Transform (Command/Ctrl-T) or it won't be recorded. The logo looks plain; let's add a layer style.

Layer styles

With your new logo layer selected, double-click the layer to bring up the Layer Styles dialogue. Check the Bevel and Emboss checkbox and adjust the settings to suit. Here we used a Chisel Hard Inner Bevel with a depth of 600%. With the final bevel and emboss effect on our logo, we are ready to stop recording the action. In the Actions palette, click the stop recording icon.

Loading the action

To load an action that you've moved to a new machine or someone has sent to you, all you have to do is double-click on the action and it will automatically load that action into your current version of Photoshop.

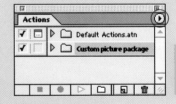

Saving your action

Saving an action is easy. Scroll to the top of the action and click the triangle to collapse all the settings. Select the folder that contains the action, and from the pop-up window select Save Actions. In the dialogue box, name the action, which will automatically be saved as a special format (.atn).

Test the action

To test your action, close the 'Promo package' page and open the same number of images remembering that the order is very important. Also note that any new images need to be the same size as the images used to record the action. Select the action and click the Play button at the bottom of the palette and watch your promo page appear.

Patching without smudging

Difficulty: Easy	Russell Brown

Photoshop 7's Healing Brush and Patch tool are great for repairing images, but they can also be used for creative uses such as making elements of an image disappear. Russell Brown shows you how to leave no evidence at the scene of the patch.

Image courtesy of Erik Aeder Studios.
(USA) **Erik Aeder Studios**
Phone: 808 572 0443
Email: eba@maui.net
http://erikaederphotography.com

Surfer away
The Patch tool allows you to repair parts of your image based on selections or channels. It also allows you to effectively clone out elements in your image much more quickly than you ever could with the Clone Stamp tool. Here we'll lose the surfer from the scene leaving just his surfboard.

Potential problem
The Patch tool is designed to heal an area of an image by blending the texture, lighting and shading of the sampled pixels to the source pixels. A potential problem when using the Patch tool is that it draws colours from adjacent areas which can 'bleed' into your selection if it comes into contact with hard-edged objects.

Starting point

Some image elements will be easier to get rid of than others. In this example we have the hard edge of the surfboard next to the area we want to remove (the surfer).

Select the Patch tool by clicking and holding on the Healing brush or use the J key to cycle between the Healing Brush and the Patch tool.

Using the Patch tool, draw a loose selection around the surfer, and try to get a nice edge against the surfboard.

Tip

You can save selections made with the Patch Tool as alpha channels (even in the middle of a patch operation) for later use.

The Patch

When you complete the path around the surfer, it will turn into a selection.

Place the cursor over the selection and you'll notice the Patch cursor will appear.

Source/Destination

The Patch tool lets you work in two directions: Source and Destination. With Source selected in the Options Bar, you can make a selection around the area that you'd like to repair, then drag your selection to a pristine area of your image to fix your originally selected area. This technique is suited to removing an object. With Destination selected, you can select a pristine image area and drag it over an area you want to repair. This technique is suited to repairing skies, or dusty areas.

Going to the source

Click inside the selected region, then with the mouse held down, move the selection to the Source area that you want to replace the original area with. When you release the mouse, the processing will begin.

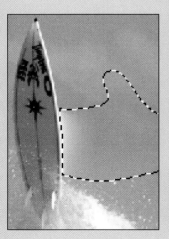

Where'd he go?

A couple of seconds after you release the mouse button, the original selection will be replaced with the Source area. Zooming in on the original selection, we can see that along the edge of the Patch selection next to the surfboard, it's trying to pull the colour and texture of the surfboard into this region. We do not want this to happen along this edge. We want this edge to be hard-edged and define the edge between the surfer and the board.

Lets start again
The secret to success is knowing that the Patch tool will only patch pixels that are visible. If we make the surfboard temporarily invisible to the Patch tool, it won't know that it's there, and won't blend the edge inward.
To do this, we'll use a layer mask. Create a path that surrounds the edge of the surfboard using the Pen tool. Next, we'll turn this path into a selection.

Select a path
Before using the pen tool, select the 'Paths' option in the Options Bar. (If the 'Shape Layers' option is selected, your path will automatically be filled as you create various points.).

Getting a good selection
When you've created your path, make sure that it's selected in the Paths palette and the correct layer is active. When working with the Patch tool, the harder the edge of the selection, the better the results. So, it's important to create a good selection from our path.
In the Paths palette, select Make Selection from the pop-out window. The Make Selection dialogue allows us to make sure there is no feathering or anti-aliasing on our selection. Set Feather Radius to 0, uncheck Anti-aliased, and select New Selection.

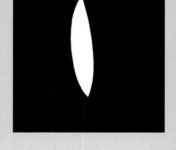

Selection from a path
In the Paths palette, select Make Selection from the pop-out window.

The layer mask
With our surfboard selection created, we can now make our layer mask.
Next, with your layer selected in the Layers palette, create a Layer Mask (Layer > Add Layer Mask > Hide Current Selection). You can also use the Add Layer Mask button in the Layers palette, and if necessary Invert (Command/Ctrl-I) the mask. Our layer mask will temporarily hide the surfboard showing only transparency.

Layer mask button
If you select the layer mask button from the Layers palette with your selection, you'll need to Invert the mask (Command/Ctrl-I) to hide the surfboard.

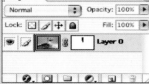

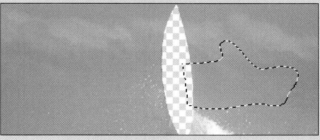

Patch it again Sam
Using the Patch tool again, draw a selection around the surfer. Be sure to extend the selection into the transparency. Now that we have our new patch selection, we want to make sure we have the correct layer targeted.

Get on the right layer
In the Layers palette, the layer mask is currently selected. You can tell this by the mask icon in the palette well. Click on the layer icon and a paintbrush will appear in the palette well. We're now ready to move our patch selection. Move the cursor inside the selection, then click and hold and then move over to the source that will be used to patch this area.

No more surfer
When you release the mouse button, the surfer will disappear again. However, this time, there is no bleeding of surfboard colour or detail into our patched area. If there are any remnants of the object you're trying to remove, simply load your selection and repeat the same patch.

Getting our board back
To bring the surfboard back into the picture, we need to turn off the layer mask. Shift-click the layer mask in the Layers palette and it returns.
In Photoshop 6, this job would take considerably longer using the Clone Stamp tool.
The Photoshop 7 Healing Brush and Patch tools considerably speed up many retouching processes and will no doubt offer more creative possibilities.

Hiding the layer mask
To bring the surfboard back into the picture, we need to turn off the layer mask. Shift-click the layer mask in the Layers palette and it returns.

Tip:
If you have no further use for the surfboard layer mask, drag the mask in the Layers palette to trash icon and click on Discard.

Natural media brushes

Difficulty: Intermediate	Adobe

Photoshop 7.0 opens up a whole new range of possibilities for creating artistic effects. With the new painting engine, you can create imagery that looks as if it was painted using natural media. Here we show you a few of the ways you can customise the Brush tool.

Choose a brush tip shape

Select the Brush tool and choose Window > Brushes to display the Brushes palette. Click on the New Brush button to create a new brush. Select Brush Tip Shape on the left side of the palette, and then select a brush tip. When you're exploring the options in the Brushes palette, it's best to choose a simple tip, such as Hard Round or Soft Round, so you can clearly see the effects.

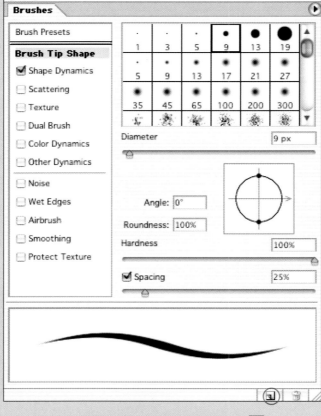

Brush Tip Shape settings

Brush diameter: 9 px

Angle: 0° (Default)

Roundness: 100% (Default)

Hardness: 100% (Default)

Spacing: 25%

Shape Dynamics settings

Size Jitter: 45%

Control: Fade (200)

Minimum Diameter: 1%

Angle Jitter: 100% (Default)

Roundness Jitter: 40%; Fade (75)

Minimum Roundness: 50%

Brushes

Brush Presets		
Brush Tip Shape	Size Jitter	45%
☑ **Shape Dynamics**	Control: Fade	200
☐ Scattering	Minimum Diameter	1%
☐ Texture	Tilt Scale	
☐ Dual Brush		
☐ Color Dynamics	Angle Jitter	100%
☐ Other Dynamics	Control: Off	
☐ Noise	Roundness Jitter	40%
☐ Wet Edges	Control: Fade	75
☐ Airbrush	Minimum Roundness	50%
☐ Smoothing		
☐ Protect Texture		

Fade the brush size

Select Shape Dynamics on the left side of the Brushes palette. Choose Fade from the Control pop-up menu below the Size Jitter slider; then enter a number of steps. The more steps you enter, the longer the stroke. You can view results at the bottom of the Brushes palette. Now try adjusting some of the other shape dynamics. Drag the sliders to add randomness to brush elements. (At 0%, an element does not change over the course of a stroke; at 100%, an element has the maximum amount of randomness.) Choose options from the Control pop-up menus to control the variance of brush elements.

Shape Dynamics settings

Scatter: 90%

Count: 2

Count Jitter: 80%

Brushes

Brush Presets		
Brush Tip Shape	Scatter ☐ Both Axes	90%
☑ Shape Dynamics	Control: Off	
☑ **Scattering**	Count	2
☐ Texture	Count Jitter	80%
☐ Dual Brush	Control: Off	
☐ Color Dynamics		
☐ Other Dynamics		
☐ Noise		
☐ Wet Edges		
☐ Airbrush		
☐ Smoothing		
☐ Protect Texture		

Add scattering

Select Scattering on the left side of the Brushes palette. The options in this section of the Brushes palette determine the number and placement of marks in a stroke. Adjust the Scatter percentage to specify the maximum percentage of scattering in a stroke. Adjust the Count value to specify the number of brush marks applied at each spacing interval. Adjust the Count Jitter percentage to add variance to the number of brush marks applied at each spacing interval.

Add texture

Select Texture on the left side of the Brushes palette.
The options in this section of the Brushes palette let you make strokes look like they are painted on textured canvas. First, click on the pattern sample at the top of the palette, and choose a pattern from the pop-up palette.
(You can load additional patterns by clicking the triangle at the top right of the pop-up palette, and choosing a pattern library from the bottom of the palette menu.)
Use the Scale slider to adjust the size of the pattern.
Now you're ready to use your brush.

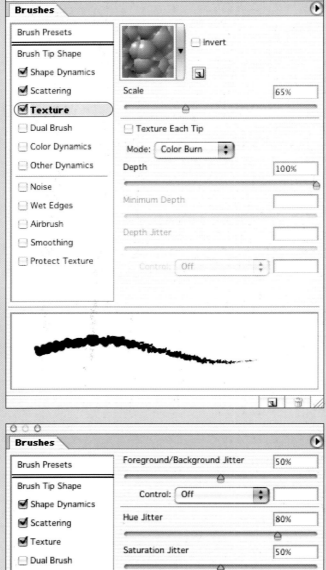

Shape Dynamics settings

Texture: Satin

Scale: 65%

Mode: Color Burn (Default)

Depth: 100%

Experiment with other options

Now that you know the basics, you can experiment with some of the other brush options.
For example, you can add colour dynamics to your brush and paint particle streaks to the fireworks we're about to create. Note: since this effect is very colorful, it may be wise to limit it to only one of the fireworks (see next page).

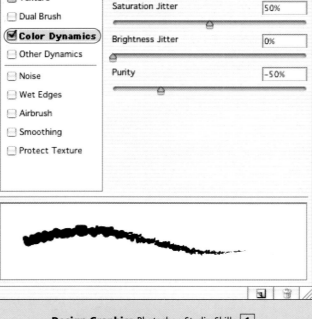

Shape Dynamics settings

Foreground/
Background Jitter: 50% (Default)

Hue Jitter: 80%

Saturation Jitter: 50% (Default)

Brightness Jitter: 0% (Default)

Purity: -50% (Default)

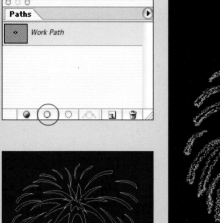

Paint in the image

You can apply a brush stroke to a path for interesting results. Create a path using the Pen tool, and make it a Work Path using the Paths palette fly-out menu. Click on the Work Path to make it active, select the Brush tool, then click on the 'Stroke Path with brush' button in the Paths palette.

Note: if your fireworks path inaccurately contains a solid stroke, select Edit > Undo, go back to your paintbrush and paint a sample stroke. Go back to your path, click on the 'Stroke Path with brush' button again, and hey presto! your stroke should appear to blaze with dramatic impact.

Layers, please

Be sure to create a new layer each time you stroke the path to keep your results on different layers. If you want to composite the fireworks on another image, create a transparent layer.

Fireworks

Change the foreground colour before applying the stroke to the path on each new layer. Vary the path's width by duplicating your original path, then with the Pen tool active, use Command/Ctrl-T to transform the path. Hit Enter to commit the transform, then use it to create new fireworks shapes.

Tip

You can get more vivid results by creating a Hue/Saturation adjustment layer and pushing the Saturation to 100%. To restrict the adjustment to only one layer, Option/Alt-click between the adjustment layer and the firework layer. The icon will change to two overlapping circles to show you that it's about to link the adjustment layer.

Tip

To mimic the brightness of the fireworks as they explode from the centre, use a radial gradient on a layer mask to vary the brightness from the centre to the outer edges. Add white 'sparkles' and motion blurs. Experiment!

Cityscape image courtesy of **Viewfinder** from **'The Australian Collection Vol 2: Sydney, Canberra & Surrounds'**. Visit: www.viewfinder.com.au

Difficulty: Intermediate	Daniel Wade

Photoshop 7 brushes

Photoshop 7 added a powerful new paint engine allowing you to simulate natural media for painterly effects. You can also create and save custom brushes using the new Brushes palette. Here we'll take a look at where everything is and how to make the most of the new brush capabilities.

Brush tool preset   Brush Preset Picker   Painting Mode   Stroke Opacity   Stroke Flow Rate   Enable Airbrush   Toggle Brushes palette

The new look Brushes palette

Photoshop 7's new paint engine allows you to simulate natural media for painterly effects. The Brushes palette will be your first stop to access the multitude of settings now available to you including: size, shape, tilt, spacing, scatter, and jitter. To bring up the Brushes palette, select Window > Brushes, or select the Paintbrush tool and click the toggle Brushes palette icon in the Options Bar. The palette can appear daunting at first glance, but all the familiar brush settings can be found here along with a new Brush stroke preview.

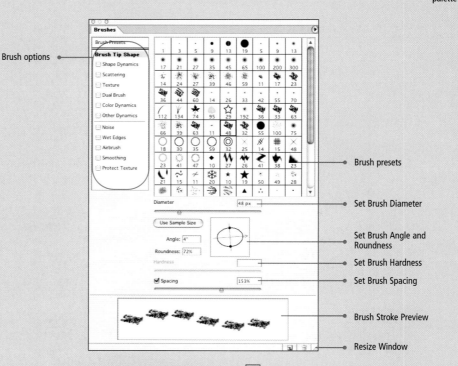

Brush options

Brush presets

Set Brush Diameter

Set Brush Angle and Roundness

Set Brush Hardness

Set Brush Spacing

Brush Stroke Preview

Resize Window

Accessing Brush presets

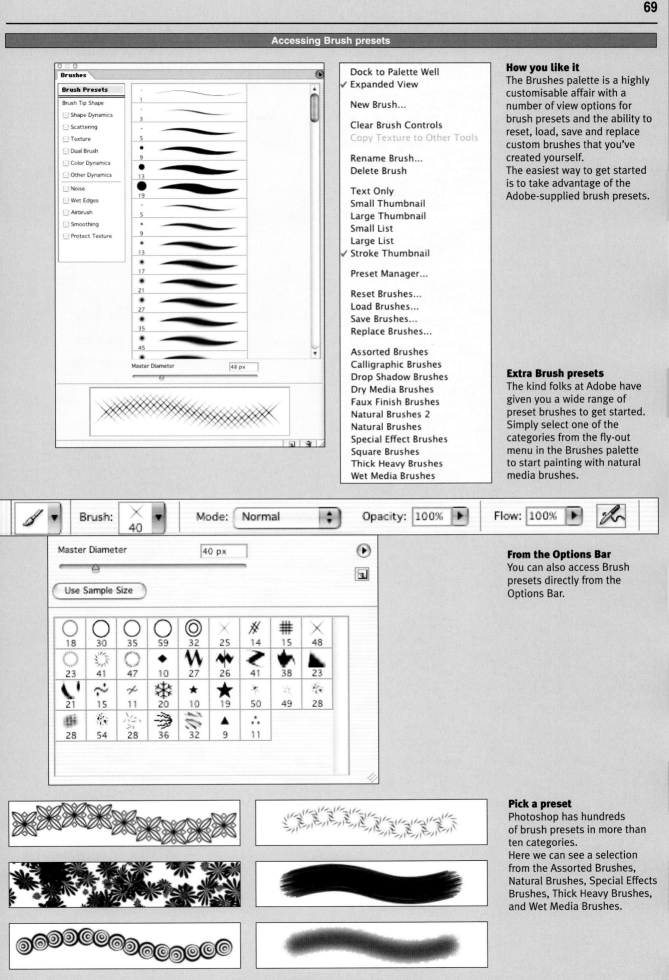

Dock to Palette Well
✓ **Expanded View**

New Brush...

Clear Brush Controls
Copy Texture to Other Tools

Rename Brush...
Delete Brush

Text Only
Small Thumbnail
Large Thumbnail
Small List
Large List
✓ **Stroke Thumbnail**

Preset Manager...

Reset Brushes...
Load Brushes...
Save Brushes...
Replace Brushes...

Assorted Brushes
Calligraphic Brushes
Drop Shadow Brushes
Dry Media Brushes
Faux Finish Brushes
Natural Brushes 2
Natural Brushes
Special Effect Brushes
Square Brushes
Thick Heavy Brushes
Wet Media Brushes

How you like it

The Brushes palette is a highly customisable affair with a number of view options for brush presets and the ability to reset, load, save and replace custom brushes that you've created yourself.
The easiest way to get started is to take advantage of the Adobe-supplied brush presets.

Extra Brush presets

The kind folks at Adobe have given you a wide range of preset brushes to get started. Simply select one of the categories from the fly-out menu in the Brushes palette to start painting with natural media brushes.

From the Options Bar

You can also access Brush presets directly from the Options Bar.

Pick a preset

Photoshop has hundreds of brush presets in more than ten categories.
Here we can see a selection from the Assorted Brushes, Natural Brushes, Special Effects Brushes, Thick Heavy Brushes, and Wet Media Brushes.

Make your own brush

Let's try making our own brush starting with the Brush tip. We'll begin by drawing a shape with the Pen tool. When you have drawn the path, create a new transparent layer by clicking the Create New Layer button in the Layers palette. Load the path as a selection by Command/Ctrl-clicking the Working Path in the Paths palette. On the transparent layer, fill the selection with black (Edit > Fill > Black). With the object still selected, Define Brush (Edit > Define Brush) and name the brush in the Brush Name dialogue. Confirm this by clicking Ok, and deselect your selection.

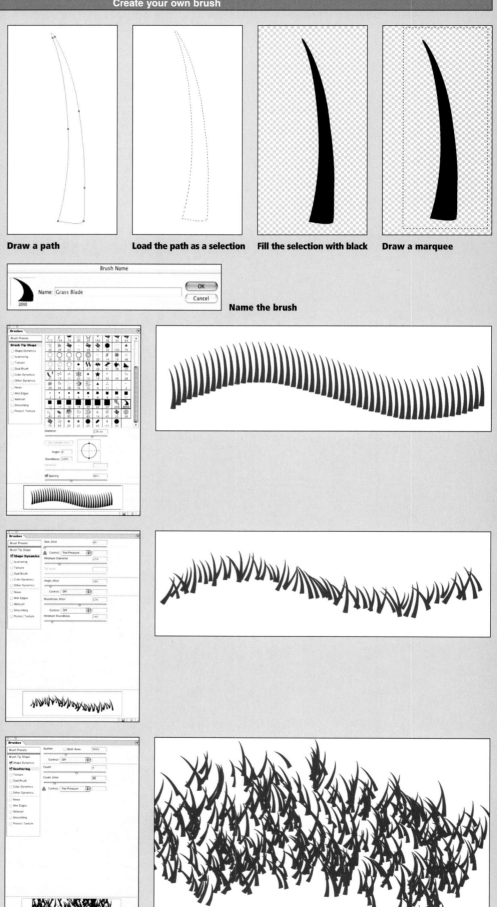

Draw a path   **Load the path as a selection**   **Fill the selection with black**   **Draw a marquee**

Name the brush

Brush tip

Select the brush tool and click on Brush Tip Shape in the Brushes palette. Our newly created brush tip will appear in the brush presets list ready to modify using the Brush palette's options. Adjust the Diameter by selecting the diameter and experient with Spacing until you're happy with the preview. Create a new document (File > New), set a suitable foreground colour and paint a few strokes to see how it looks.

Brush Shape Dynamics

Select Shape Dynamics in the Brushes palette. (Ensure that this option is not only ticked, but highlighted too.) Here we can alter the size, Angle, Diameter and Roundness of the brush shape. Here we use a Size Jitter of 50% with a Minimum Diameter of 25% which alternates the size of each brush tip. An Angle Jitter of 10% rotates the brush shape a little as you paint a stroke and the Roundness Jitter flattens the brush shape by 57% but not below 14%.

Brush Scattering

Click on Scattering in the Brushes palette.
You can scatter the brush shape by a percentage and also specify the amount of brush shapes that will appear. Here to give the feel of dense grass we use a scatter of 360%, a count of 9 to multiply the amount of grass blades and a Count Jitter of 18% to vary the density.

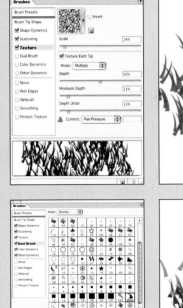

Brush Textures

Click on Texture in the Brushes palette.
You can select a Texture preset to texture your brush shape, and specify the blending mode, Depth and Depth Jitter to vary the texture for each brush shape. Here we use a Scale of 43% so the grass doesn't have too much texture. A Depth of 50% with a minimum variation of 11% gives a subtle result.

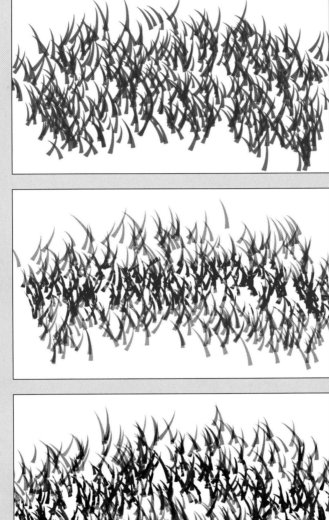

Dual Brushes

Click on Dual Brush in the Brushes palette. Dual Brush overlays an additional brush over the selected brush shape with the ability to vary blend mode, Diameter, Spacing, Scatter and Count.
Here we've selected the same settings as the original brush with a blending mode of Overlay.
The main use for this feature is to distress your brush shape, which you may or may not want.

Color Dynamics

Click on Color Dynamics in the Brushes palette.
Here you can specify variations in the colour between brush shapes. Though you only see a greyscale preview, depending on the foreground/background colours selected, the brush shapes will vary according to Hue, Saturation, Brightness and Purity Jitter.
In addition to a foreground colour of green, we set the background colour to black to add some depth.

Other Dynamics

Click on Other Dynamics in the Brushes palette.
Here you can vary the Opacity of your brush shapes according to a Jitter percentage.
The Brightness Jitter works much the same, but with the brightness of the brush shape.

2

Paths, Selections, Masks & Channels

Difficulty: Intermediate	Colin Wood

Working with difficult hair

Separating a picture from its background can be difficult, especially if the image has problem areas, such as spiky hair. Using a path can be almost impossible and may not always provide a realistic final result.

Here's another method that uses the multiply blending mode.

A bad hair day
This shot was taken in a studio against a plain background but we might want to place these figures on another background. To do that we will need a mask that will allow a new background to show through without losing too much of the image. The problem area will be around the edges of the hair.

The solution will rely on two things: making a good mask, and using the multiply blending mode on the edges of the hair to allow it to blend in with the new background.

First let's make a good mask using one of the channels as a starting point.

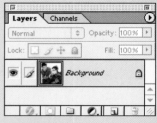

Photograph courtesy
George Fetting

Channel choice
Choose the channel that has the most density in the hair. In this case it is the Blue channel.

Red

Green

Blue

Mask metamorphosis
Duplicate the Blue channel as an alpha channel. We will use this channel to make the mask.

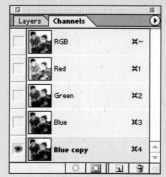

Technique overview
This technique uses two copies of the same image placed on a new background. The top layer is the contoured image in Normal blend mode. It has a layer mask that removes the edge by just a couple of pixels.

Multiply layer
Between the top layer (our main image) and the background there is the same contoured image (but this time the edge is still visible). This layer is in Multiply mode to combine it with the background. You will only see the edge in the final result.

New background
The new background will combine with the Multiply layer.

Final composite
The three layers will combine smoothly.

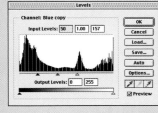

Making a mask
Use Levels (Command/Ctrl-L) and adjust the highlight slider until the background goes white (especially around the figures). Adjust the shadow slider to darken the figures as much as possible without the background becoming 'dirty'.

Tip
Don't bring the sliders together or you will delete the anti-aliasing around the figures, giving the masked image too hard an edge.

Edges rule!
Paint out the inside of the figures until you have a 'shadow mask'.

Transition pixels
A good mask will have some grey pixels around the edge that will act as 'transition' pixels between the foreground and background.

Work on sections

Some sections of your mask may require special attention. Use selections to work on particular parts of the mask.

Fine hair

This section of hair is much finer and will require special attention.

Make a selection around the section needing attention, being careful to include complete areas.

Anti-aliasing

In the Levels dialogue box, note that the values between 0 and 255 indicate the shades of grey around the edge.

If you clip them all away, you will be left with a bitmap image (and a very hard edge).

Make two masks

Here is our new mask.

In addition we will need a second mask, one that fits 'inside' this one. That is, one with a smaller sillhouette of the figures.

Duplicate your new mask and rename them 'Large' and 'Small'.

Composite view

This is a diagramatic view of the amount we need to trim off our second mask. The grey line around the figures shows the difference between the two masks.

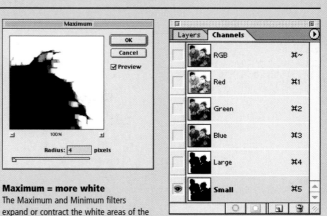

Maximum = more white

The Maximum and Minimum filters expand or contract the white areas of the mask respectively. If our mask had been the reverse (negative) of what it is, we would have needed to use the Minimum filter.

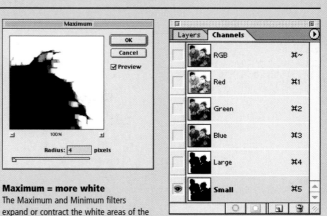

Maximum filter

We now need to make the 'Small' mask fit tighter around our figures.
Use Filter > Other > Maximum to enlarge the white part of the channel.

Which setting?

The Maximum filter works in whole pixels only (no fractions of a pixel).
Use the preview window in the Maximum dialogue box to see the result you will get.
Frequently you will find that a setting of one pixel is sufficient. Remember, you can always do it again but it is harder to undo. The radius will depend on the resolution of the image but it will probably be between 1 and 4 pixels.

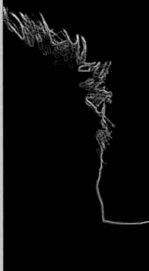

The difference

This picture shows the difference between before and after running the Maximum filter.

Invert the masks

Because we started with a copy of the Blue channel (black figures on a white background), we now need to invert both of the masks we have made (Command/Ctrl-I).
This is the (larger) mask we will use for the Multiply layer.

Mask for top layer

This is the (smaller) mask we will use for the (top) Normal layer.

Duplicate your image

Double-click on the background layer to turn it into a layer.
Duplicate the layer.

Add a new background

Create a new background and place it on a new layer.
Drag this to the bottom of the layer stack.
You are now ready to add the layer masks.

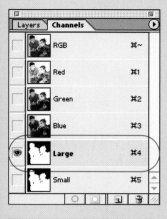

Add a layer mask

Command/Ctrl-click on the 'Large' channel to load it as a selection.

Click on the 'Multiply' layer to make it active and then (with the selection loaded), click on the Layer Mask icon.

A layer mask will be added to the 'Multiply' layer.

Then change the layer blending mode to Multiply.

You will be able to see the background through the main image.

Add another layer mask

Command/Ctrl-click on the 'Small' channel to load it as a selection.

Click on the 'Normal' layer to make it active and then (with the selection loaded), click on the Layer Mask icon.

A layer mask will be added to the 'Normal' layer.

At this stage the figures look fine against their new background.

There is just one final tweak to make to complete the illusion.

Final tweak

There is one final touch that will complete the illusion.

To smooth away any remaining hard edge, it is sometimes good to soften the edge of the mask on the Multiply layer.

Click on the layer mask to make it active. Use Filter > Blur > Gaussian Blur to bring up the Gaussian Blur dialogue box. Blur the mask by a small amount. As the RGB image is visible while the layer mask is active, you will be able to see the result before you commit.

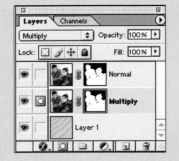

Before Gaussian Blur on the layer mask

After Gaussian Blur on the layer mask

Good hair day
Never be afraid of whispy hair again!
Once you get into the swing of this technique you will find it relatively quick and easy to do, and well worth the effort.

Final composite

Difficulty: Easy	Colin Wood

Manipulating selections

When you need to mask out a shape that has regular curves, do you trust your painting skills? How steady is your hand? If the shape is a circle, the job is easy. But it's not so easy when the circle is on an angle and you have an ellipse to deal with. Your secret weapon is Transform within Quick Mask.

There are many occasions when you need to make selections that are not quite a regular geometric shape. Here's a way to use the built-in features of Adobe Photoshop to create a precise irregular selection. You'll find that it's not only easy, but saves a lot of time too.

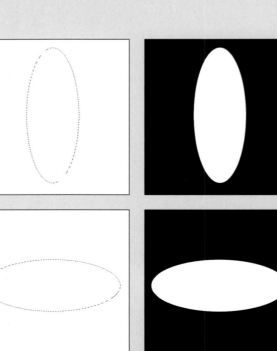

Vertical selection
One of Photoshop's limitations is that the standard tools only create selections in horizontal or vertical orientations. Here is a vertical ellipse shown as both a selection and as a channel.

Click here to turn a selection into a Quick Mask.

Horizontal selection
And here it is in the only other orientation—horizontal.
A selection can be saved as a channel and can also be made into a Quick Mask.
A Quick Mask is a little like a layer mask that can be 'painted' to make alterations.

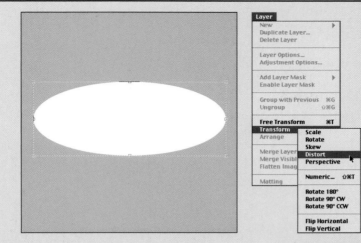

Transformation trick

Now here's the magic! You can use the Transform command on a Quick Mask to make it into an irregular geometric shape.
To transform your Quickmask selection, go to
Edit > Transform (Cmd/T). This creates a bounding box around the selection with handles on the corners and sides.
Once you have the transform bounding box, you can simply pull out the corner or side handles to change the shape of your selection.

Note: A drop-down list of individual Transform functions (such as Scale, Rotate, etc.) can be accessed via Edit > Transform.

Transform Options

You can also be more precise when using the Transform command. Using the Tool Options Bar, you can specify numerical values of your choice. Here we were able to accurately rotate the selection 45° (which is counter clockwise).

Carrying out the Transform function on a Quick Mask is much the same as applying it to a channel. However, in Quick Mask mode you can see the image you are working on at the same time, allowing accurate adjustments to be made.
In this example only the Quick Mask is shown for clarity.

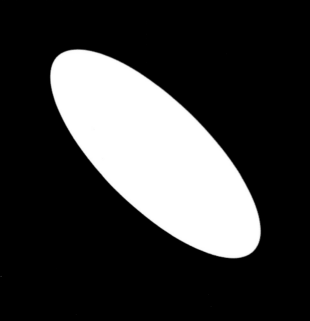

A mask created in Quick Mask mode can be converted into a selection (above), and it is always a good idea to save a selection as a channel (right).

Turn the page for a typical application of this technique.

Background to Layer

It is possible to carry out the Quick Mask technique shown here, and save the selection as a channel, if your file is only a background layer.

But if you intend to use the selection as a layer mask, you will need to double-click your background to turn it into a regular layer.

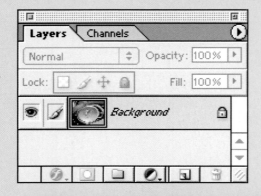

Ellipse

Here is a typical image from which you may wish to extract a circular item. The problem is that almost all circular objects in the real world aren't circles at all. They're ellipses.

How do you mask them?

Quick Mask to the rescue!

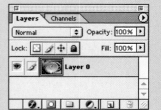

Make a selection

Choose the Elliptical Marquee Tool from the Tool palette and create an elliptical selection. Make one that is complete (doesn't run off into the pasteboard) and is as large as will easily fit into your image size.

Quick Mask

In the Tool palette, change to edit Quick Mask Mode. Your image will now look like this.

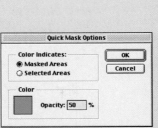

Quick change
The default colour for a Quick Mask is red. If you'd like to change the colour, double-click on the Quick Mask icon in the Tool Palette to bring up the Quick Mask Options.

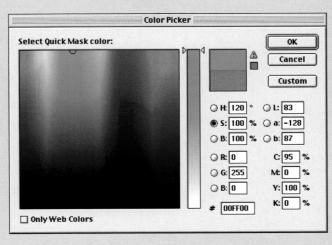

It's easier being green
Then click inside the sample colour patch to bring up the Color Picker.
You will find that 100% green is easier to see than red in most cases.
Change the Red to zero and the Green to 255.

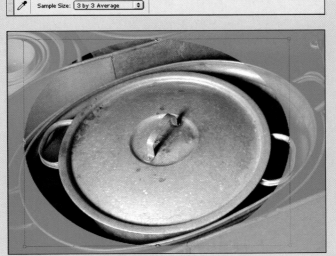

A different angle
In Quick Mask Mode, use Command/Ctrl-T to bring up the Transform marquee.
All of the Transform variations are available.
In order to fit the ellipse over the shape, the marquee handles must lie on the 'x' and 'y' axes.
Move the cursor near the corner handles to bring up the rotation cursor to change the angle.
Move the side handles to change the size.

Harder than it looks
Even a trained eye can find it tricky to line up the handles with the axes first time.
The trick is to move one of the sides close to the object and see which way the shape bulges away from the object.
The red lines show the 'x' and 'y' axes which is where we want to end up.

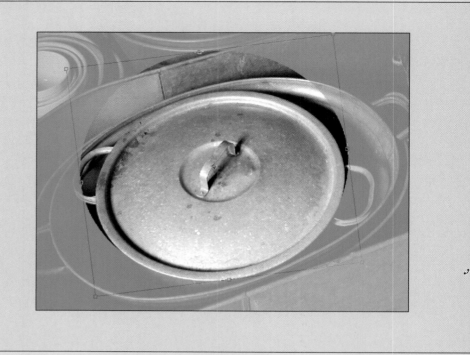

Touch down
Get one handle in place first in such a way that the bulge is symetrical against the object.

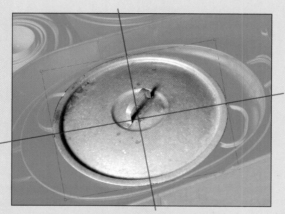

Closing in
By adjusting side and corner handles and tweaking the rotation, you will be able to close in on your target. Hit Enter to commit the transform.

Final adjustment
Once you have committed the transform it is possible to make a further transform, but the marquee will be at right angles to the image frame.
Thus you cannot 'undo' a transform in that way. But you can make limited adjustments.

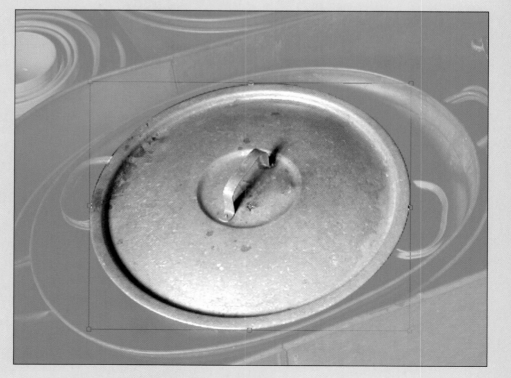

Final selection

In the Tool palette, click the icon to change back to Edit in Standard Mode.
Your new selection will appear. Now, before you do anything else, save the selection as a channel and then immediately save the file.

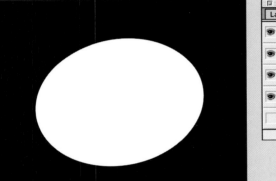

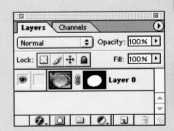

Save as channel

To save the selection, in the Channels palette, click on the Save Selection as Channel icon.

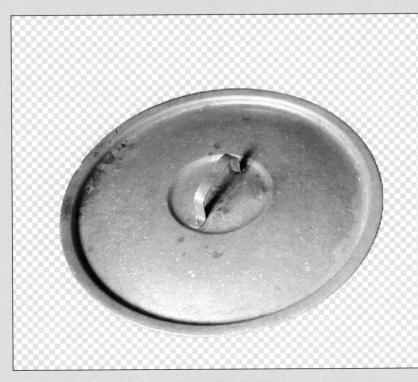

Add a layer mask

With the selection loaded and the target layer active, click on the Add Layer Mask icon to add the selection as a layer mask, thus hiding all the areas that are black on the mask.

You need never be afraid of odd circular selections again.
Just remember to use the transform function within Quick Mask to home in on your target.

Colin Wood

Creative Calculations

Difficulty: Intermediate

Calculations can make the task of producing complicated alpha channels as easy and quick as clicking a button. Photoshop's live preview allows you to see the result you will get, blending modes give you flexibility and the addition of a mask widens your creative possibilities.

Image Calculations is an area of Photoshop that most people seem to stay away from. They think it's hard. You may think that you have to do mathematical calculations yourself. You don't. Photoshop does that for you and makes it easy to see what's happening due to the live preview.

In this tip you will see how Calculations work, how to use blending modes in Calculations and how to modify the result with a mask.

Finally you will see how to use a Calculation with a mask to expand your creative possibilities.

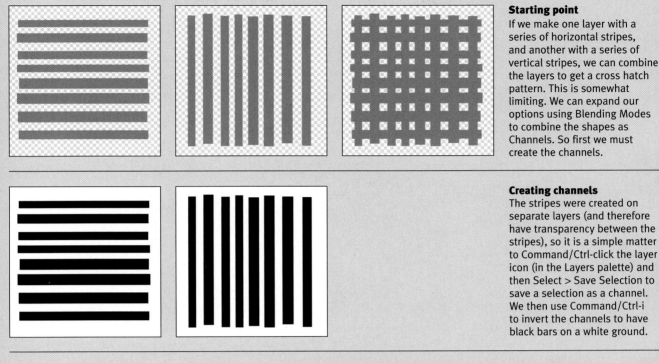

Starting point

If we make one layer with a series of horizontal stripes, and another with a series of vertical stripes, we can combine the layers to get a cross hatch pattern. This is somewhat limiting. We can expand our options using Blending Modes to combine the shapes as Channels. So first we must create the channels.

Creating channels

The stripes were created on separate layers (and therefore have transparency between the stripes), so it is a simple matter to Command/Ctrl-click the layer icon (in the Layers palette) and then Select > Save Selection to save a selection as a channel. We then use Command/Ctrl-i to invert the channels to have black bars on a white ground.

Name your channels

Rename the channels so that you can identify them easily in the Calculations dialogue box.

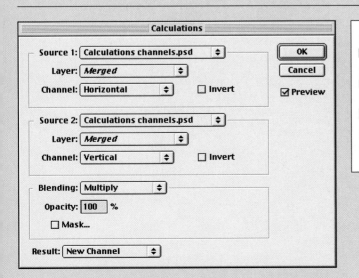

Calculations default

Use Image > Calculations to bring up the Calculations dialogue box.

Your preview will look like this using the Multiply blend mode. This simply combines the stripes of each channel and puts the combination in a new channel.

Now we are ready to experiment with the blend modes.

Calculations – The basics using blend modes

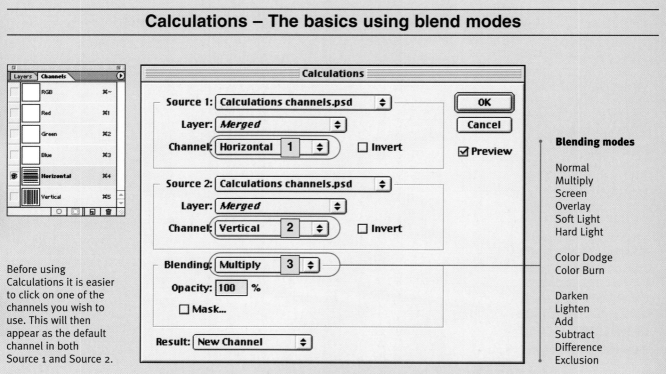

Blending modes

Normal
Multiply
Screen
Overlay
Soft Light
Hard Light

Color Dodge
Color Burn

Darken
Lighten
Add
Subtract
Difference
Exclusion

Before using Calculations it is easier to click on one of the channels you wish to use. This will then appear as the default channel in both Source 1 and Source 2.

Select the two channels you wish to use (interact) using the pull-down menus under Source 1 and Source 2.
Then select a blend mode. The preview will show the result, which can be a new document (very useful if you have run out of channels), another channel or a selection. Here are the results of combing our horizontal and vertical stripes using all of the available blend modes (Dissolve, Hue, Saturation, Color and Luminosity are not available in Calculations).

Normal	Multiply	Screen	Overlay
Soft Light	Hard Light	Color Dodge	Color Burn
Darken	Lighten	Add	Subtract
Darken	Exclusion		

Working with masks

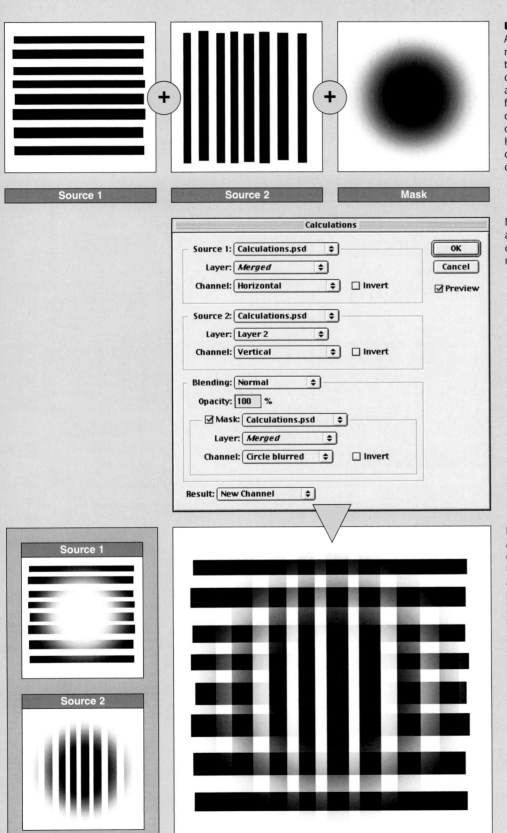

Source 1 + **Source 2** + **Mask**

Source 1

Source 2

Using a mask
A third channel can be used to modify the result of combining two channels. This third channel can be from the current file or another file. It can be made from the file's layers singularly or merged, any of the channels or a current selection.
Here we have created a blurred circle to demonstrate the effect of a mask on a calculation.

Note that when you select a different layer, the mask channel resets itself and must be reselected.

How a mask works
A mask works in opposite ways on the two source channels. Using the Normal blend mode, it acts as a positive mask on Source 1 (just like adding the blurred circle as a layer mask) and a negative mask on Source 2. Different blend modes give different results.

Let's compare

Let's see how straight two-channel calculations compare with some using a mask. Here is our original image that we will use to create an alpha channel to be used in combination with a second channel.

Original

Calculations (no mask)

Source channels

We have taken the channel with the biggest range of tones (in this case it is the Red Channel) and copied it as an alpha channel. We will use this as one of the source channels for the calculations.

We have prepared a 'tunnel' of concentric squares in another alpha channel that we will use as the second source channel.

Source 2

Source 1

Calculations without a mask

While a variety of combinations are possible using blend modes, there are almost no calculation examples in which all of the tunnel and the butterfly can be seen together.

This is because the tunnel is solid black and white. The only exceptions are Difference and Exclusion.

Screen

Overlay

Soft Light

Subtract

Multiply

Difference

Togetherness

The Multiply blend mode gives an interesting result but the butterfly and the tunnel share some black areas.

Confusing alternation

The Difference blend mode gives some interesting results, although the alternating blacks and whites can be confusing.

Design Graphics Photoshop Studio Skills 1

Calculations using a mask

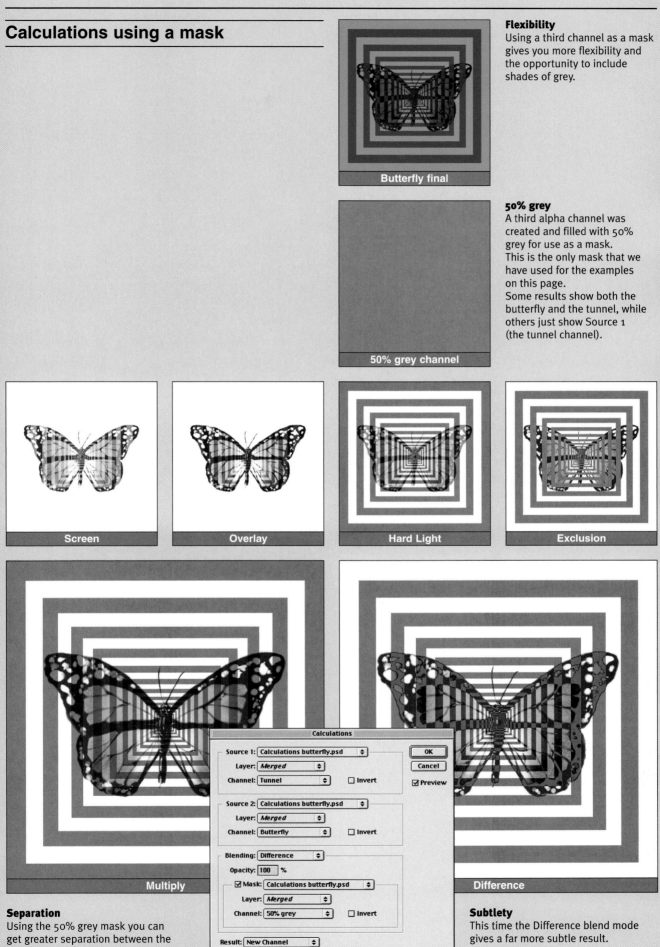

Butterfly final

Flexibility
Using a third channel as a mask gives you more flexibility and the opportunity to include shades of grey.

50% grey channel

50% grey
A third alpha channel was created and filled with 50% grey for use as a mask.
This is the only mask that we have used for the examples on this page.
Some results show both the butterfly and the tunnel, while others just show Source 1 (the tunnel channel).

Screen

Overlay

Hard Light

Exclusion

Multiply

Difference

Calculations

Source 1: Calculations butterfly.psd
Layer: Merged
Channel: Tunnel   ☐ Invert

Source 2: Calculations butterfly.psd
Layer: Merged
Channel: Butterfly   ☐ Invert

Blending: Difference
Opacity: 100 %
☑ Mask: Calculations butterfly.psd
Layer: Merged
Channel: 50% grey   ☐ Invert

Result: New Channel

OK
Cancel
☑ Preview

Separation
Using the 50% grey mask you can get greater separation between the two source channels.

Subtlety
This time the Difference blend mode gives a far more subtle result.

Design Graphics Photoshop Studio Skills 1

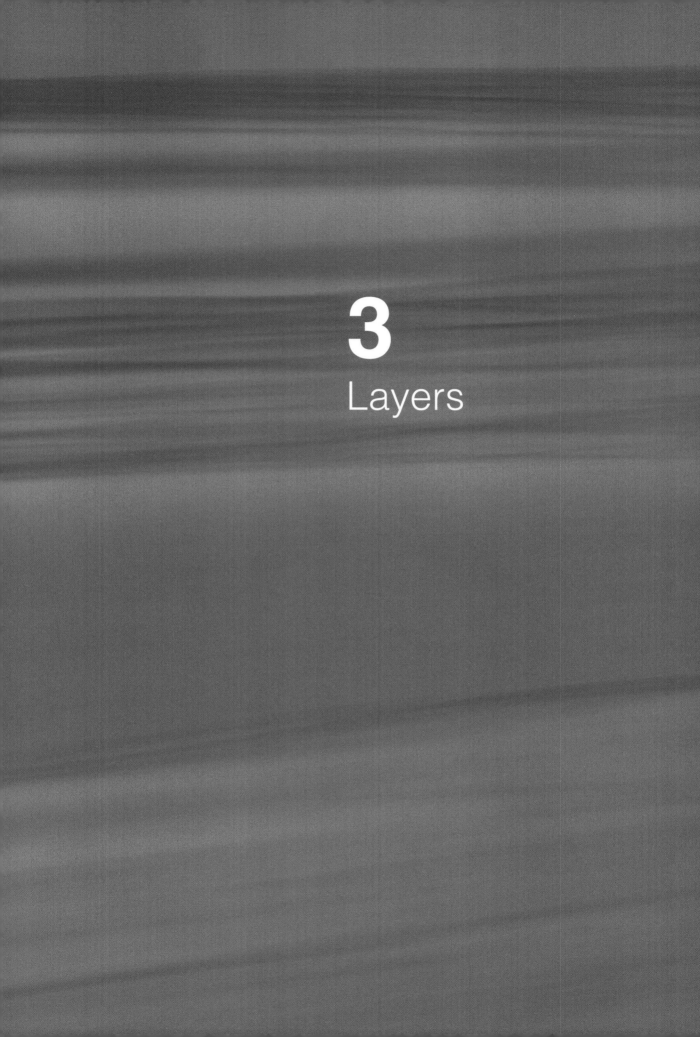

3
Layers

Difficulty: Easy	Colin Wood

Pasteboard blues no more

In Photoshop, what you get is sometimes not what you see. This is particularly true if your original image extends beyond the image boundaries onto the 'pasteboard'. Although you are not actually seeing the entire image, it is all there. Out of sight should not be out of mind!

Starting with a white square
What you see is this.
But what you don't see
may affect what you do.

Pasteboard — Image — Pasteboard

Tip:
To take advantage of Photoshop's ability to 'hide' elements on the pasteboard, you'll need to float the background layer. Double-click on the Background layer and click Ok.

Now you see it ...
During work on your image, the pasteboard can get quite full. Here we have assumed that our white square is surrounded by a black frame that we can only see with the Reveal All command (Image>Reveal All).

The Photoshop pasteboard is not like those in other applications such as QuarkXPress, PageMaker, Illustrator, FreeHand and so on in that you cannot see it (unless you use the Reveal All command).
Items can be dragged back into view in the image window but cannot be viewed, even by zooming out.

Pasteboard

Image

Pasteboard

Blurred vision
If you blur what appears to be a white square, expect the unexpected!
The black on the pasteboard has blurred into view.

Gaussian Blur
OK
Cancel
☑ Preview
17%
Radius: 100 pixels

This is how our complete image looks including the pasteboard which is out of sight.
(above)

All we can see is the centre section.
(right)

The implications
The influence of the 'pasteboard' has serious implications for the shapes of things in your image.
For instance, you may wish to add a drop shadow to a layer. So you select all of the pixels on that layer (Command/Ctrl-A), click on the layer in the Layers palette, make a new layer and fill that selection with your shadow colour. This is ok as it will make a selection of only the pixels that you see.
But, if you copy the complete layer, you take the pasteboard as well.

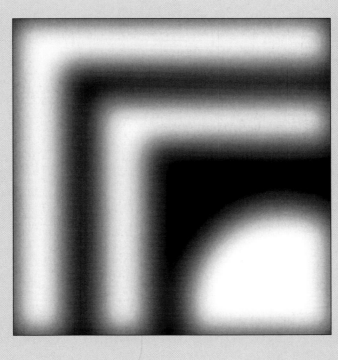

Out of shape
After applying a Gaussian Blur to the image, the 'L' shapes have rounded ends and the circle has become decidedly oval.
By copying the layer into the new image we have taken the pasteboard with it.
(You will see this if you select Image > Reveal All).

So how do we fix this problem?

The solution

Before applying the Gaussian Blur, make sure that there is nothing on the pasteboard on the layer to be blurred.

This is achieved by selecting all (Cmd/Ctrl A) and cropping (Image > Crop) the image.

Note: The Crop command applies to all layers in your file, including those not currently active.

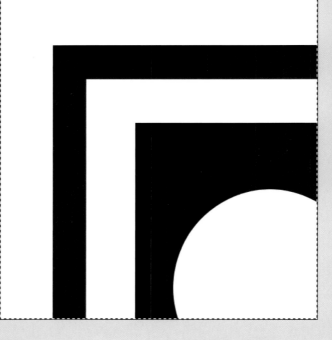

Reveal All

Reveal All helps you see what lies beyond the boundaries of your image. But there's one small problem: if you do some work on the image you cannot go back to its previous crop state (before Reveal All was applied). Solution: Create an extra layer of your image as it extends to the pasteboard and fill the area that you have cropped with a flat colour, then Add guides to the area that was originally cropped. Crop your image by altering the canvas size (Image > Canvas size) instead of the Crop tool. It's perfect as, unlike the crop tool, it won't throw away any pixels on any layer.

All correct

Now everything on the pasteboard has disappeared. Use Reveal All (Image > Reveal All) to check.

Notice that the Gaussian Blur filter has affected only the pixels that you can see.

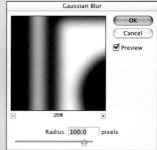

Example
Done incorrectly, this drop shadow includes parts of the unwanted image on the pasteboard.
So why have this ...

The example below shows what happens if you offset the shadow layer after cropping it - the bottom edges of the image which are necessary for a satisfactory blur are missing.

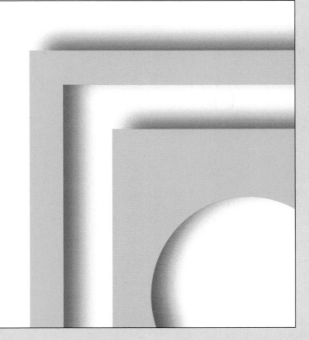

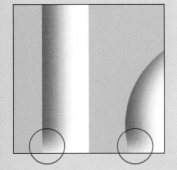

... when you can have this?

Correct drop shadow
To achieve the correct drop shadow (right), it was necessary to offset the shadow layer first and delete unwanted parts of the image that had moved in from the pasteboard.
It was then a simple matter to crop the image as described previously before applying the Gaussian Blur.

In this tip we show you how to restore the image canvas size and position within Reveal all. (mentioned earlier)

Work in progress
So here is your work in progress. A file with four layers, two of which extend beyond the canvas size, with neither of the other two touching all sides.

Reveal All
You want to see what you have on the pasteboard so you use Image > Reveal All. Photoshop does a great job of revealing every pixel on every layer.
If you want to back up (immediately) to the smaller size you can use Undo (Command/Ctrl-Z) or the History Palette. But if you do some more work on the image you cannot back up to the previous crop state without losing your recent work. Photoshop does not cache the canvas size.
However, all may not be lost.

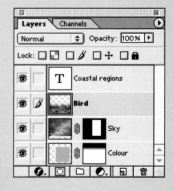

Thinking ahead
If we had thought ahead we would have created an extra layer and filled it with a flat colour.
Or we could have created an alpha channel filled with white. When the canvas size is increased the new area will fill with black.

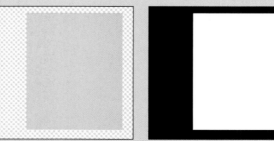

Save with a different name
One way out of this dilemma is to save your file with a different name. Then you can use the previously saved version as a reference.
If you hadn't yet saved the file, guides are your best choice.

Strategy
Our strategy will be to locate guide lines at the previous edges.

Tactics
Assuming that we did not think ahead, we are left to find ways of locating guide lines at the edges of the previous canvas size.

Clues
Let's examine the layers to see how they can help.

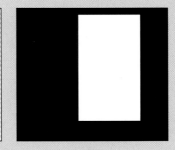

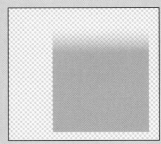

Bird
The bird gives us no clues at all. It was brought in as a complete image before we decided which portion to use.

Sky
The sky gives nothing but …

Sky layer mask
… its layer mask (being white where you see the image) has a black border due to the extended canvas size. A selection based on this channel will give us the top edge.

Colour
This is the best as it gives us the left, right and bottom edges.

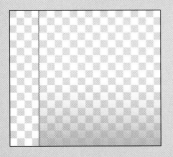

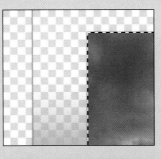

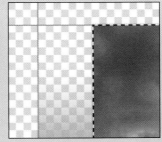

Add guides
There are two qualities about guides that you can use:
• Guides will snap to pixels on the current layer.
• Guides will snap to selections. For layer masks, Cmd-click on the channel layer mask to load the mask as a selection.
• In both cases, guides will snap to the mid-point of blurred areas.

Tips for Guides
• To access the guides, use View > Show Rulers (Cmd/Ctrl-R) and simply click and drag guides from the rulers.
• Guides will snap to the edges of an image on layers but not on a background layer.
• Guides snap to pixels on the current layer, not pixels that are on other layers.
• If you have an active selection, guides will snap only to that selection (even on a background layer).
• The Marquee and Crop Tools snap to visible guides. If the guides are hidden (View > Hide Rulers or Cmd/Ctrl-R) no snapping takes place.
• Guides will snap to the mid-point of a blurred selection.

Crop tools - destructive
• With an active selection created with any of the Marquee Tools, Image > Crop will reduce the canvas size (to a rectangle) and throw away all pixels outside that rectangle on all layers.
• The Crop Tool may also throw away pixels outside the resulting cropped image (with the Delete option selected), or preserve them (with the Hide option).

Crop Tools - non-destructive
• Altering the canvas size (Image > Canvas size) does not throw away any pixels on any layer. This is why it is perfect for this problem.
• The Crop Tool can also be used to enlarge the canvas.

Crop Tool finale
Use the Crop Tool which will snap to the guides and shield the area to be cropped.
Select the Hide option in the Options Bar to preserve image areas on the pasteboard.
Caution: ensure that the Delete option is not selected.

Difficulty: Easy	Julieanne Kost

Just passing through

There's a new blend mode in town called Pass Through and you're going to want it. Available when using Photoshop 6.0's (or later) Layer Sets, it offers the ability to control how layers interact with each other. Julieanne Kost shows you where you'll want to use it.

Layer Sets
Adobe Photoshop 6 introduced Layer Sets allowing layers to be grouped together. The advantage of being able to group layers is that you can move them as a group, apply attributes or a mask to the group, or collapse the group to save palette space.

Blending modes
Layer Sets also offer to double your pleasure by being able to apply blending modes to an entire layer set.
This is in addition to applying blending modes to individual layers.
What's more, you can do both at the same time!
So you can use two blending modes simultaneously.

Pass Through & Normal
The Pass Through blending mode is unique to layer sets (individual layers don't have it) and is selected by default. This means that the layer set has no blending properties of its own.

Layers and adjustment layers inside a layer set in **Pass Through** mode appear the same as they would outside of the layer set.
They also interact with the layers underneath the layer set.

Layers and adjustment layers in a layer set in **Normal** blending mode do not interact with layers outside of the set.
This can give you a wide range of opportunities.

Blending mode and sequence
Changing the blend mode of a layer set changes the order in which your image is composited.
Layers within a set are composited first, then composited as a single image with the rest of the layers in the image using the selected blending mode.

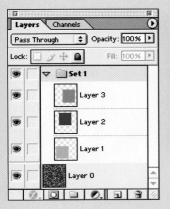

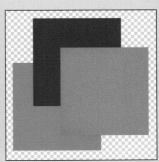

Layer set

Here we have a file with three layers in a set plus a background.
The layer set is set to the default Pass Through blending mode.

Everything is normal

If we view all of the layers and have them all in Normal blending mode, the file will look like this.

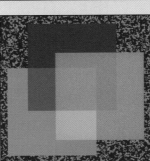

Hard Light layers

Now we have the red and purple squares in Hard Light blending mode. The cyan square is in Normal mode.
The layer set is also in Normal mode.
The layers in the set interact with each other, but not with the background.

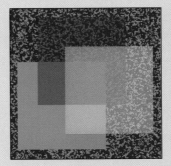

Pass Through layer set

The layers within the set are as they were above, but this time the layer set is in Pass Through mode.
The two squares that are in Hard Light mode interact with the background.
The cyan square, being in Normal mode, does not.

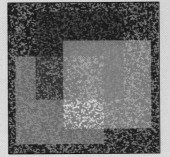

Pass Through layer set

Everything stays the same as above except that the layer set is now in Hard Light mode.
This time all layers interact with background.

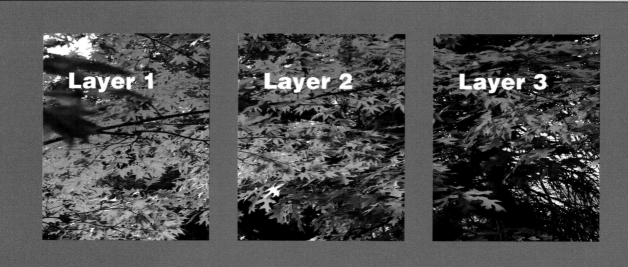

Three into one

Here we have three elements on separate layers that combine to form one image, a triptych of autumn leaves.
So that we can treat the layers as one element, they are together in a layer set.
They sit against a grey background.
For creative effect we wish to change the colours of the leaves.

Hue/Saturation

To adjust the colours of the leaves we can add a single Hue/Saturation adjustment layer within the layer set.

Default mode

Notice that the default blending mode for the layer set is Pass Through.

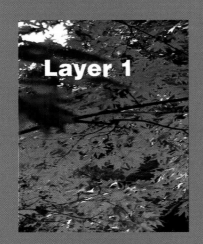
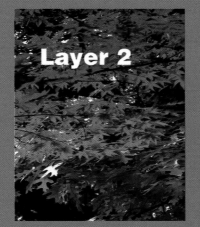
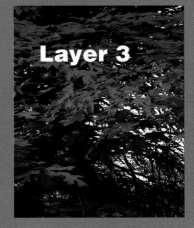

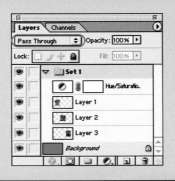

All change

The colours of the leaves have changed; but so has the colour of the background!
Because the layer set blending mode is Pass Through (the default setting), the Hue/Saturation adjustment is affecting the background too.

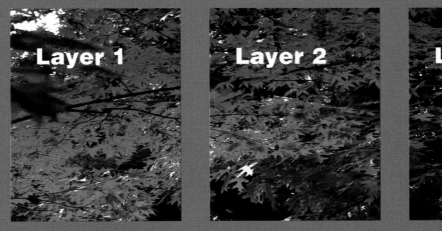
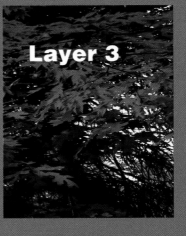

Ah, that's better!

By changing the layer set to Normal blending mode, the Hue/Saturation adjustment now affects only the layers within the layer set, leaving the background unaffected.

4

Colour Effects & Correction

Adding body

Difficulty: Intermediate	Colin Wood

When an image is slim on tonal range, a simple levels adjustment can throw away detail and add too much contrast. Here's how to use multiple layers of an image using blending modes to add body, curves to add contrast and saturation to bring out the color. It's a natural!

**Take a tour of the various steps of image refinement and learn how an image lacking life and lustre can be transformed into one that is bright, more colourful and has more contrast. The key to this quick fix?
Soft light, curves, hue/saturation and a touch of the original.**

Play misty for me
The problems with this image are evident in the Levels histogram: no black or white points, just shades of gray.

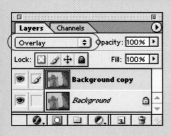

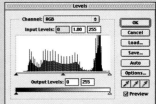

If you need some body
Duplicate the background layer and change the blending mode to Overlay. This will make the dark areas darker and the light areas lighter. This will add contrast and extend the tonal range at both ends. At 100% opacity it can be a little harsh.

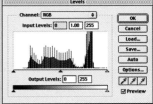

Soften up
The Soft Light mode can be used to create an effect similar to Overlay, but less harshly. The histograms tell the story. This is sometimes sufficient to improve an image.
But what if you want to add even more contrast?

110

Cautious of Curves?

Many people stay away from Curves adjustments as they don't understand it and it looks so simple that it must be really complicated!

Curves adjustments are very powerful and some people would use nothing else.

The main problem is that there is no 'make better' button. Even using the 'Auto' function leaves the RGB curve unaltered. Quite baffling!

However, there are some quite simple adjustments that can be made. One such is the 'S' curve.

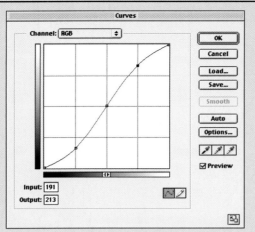

The 'S' curve

The 'S' curve will add contrast and saturation, so it is the ideal tool to add body to a feint image.

Click in the middle to lock the mid-point. Push the highlights up and the shadows down as shown.

Curves adjustment

Make a Curves adjustment layer and create an 'S' curve as shown above.

You can always check the histogram in the Levels dialogue box to check your progress.

How are we doing?

The adjustments we have made increase contrast and saturation, and therefore can introduce some unwanted characteristics.

To check the colour shift, create a Hue/Saturation adjustment layer and increase the saturation to +100.

You may be surprised what you see but it will give you a good idea of the direction your image is travelling.

Remain in the Hue/Saturation dialog box as you will now be inserting a more realistic value.

For checking purposes only

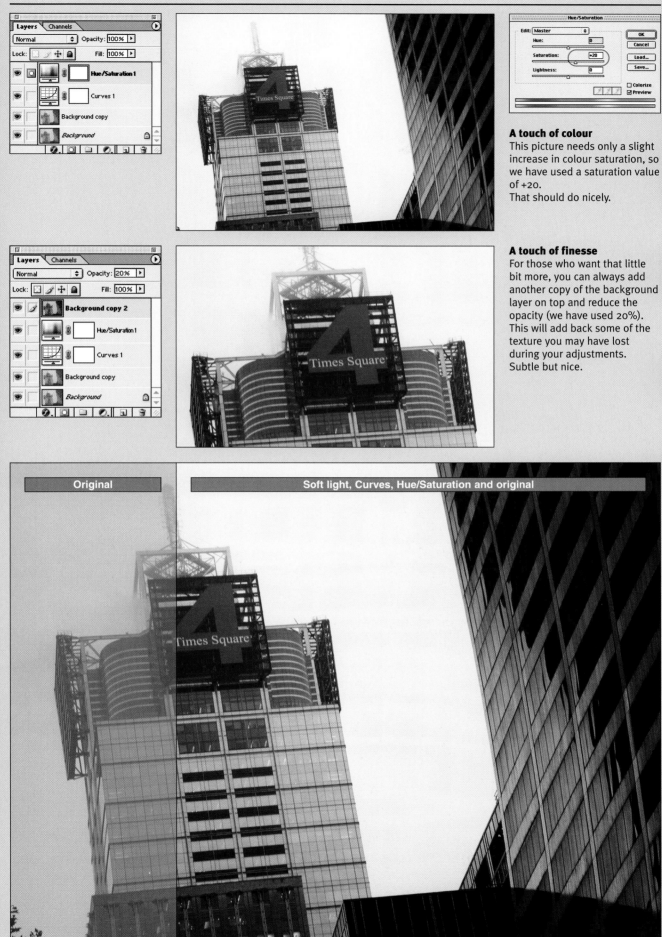

A touch of colour
This picture needs only a slight increase in colour saturation, so we have used a saturation value of +20.
That should do nicely.

A touch of finesse
For those who want that little bit more, you can always add another copy of the background layer on top and reduce the opacity (we have used 20%). This will add back some of the texture you may have lost during your adjustments. Subtle but nice.

Original

Soft light, Curves, Hue/Saturation and original

	Difficulty: Easy	Carl Stevens
Sepia tints	There are a number of ways to convert a greyscale image into a sepia toned image for reproduction using four-colour process printing. Carl Stevens shows us one of his favourite techniques, which will enable you to save your settings and apply these same effects to other images for greater consistency.	

Sepia tints add an emotional quality that is especially useful for certain images. It softens, it ages, it can distance the image from the hustle and bustle of modern urban life.

Afghanistan - photograph reproduced courtesy of **George Fetting.**

Creating a Sepia Tint

If your chosen image is RGB or CMYK, for best results you must first convert it to greyscale.

Scanning

The first step, of course, is to scan in the original black and white image as a greyscale— remember that the better quality scan you begin with, the better the final sepia result.

Select all and Copy. It is important to Copy at this stage so that you use the greyscale image to create CMYK channels.

CMYK

The next step is to change the mode to CMYK.
From the Image menu, select Image > Mode > CMYK Color.

Select all and delete the image. Your screen will look like this, but don't panic! You have an image on the clipboard.

04 - Colour effects & Correction

Changing channels

Go to the Channels palette and select the Magenta channel. Paste the (greyscale) image you originally copied onto the clipboard into the Magenta channel.

Two more channels

Now do the same for the yellow and Black channels. You should have three channels where you have pasted the original image. Using only three channels provides the best sepia brown.

Adjusting the Curves

So far so good, but the image looks a little muddy.

Now we will adjust the curves on each channel separately until we have the desired result.

Choose the CMYK composite channel in the Channels palette. Select Curves (Image > Adjustments > Curves).

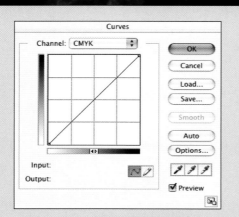

Adjusting curves

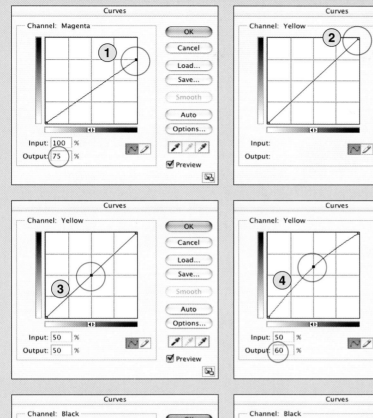

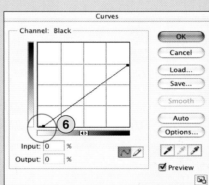

It is important that you make all of the channel curve adjustments in one operation. In this way you can double-check your progress as the results will be shown progressively in your image. Use the drop-down Channel menu to adjust the curves of each channel individually.

Magenta
1. Reduce the shadows to 75%.

Yellow
2. Leave 100% in the shadows.
3 & 4. Pull up the curve in the midtones to increase it by 10% to an output level of 60%.

Black
5. Reduce the shadows to 75%.
6. Reduce highlights by 5%. You can also pull down the midtones in the Black so that the colour will show through more in the mid and quartertones.

Because the changes are shown progressively on screen, you can make minor adjustments in any channel until you have the desired effect.

Saving curves
If you wish to apply these curves to more images, you need to save the settings before you close the dialogue box.

You will also find that different clients will have different ideas on what looks best, so you can save each set of curves with the client's name.

The final result will give you a sepia tone that is rich in colour and ready for output in CMYK.

Difficulty: Easy	Carl Stevens

Removing colour casts

Finding the ideal image may require some extra work to suit your purposes. The lighting may not give you the effect you want, or there may be a colour cast. Carl Stevens shows you how to use Photoshop's Curves to quickly colour correct an image.

Image courtesy of **Photoessentials** from the **Real Australia** collection.

Too warm

You've received a picture to be used in an ad campaign. It's a nice sunset shot, though we don't want the scene or the people's flesh tones looking so warm.

Note
The following technique works best with RGB images.

Curves

We want to make the scene a little cooler, so select Curves (Image > Adjustments > Curves). Curves allows you to adjust the tonal range of an image by either manually adjusting the tonal curve or choosing white, black and midpoints.

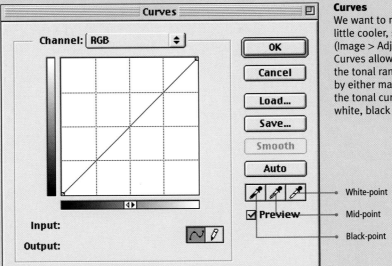

Curves

Channel: RGB

OK
Cancel
Load...
Save...
Smooth
Auto

Preview

Input:
Output:

White-point
Mid-point
Black-point

In the Curves dialogue we'll use the black, white and midpoints to correct the colour for this image. First look for a reference in your image that you have a good idea what the colour should be. Feel free to experiment with different points in the image. You can easily undo a selection and try another point.

Setting the midpoint	Setting the black point

Setting the mid-point
In this case, we want to set the midpoint (neutral grey) which could either be the water tank in the background or the man's trousers.
To set the midpoint, click on the midpoint eyedropper, then click on the part of your image you want to be neutral grey (the side of the water tank).

Setting the black-point
In this case the shadows under the water tank look to provide the darkest area of the image. Click on the black-point eyedropper, then click on the part of your image you want to be neutral grey (beneath the water tank).

Setting the white point

Setting the white-point
There are a few options here:
the man's shirt, the woman's
dress or even the highlight
on the water tank.
Click on each of the points
to see which gives the best
result. In this case, we set the
white-point on the man's shirt.

Ready for any purpose
Setting the three points in the
image neutralise the warmth
of the sunset in the image.
If we wanted to take just the
man from the background,
he would happily sit on a
coloured background without
looking out of place.

| Difficulty: Easy | Carl Stevens |

Tonal range improvement

Carl Stevens takes the next step with Photoshop's Curves to improve flat images that lack dynamic tonal range. By setting black (shadow) and white (highlight) points, he uses Curves and adjusts the HSB brightness value to improve the image considerably. Judge for yourself!

As you can see with the histogram of the original image, the majority of image data is in the shadow end which corresponds with the darkness of the image.

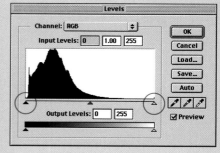

Auto in Curves
Our original image is flat with the face in shadow judging from the light on the girl's shoulder.

Using Auto in Curves
does not improve the image significantly. While the automatic adjustments have been made taking the whole picture into account, it is the face that we wish to correct.

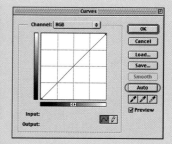

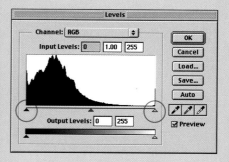

By selecting Auto in the Curves dialogue, Black and White points are set. However, as you can see by the result, there is not a great deal of difference between the two images.

Image courtesy of **PhotoEssentials**
(number 011): **'Images of the World'**.

Auto Curves
Start by selecting Auto in the
Curves dialogue to set white
and black points. Now double-
click on the highlight eye
dropper.
The default reading should be
255 in each of R, G and B and 0,
0, 0, 0 in CMYK *(below)*.

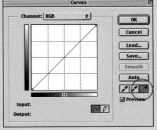

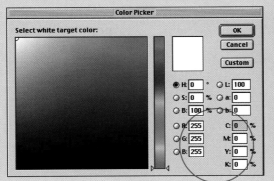

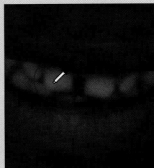

Sample a white point
When the Color Picker is
active, the cursor changes
to an eyedropper. Click the
eyedropper in the teeth to take
a reading of the pixel colour.

The colour will appear in the
Color Picker together with four
colour space values (HSB, LAB,
RGB and CMYK).

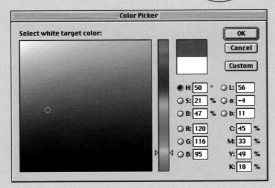

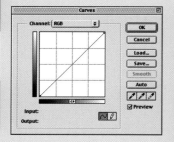

There are many times when colours are not what you think they will be. In this case the colour of the teeth (as it appears in the image) is quite dark. We know that in real life the colour will be much lighter. Seeing is believing; but always be cautious when making comparative judgements concerning colour.

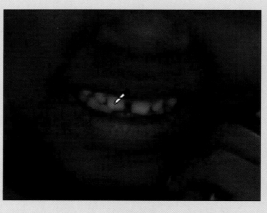

The Curves dialogue box will still be open to access the Color Picker during the following operations.

The original colour of the teeth is quite dark, mainly because the face is in shadow. The Brightness reading is 50%.

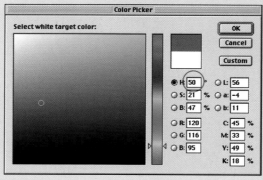

Increase the brightness
To brighten the image we will raise the Brightness percentage in the Color Picker to 80%. This will brighten the entire image. Notice that, with this change, the Hue and Saturation remain unaltered. However, the CMYK values will change.

Click OK to commit the change. This will return you to the Curves dialogue box.

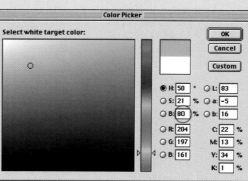

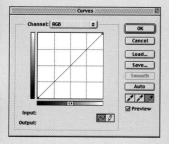

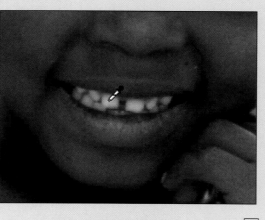

The new, lighter colour is still within the hue range of the original.

With the highlight eyedropper still selected, click in the same spot on the teeth. The result is a brightening of the image overall.

Before and after
The before and after shots show how
dark the original image is and the obvious
improvement in the final result.
Experiment with brightness values on
a case by case basis for the best results
on different images.

Difficulty: Easy	Carl Stevens

Using Curves on midtones

Over the years too many people have used Curves and Levels simply by hitting the 'Auto' button, often destroying any mood that was in the original shot. In this article Carl Stevens takes the mystery out of Curves, demonstrating how to achieve improvements and special effects in minutes.

You start with this

Applying Auto Curves you get this

We show you how to get this

Image courtesy of **PhotoEssentials**
(number 064): **Ganges River, Varanasi.**

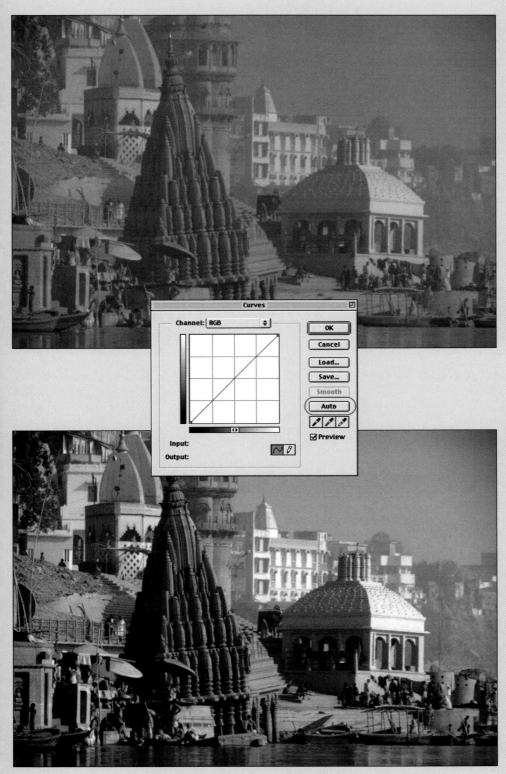

Setting the points

Here is picture waiting to become a problem. The colour palette is a mixture of sympathetic hues and tones. We would like to take out some of the cast and give the image a greater dynamic range so that it will print with truer white and black points.

Curves

Start by opening the curves dialogue box (Command/Ctrl M). Hit the Auto button and see what happens.

Auto Curves

The outcome is that the blacks are now balanced and the whites neutral but to achieve this result, the mood and lighting of the shot have been lost. Morning and afternoon light each have specific characteristics and our original, shot in dusky, pink light, has colour and mood characteristics that we want to retain.

But don't despair. Photoshop has a built-in feature to help you replace the original lighting once you have corrected the black and white points.

Save this image with a different name so that you can compare the results.

Grey balance
Open the Curves dialogue box
again but this time, before using
Auto, double-click on the grey
balance eyedropper.
This brings up the Color Picker.

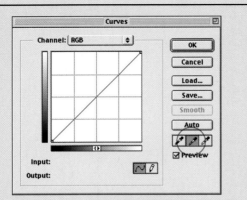

Color Picker
You will notice that in the Color
Picker, the RGB values for the
midtones are all set at 127.
Which makes sense because,
for RGB images, the Curves
dialogue box shows brightness
values from 0 to 255.

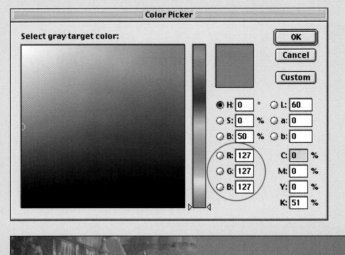

Sample a midtone
With the Color Picker still open,
move the cursor back over the
image. The cursor will change to
an eyedropper and you can
sample a typical midtone. We
have chosen a spot on the side
of the building as shown.

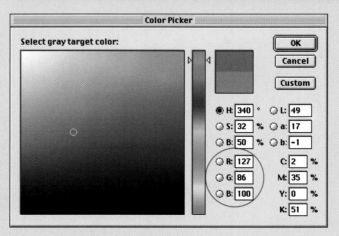

New values
Look at the Color Picker, and
you will see that the RGB values
have now changed to show the
values for the area sampled.

Click OK to close the Color
Picker.

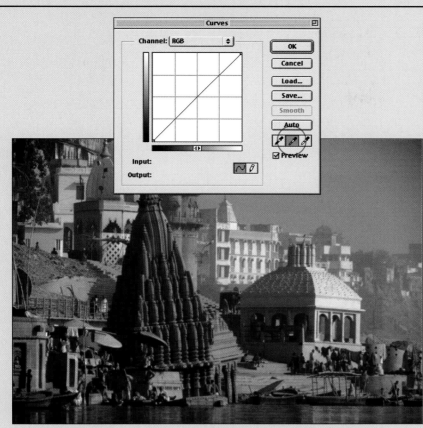

Auto again

The Curves dialogue box will still be open. Click on Auto to adjust the image in the same way as before.

But wait a minute, there's one more step. We need to tell Photoshop where to apply the midtone value we sampled.

Re-sample

With the grey balance dropper still highlighted, click on the same area of the image that was sampled in the first step.

Presto! The midtone values of the original image have been re-applied, restoring much of the mood and lighting of the original. The Auto corrections to black and white points have also been retained.

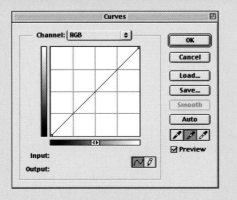

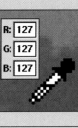

R: 127
G: 127
B: 127

Auto

The pictures on the **left** show the results of applying the standard mid-tone RGB values of 127 to different areas in the image after Auto Curves have been applied.

This tip is not only useful in correcting a cast, it is a great way to create special mood effects. Here we show what can be done by applying standard and sampled midtone values to different areas of the image.

The pictures on the **right** show the results of applying a sampled midtone value to different areas in the image after Auto Curves have been applied.

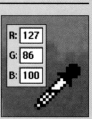

Try, Try again
Experiment as much as you like, but remember to set the grey balance back to its original values when you have finished. It won't affect what you do with the Auto button, but it will affect corrections to other images using this method.

This technique also works using Auto Levels in the Levels dialogue box.

Difficulty: Intermediate	Julieanne Kost

Colour correction by numbers

Colour casts can be introduced as a result of the time of day that a photo was taken, reflected light illuminating a scene or even the type of camera you're using. Julieanne Kost shows you how to expel a colour cast using a combination of Adjustment Layers, Color Samplers and the Info palette.

Open the file
Select File > Open to navigate and open the RGB file that contains a colour cast that needs to be corrected.

Note
Sometimes images have desirable overall colours such as at sunset which don't need to be corrected.
However, in this image, the magenta colour cast needs to be eliminated for the food to look appetising and the tablecloth to look as we know it to be: basically white.

Note

If you base all of your colour correction on a point sample, and that one point isn't representative of the rest of the image, you might get unexpected results.

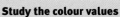

Using the Color Samplers

To read the average value of the specified number of pixels within the area you click, set the options for the Color Sampler tool to measure either a 3x3 or 5x5 pixel average.
Click on the Color Sampler tool in the tool palette to access its options via the Option Bar.

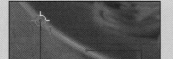

Preferred white-point   Catchlight

Tip

Some images may lack a true white-point, but instead have a catchlight (specular highlight) which is a reflection from another lightsource. The catchlight is 'whiter than white' so is not a good white-point. Look for another point nearby that is not reflecting a major lightsource.

Measuring colour values

Using the Color Sampler tool, click in the highlight area of the image.
Setting a Color Sampler allows you to measure the values of the highlights in the Info palette and make the necessary changes.
Click again to set a Color Sampler in the shadow area.
In this example, the shadow area is in the darkest area of the spaghetti sauce.

Study the colour values

Open the Info palette (Window > Show Info).
The Info palette displays the colour values for each of the Color Samplers that were set in the highlight and shadow areas of the image. Notice the different values of red, green and blue for each of the samplers.
If the highlight or shadow values were all the same, the image wouldn't have a colour cast since equal amounts of RGB result in neutral tones.
In the Info palette, look at the values for red, green and blue for Color Sampler number one (the highlight area of the image). Find the colour with the lowest value. In this example, the lowest value is for G (green).

Add an adjustment layer
Create a new Levels adjustment
layer from the pop-up at the
bottom of the Layers palette.

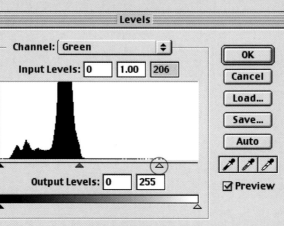

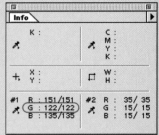

Adjusting Levels
From the Channel menu,
select the channel that has
the lowest measured value
from the previous step (122).
In this case Green.

Neutralising the highlights
While watching the values
from the Color Sampler
number one in the Info palette,
begin dragging the white
triangle in the Levels
Adjustment layer dialogue
to the left.
The Info palette displays
an adjusted value for
the colour samplers.
Keep dragging the triangle
until the value matches
the highest value (151) for the
highlights (Red in this case).

Note:
Input values in Levels do not correlate
with those in the Info palette. Instead,
they serve as a guide – as you move
input values on the slider, the Info
palette will provide a different reading.

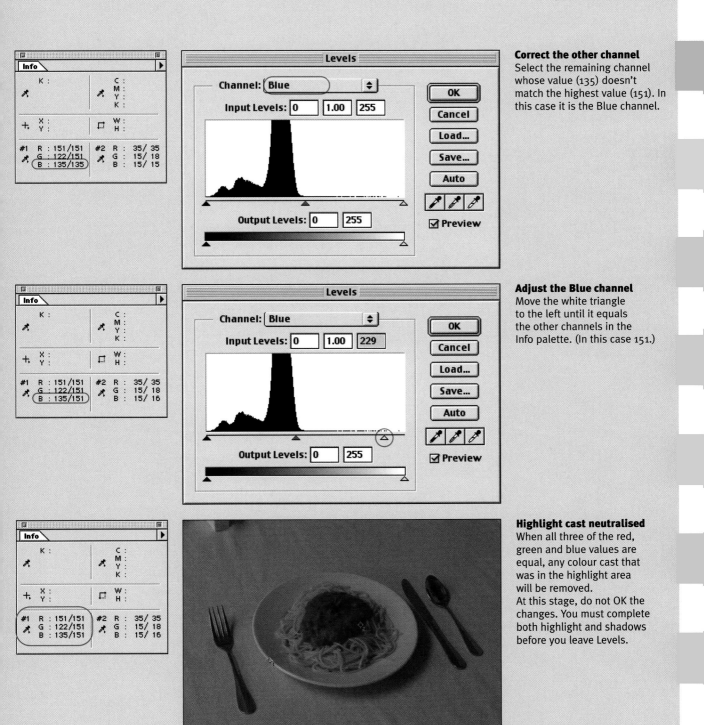

Correct the other channel
Select the remaining channel whose value (135) doesn't match the highest value (151). In this case it is the Blue channel.

Adjust the Blue channel
Move the white triangle to the left until it equals the other channels in the Info palette. (In this case 151.)

Highlight cast neutralised
When all three of the red, green and blue values are equal, any colour cast that was in the highlight area will be removed.
At this stage, do not OK the changes. You must complete both highlight and shadows before you leave Levels.

Moving into the shadows
With the cast removed in the highlights, it's now time to work on the shadows.

Neutralising the shadows
While still in the Levels Adjustment layer dialogue, select the channel that has the highest value for the second Color Sampler (the one in the shadows). In this case, the Red channel.

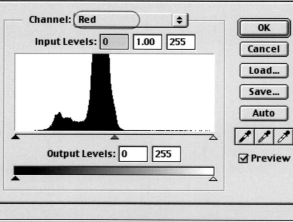

Adjust the Red channel
Drag the black triangle to the right until it matches the lowest value in the Info palette (16). In this case, it is the Blue channel).

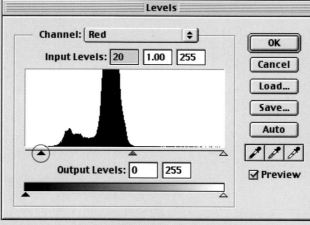

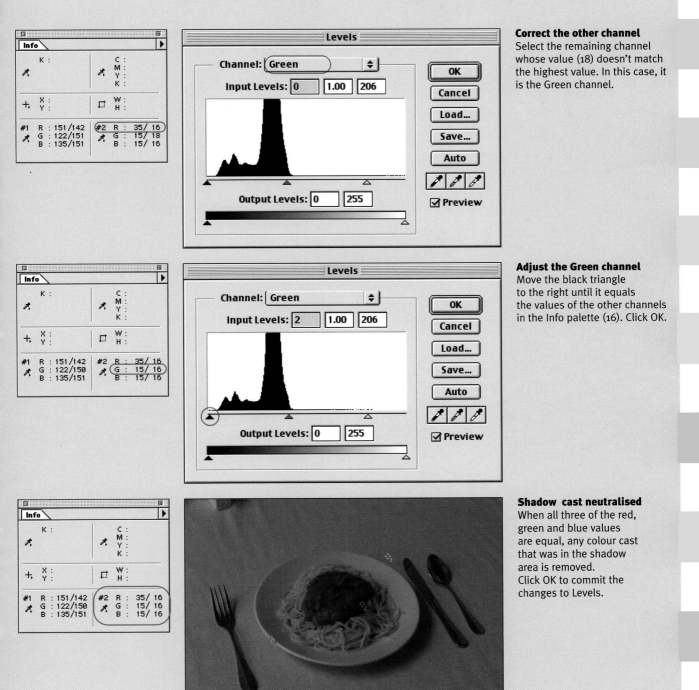

Correct the other channel
Select the remaining channel whose value (18) doesn't match the highest value. In this case, it is the Green channel.

Adjust the Green channel
Move the black triangle to the right until it equals the values of the other channels in the Info palette (16). Click OK.

Shadow cast neutralised
When all three of the red, green and blue values are equal, any colour cast that was in the shadow area is removed.
Click OK to commit the changes to Levels.

Neutralise the mid-tones

Even with the shadow and highlights neutralised, a colour cast still remains in the image's mid-tones. Add another Color Sampler in a midtone area of the image that should have a neutral value (in this case, the tablecloth).

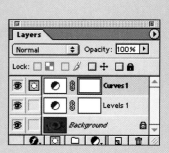

Adjusting the Curves

Create a new Curves adjustment layer using the pop-up at the bottom of the Layers palette.

Selecting and modifying

While watching the Info palette, select and modify each of the channels by raising or lowering their curve until they all match in value.
In this case, we raised the Red channel's curve and lowered the Green channel's curve to match the Blue channel's measured value. Click OK.

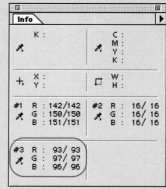

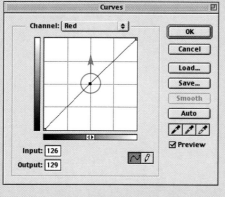

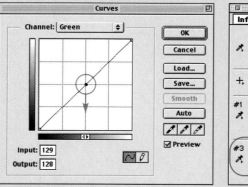

Midtones cast neutralised

When all three of the red, green and blue values are equal, any colour cast that was in the mid-tones is removed.

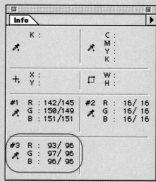

Cast away
By colour correcting by numbers using the Color Samplers and Levels and Curves adjustment layers, we have taken the magenta colour cast out of the highlights, shadows and mid-tones. The image is still a little dark, so let's lighten it using another Levels adjustment layer.

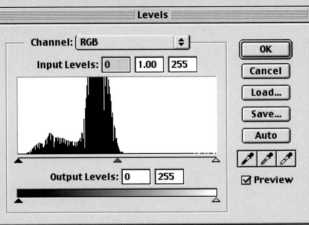

Add an Adjustment layer
Create a new Levels adjustment layer using the pop-up at the bottom of the Layers palette. Notice that there is very little tonal information beyond the grey slider.

Levels
Expanding the tonal range of the image creates white and black points and redistributes the tonal information of the image between these two points.

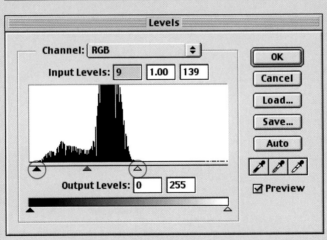

Moving towards the light
By dragging in the highlight slider, we are expanding the tonal range of the image making some part of the image white. Similarly, we can create a black point, adding contrast to the entire image by bringing in the shadow slider.

Ready to serve
The image is now ready for consumption without the colour cast which would have dissuaded even the bravest connoisseur from ordering the spaghetti.

Difficulty: Intermediate	Colin Wood

Posterising colour shapes

If you need coloured roundals or targets in a hurry, the Posterize command is here to help. When combined with a Gradient Map, the process is quick and easy. Here's how to make coloured regular shapes in three easy, non-destructive steps using adjustment layers and your imagination.

Convert your gradient into concentric circles using posterize and then apply a Gradient Map to add your preferred colour.

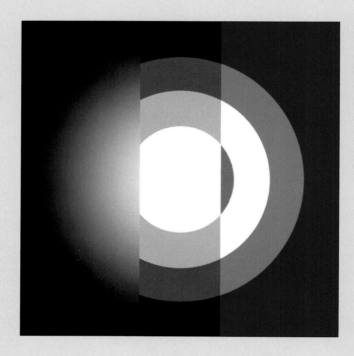

What is posterisation?

Posterisation involves taking a range of tonal levels and mapping them to a smaller amount of solid tonal levels. If you have a greyscale image with 256 tonal levels and you use the Posterize command to reduce the image to four levels, then the 256 levels will be mapped to the four levels, reducing your tonal range to white, light grey, dark grey and black.

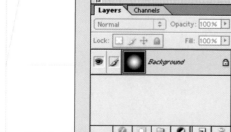

Our radial gradient contains all the greyscale shades from white to black. What we would like are just four graduated shades including the background. We can use an adjustment layer to do this.

Use the adjustment layer pull-down menu.

Make a radial gradient

Open a new RGB document. Find your centre point using rulers and guides. (See page 28 – Photoshop Actions.) In the tool palette, select the default foreground and background colours (white and black). Select the Gradient tool and choose radial gradient from the Options Bar. Position your cursor from the centre point of your document, dragging outwards.

Smooth radial gradient
Your image will now look like this.

Posterising

Add a Posterize adjustment layer from the pull-down menu. Use a value of 4 levels.

Posterize

Levels: 4   OK
            Cancel
☑ Preview

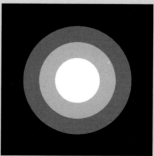

Posterised
Your image now consists of four grey levels.

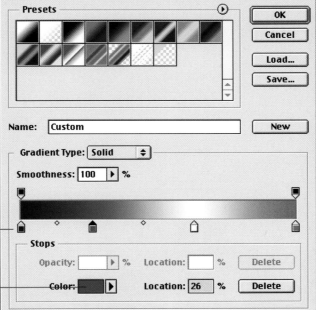

What does a Gradient Map do?
The Gradient Map command maps the equivalent colours specified to the existing grayscale range of an image. A two-colour gradient fill, for example, will apply shadows in the image map to one of the endpoint colours of the gradient fill, highlights to the other endpoint colour, and midtones to the gradations in between.

Colour stops ●

To change colours, click on a colour stop and then click here to bring up the Color Picker.

Adding colour
We will use another adjustment layer to add colour to our image. Add a Gradient Map adjustment layer from the pull-down menu. The colours in the Gradient Map dialogue will be white and black (your current foreground and background colours).
Click in the gradient to bring up the Gradient Editor.

Custom gradient
So that we can have a different colour for each of our posterised tones, we need to create a gradient with four colours. Add two 'colour stops' by clicking beneath the gradient. Then click on individual colour stops to bring up the Color Picker and select your colours.

Tip
If you select Gradient Map colours and your image is a series of greys, your document is probably in greyscale mode.

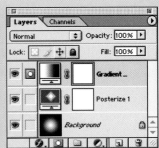

Bull's eye!
A coloured target from a greyscale radial gradient.

Playing with posterisation

Variations
Our Gradient Map will produce different effects depending on the number of levels in our posterisation.

No posterisation
If the base layer is a stepless blend, the colours of the gradient map will appear as a gradual transition from colour to colour.

2 levels
If our base layer has only two tones (white and black), our image will show only those colours at the ends of the gradient.

6 levels
This is the result of posterising our base layer to 6 levels.

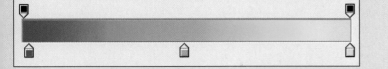

Choose a colour
A gradient map can contain more colours than you will ever need.

Diamond bright
Here is a square rotated through 45 degrees, posterised using the Gradient Map shown above.

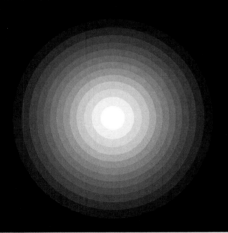
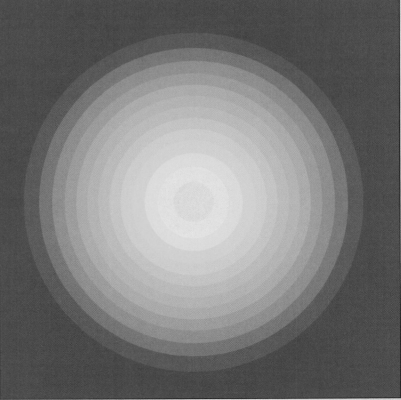

That's all folks!
This technique will save you hours and amaze your friends.

04 - Colour effects & Correction

Creating a digital master

Image editing in Photoshop can be a series of compromises as each correction stretches the tonal range of your image, creating gaps in your histogram. One solution is to capture and correct your images in 16-bit then convert to 8-bit as a last step retaining you image's tonal range.

Why 16-bit?

In the beginning, the pixel was monochrome which meant that it could only be represented in shades of grey. This legacy can be found in Photoshop where RGB and CMYK images consist of individual colour channels which are represented as greyscale. The standard bit-depth for most Photoshop users is 8-bit, which is the amount of bits taken to represent each colour channel. This provides a range of 256 shades of grey which go to make each colour channel. 16-bit images are represented by 65,536 shades of grey which give you a greater tonal range to work with.

Though the tools have been available for a few versions of Photoshop, 16-bit editing (also known as high-bit editing) has not enjoyed much acceptance. The slow takeup of 16-bit editing is potentially due to the fact that not all of Photoshop's editing tools are available in 16-bit and also because the files are typically twice the size of their 8-bit counterparts. So why would you opt to edit in 16-bit mode and what purpose is it best suited to? The simple answer is to create a high quality original image which you can repurpose for multiple mediums and requirements.

What works in 16 Bits/Channel

Tools
Marquee tools
Lasso
Polygonal Lasso
Crop
Healing Brush/Patch
Clone Stamp
Path Selection/Direct Selection
Pen/Freeform Pen/Add Anchor Point/Delete
Anchor Point
Note/Audio Annotation
Hand
Move
Magic Wand
Slice/Slice Select
History Brush
Horizontal Type Mask/
Vertical Type Mask

Shape tools (for drawing work paths only)
Eyedropper/Color Sampler/
Measure
Zoom

Adjustments
Levels/Auto Levels
Auto Contrast/Auto Color
Curves
Color Balance
Brightness/Contrast
Hue/Saturation
Channel Mixer
Gradient Map
Invert/Equalize

Filters
Blur > Gaussian Blur
Noise > Add Noise/Dust
& Scratches/Median
Sharpen > Unsharp Mask
Stylize > Solarize
Other > High Pass

Channels
Saving a selection (Selection > Save
Selection) creates a new document
with just the channel information.
You can select individual channels
for global colour corrections.

History
Step forward and backward through
history and create snapshots.

Paths
Save Path/Delete Path/Make Selection

Save As
Photoshop (.PSD)/RAW/TIFF

Selections
Inverse/Feather/Transform
Selection/Save Selection
Modify > Border/Smooth/
Expand/Contract

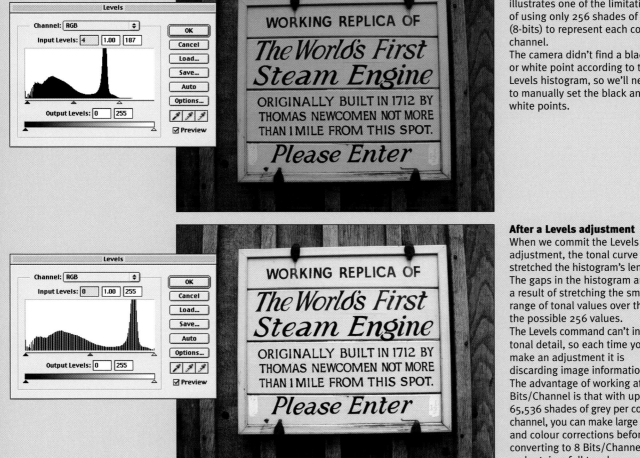

The problem with 8-bit
A typical digital camera shot illustrates one of the limitations of using only 256 shades of grey (8-bits) to represent each colour channel.
The camera didn't find a black or white point according to the Levels histogram, so we'll need to manually set the black and white points.

After a Levels adjustment
When we commit the Levels adjustment, the tonal curve is stretched the histogram's length. The gaps in the histogram are a result of stretching the small range of tonal values over the the possible 256 values.
The Levels command can't invent tonal detail, so each time you make an adjustment it is discarding image information. The advantage of working at 16 Bits/Channel is that with up to 65,536 shades of grey per colour channel, you can make large tone and colour corrections before converting to 8 Bits/Channel and retain a full tonal range.

What doesn't work in 16 Bits/Channel

Tools
Magnetic Lasso
Pattern Stamp
Eraser
Magic Eraser
Background Eraser
Blur/Sharpen/Smudge
Brush
Pencil
Art History Brush
Gradient
Paint Bucket
Dodge
Burn
Sponge
Horizontal Type
Vertical Type

Adjustments
Desaturate
Replace Color
Selective Color
Threshold
Posterize
Variations

Filters
All filters except Gaussian Blur, Add Noise,
Dust & Scratches, Median, Unsharp Mask,
Solarize and High Pass

Layers
No layers, no adjustment layers,
no blend modes, no layer-based
sharpening or blurring.

Channels
16 Bits/Channel images do not
support the creation of channels

History
Fill from History

Paths
Fill Path/Stroke Path/Clipping Path

Save As
No options except Photoshop
(.PSD)/RAW/TIFF

Selections
Color Range/Grow/Similar/
Load Selection

Start with a scan

Many current scanners allow you to scan at 16-bits per channel (also referred to as 48-bit: 16-bits per channel for R, G and B). Within your scanner driver, select the 16-bit (48-bit) option and scan your image at the highest optical resolution of the scanner. In Photoshop, check that you are in 16-bit mode by viewing the Mode menu (Image > Mode). The 16 Bits/Channel option should have a tick next to it.

Crop

Before we tackle the colour correction of our image, we want to crop the transparency border from the image.
If we retain the border, it will skew our Levels adjustment as the blackest part of the image. The Crop tool happily works on 16 Bits/Channel images.

Levels

Photoshop gives you a basic set of Image Adjustments in 16 Bits/Channel mode including Levels, Auto Levels, Auto Contrast, Auto Color, Curves, Color Balance, Brightness/Contrast, Channel Mixer, Hue/Saturation, Gradient Map, Invert and Equalize.
We'll start with Levels to set our highlight and shadows.

Tip
To access the last settings that you used in Levels, hold down the Option/Alt key before selecting Levels
(Image > Adjustments > Levels).

Set the black point

The Levels dialogue allows us to set the Shadow (Black) and Highlight (White) points in our image, but how can you tell where these points are? By holding down the Option/Alt key and dragging the Black (Input Levels) slider to the right, our image will change to show us the darkest parts of the image. Ignoring the sky, dark points in the image will appear to show the points of greatest detail. Adjust the slider until it is at the point where the darkest details appear. Release the Option/Alt key to see effects.

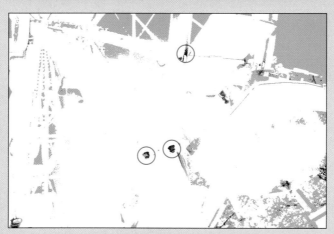

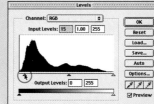

Set the shadow (black) point

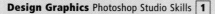

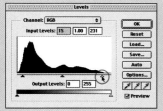

Set the highlight (white) point

Set the white point

Hold down the Option/Alt key and drag the White slider to the left, to show the lightest parts of the image.
Ignoring the specular highlights (where the sun is reflecting off an object's edge), adjust the slider until it is at the point where the lightest details appear such as the door of the gondola. Release the Option/Alt key to see effects. Click OK to apply the Levels correction.

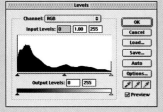

Check the histogram

Select Levels again to see the change to the histogram based on our Levels adjustment. You'll notice that the tonal curve has stretched out to meet the left and right of the histogram, but there are no tell-tale gaps that would typically appear when working in 8 Bits/Channel mode.

Color Balance

In this example there is a blue cast which we'd like to remove. Thankfully, the Color Balance command works in 16 Bits/Channel mode.

Removing a cast

The next step is to remove the blue cast in our image. The Color Balance command is available to us in 16 Bits/Channel mode, which will do nicely. Select Color Balance (Image > Adjustments > Color Balance), then drag the Yellow-Blue slider towards the Yellow.
This does the job of removing the blue colour cast.
Next we'll concentrate on the sky.

Excuse me while I change the sky

It's a well-known fact that you can't use your regular selection tools in 16 Bits/Channel mode. So how do you make selective colour corrections to your image? Jeff Schewe came up with a great technique providing the power of selections when they're needed. Duplicate your 16 Bits/Channel image (Image > Duplicate), then change to 8 Bits/Channel mode. In this case, we want to select and colour the sky. Choose Color Range (Select > Color Range), then Shift-click around the sky with the eyedropper to make a selection. Click OK.

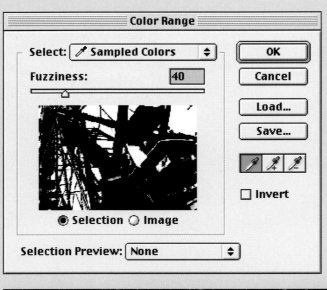

Jeff Schewe
To see the work of this Photoshop guru, visit: www.schewephoto.com

A selection to work on

Color Range gives us a good selection to start with, but we want to refine it a little using a channel.

Into the channel

Create a channel based on your selection by clicking the Save Selection as Channel button in the Channels palette.
Spot clean the channel with a brush with a hardness of 85% to clean up the edges.

Using 8 Bits/Channel selections

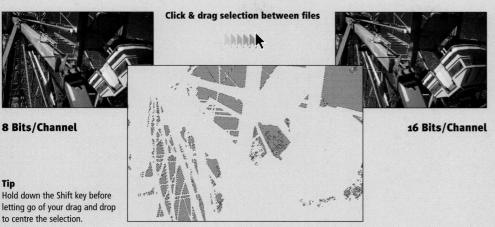

Click & drag selection between files

8 Bits/Channel

16 Bits/Channel

Tip
Hold down the Shift key before letting go of your drag and drop to centre the selection.

Transfer the selection
To load your new selection, Command/Ctrl-click the channel in the Channels palette.
With the refined sky selection, we're now ready for clever part of Schewe's technique. Select the Marquee tool (m), then drag the selection from your duplicate image (8 Bits/Channel) into the original 16 Bits/Channel image holding down the Shift key to centre the selection.

Tip
The History command is available in 16 Bits/Channel mode which also allows you to create Snapshots at different stages of the editing process.
This in a small way makes up for the absence of layers and adjustment layers.

Hue/Saturation

Edit: Master

Hue: -121

Saturation: -21

Lightness: +2

OK
Cancel
Load...
Save...

☐ Colorize
☑ Preview

Making use of the selection
Back in our 16 Bits/Channel original image we have a selection that could not have been created with the selection restrictions in 16 Bit/Channel mode, but can now be used to selectively colour our sky. Choose Hue/Saturation (Image > Adjustments > Hue/Saturation) and adjust the Hue and Lightness sliders to create a green sky. Click OK to commit the adjustment.

New sky
The sky is now a lovely shade of green (for illustrative purposes), and we are still working in 16 Bits/Channel mode which means that we haven't thrown information away that will be visible when we finally convert to 8 Bits/Channel.

16 Bits/Channel

The histogram of the 16 Bits/ Channel image is unbroken even after Levels, Color Balance and Hue/Saturation adjustments and a final conversion to 8 Bits/Channel.

Though you can't use a 16 Bits/Channel image in QuarkXPress or InDesign layout, the advantage is that you start out with a high-quality 8 Bit/ Channel image with a solid tonal distribution.

Levels

Channel: RGB

Input Levels: 0 1.00 255

Output Levels: 0 255

OK
Cancel
Load...
Save...
Auto
Options...

☑ Preview

8 Bits/Channel (24-bit)

8 Bits/Channel

The histogram of the 8 Bits/ Channel image shows gaps in the histogram after only Levels, Color Balance and Hue/Saturation adjustments. The more adjustments you commit to an 8 Bit/Channel image, the more information you lose which eventually shows in its reproduction.

150

	Difficulty: Power User	Colin Wood
Better seas	The scene you see when you take the photograph so often fails to appear in the image quite as you remember it. For example, a bright blue sea can end up as a green sludge. We show you how to clean up the high seas, adding depth and modelling.	

After balancing the colour, this tip shows two ways to add contrast through blending a monochrome with the original.

First we make a monochrome version using luminance values and then show how to do the same using the Channel Mixer.

This is the problem
A 'flat' sea with little contrast. In order to give this sea some life we need to make it cover a much greater range of tones.
However, we can't simply stretch the existing image as there is not sufficient information. We need to add something without distorting it unrealistically.

Our solution
As we need to add tones (highlights and shadows) we will make a greyscale version of the image and blend it with the original.
Our greyscale will need to have much more contrast than the original.

The two together
When we blend the two together we will have given the sea a wider dynamic range (as shown in a Levels histogram) without affecting the basic colour and without increasing the colour saturation.
All aboard!

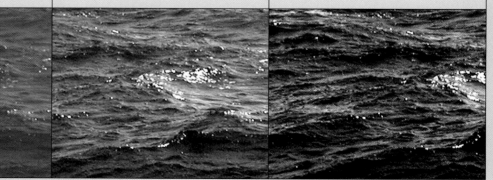

What does not work

A very flat sea
Here is the offending image, taken at Venice Beach, California on a sunny Sunday. There is a hint of Los Angeles smog in the air and the water looks like a lifeless green soup. Not quite what we thought we saw on the day.
There are many ways that Photoshop can help us improve this image.
We will concentrate on giving the sea more contrast.

Auto Levels | **Auto Contrast** | **Auto Color***

Image > Adjustments > Auto Levels, Auto Contrast and Auto Color usually do a good job but in this case they fall short.
The reason is that the sea consists of a relatively narrow band of values, which is why it looks so flat and lacking in contrast.
None of these Auto adjustments have done a good enough job, so let's move on and try a manual Levels adjustment.

* Auto Color only available in Photoshop 7

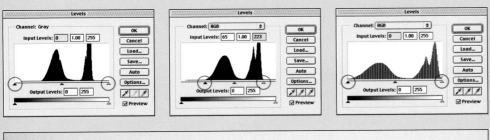

Levels adjustment
The first histogram shows the Levels dialogue box when it is first opened. Note the two humps: the left hand one denotes the sea, the right hand one is mainly the sky but does include the sea's highlights.
The second shows a typical adjustment you might make.
The third shows how that adjustment will spread the tones across the full dynamic range.
Note that it is usual for adjustments to the shadow slider (the black slider) to increase saturation.

Not bad, but could be better
Doing the usual Levels adjustments manually on the entire image expands the dynamic range but the sea still looks flat. We have more colour but it is not convincing.
There is a better way overleaf.

Colour balance

Get the basic colour right first

It is usually a good idea to get the levels right before improving the colour. But in this case we'll get the colour right first.

If we use a Color Balance adjustment layer we can always tweak it later on.

In this case we will move the predominant colour from yellow towards blue using a Color Balance adjustment layer. We moved the blue slider to +14.

Original   Colour balanced

Method One - Using a Luminance layer

Selecting the luminance

The first trick is to use Option-Command-~ (tilde) for Mac (or Option-Ctrl-~ for Windows) to load the image luminance as a selection.

This will be a better greyscale representation of the image you are working with.

We have been used to loading one of the RGB channels but none of these contain the overall image brightness.

Save the selection as a channel.

Paste the channel as a layer

Copy the channel to the clipboard, change to the Layers palette and then paste (Command/Ctrl-V).

Photoshop will automatically create a new layer in your RGB file that will appear as monochrome (it converts from greyscale to RGB during the paste).

The histogram shows two distinct ranges, one mainly for the (lighter) sky and another mainly for the (darker) water. Some of the water highlights will be in the lighter tones with the sky.

Levels adjustment

Use Image > Adjustments > Levels (Command/Ctrl-L) to spread the tonal range of the sea over all 256 tonal levels. In this case the (lighter) sky and the (darker) water are easy to identify in the histogram, although you will be clipping some of the highlights in the water with the settings we have used here. For added flexibility you can use a Levels adjustment layer and group it with the monochrome layer.

The next step will be to blend the monochrome layer with the original.

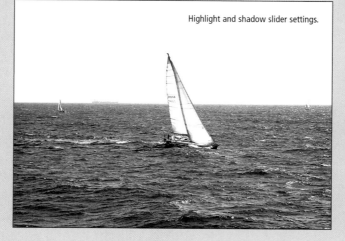

Highlight and shadow slider settings.

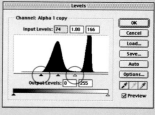

Method One - Using a Luminance layer

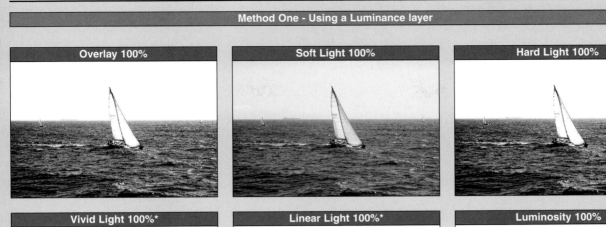

| Overlay 100% | Soft Light 100% | Hard Light 100% |
| Vivid Light 100%* | Linear Light 100%* | Luminosity 100% |

Using the Luminance layer
With the monochrome layer above the original image, you can try out various blend modes.
Here are the results of six modes all used at 100% opacity.
* Blend mode only available in Photoshop 7

Overlay wins
The Overlay mode is a combination of Multiply and Screen, with 50% being the break point. So our monochrome layer is darkening the darker tones and lighting the lighter ones, thus adding contrast.

No increase in saturation
Overlay adds contrast without increasing the colour saturation.
By comparison, when making a Levels adjustment, the shadow slider tends to increase colour saturation.

Decrease the opacity
You will probably find that any of the blend modes will be too strong at 100% opacity. This image looks great with the Overlay layer reduced to 50% opacity, allowing more of the original image to show through.

It's sharper too
As well as adding contrast, this effect appears to add some sharpness too. It does this through adding contrast, not by emphasising edges. Thus it is very kind to images that would become pixelated when sharpened using Unsharp Mask.

Overleaf we show another method, adding more flexibility with the Channel Mixer.

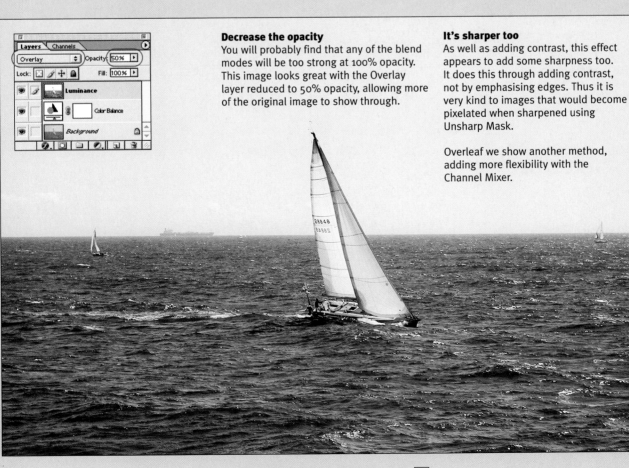

04 - Colour effects & Correction

Added flexibility
If you use a Channel Mixer adjustment layer instead of the Luminance 'greyscale' layer, you can still use a greyscale layer but have the added flexibility of the Channel Mixer.

This method is also useful if you have run out of alpha channels.

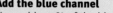

Check for monochrome
Here is our image with a Channel Mixer adjustment layer checked for monochrome. At this stage it is basically the information in the Red channel.

Add the green channel
Our aim is to make a monochrome version of our image (in much the same way as selecting the luminance), so add 100% of the green channel. The image goes lighter because we are adding more information.

Add the blue channel
Now add 100% of the blue channel. The image looks as if it has blown out completely, but don't despair.

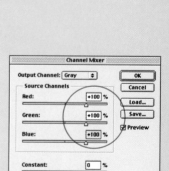

Reduce the Constant
Modulate the effect by reducing the Constant. This will make the image darker again and have much more contrast.
Here we show a Constant of -90.

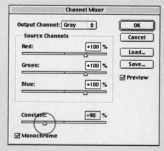

Method Two - Using the Channel Mixer

Test different settings
You may find that your first attempt overcooks the image somewhat.
Try various settings until you get a good greyscale with plenty of contrast.
It doesn't matter if it is not perfect because you will be tweaking it later.

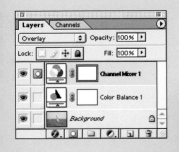

Overlay blend mode
Now change the blend mode of the Channel Mixer to Overlay. The opacity will be 100% and the image will looks like this. The next step is to reduce the opacity until you are happy with the result.

Original

In practice you would probably change the blend mode of the Channel Mixer adjustment layer sooner and carry out the adjustments in 'real-time'.

The final image
Here we show the image with an opacity of 70% for the Channel Mixer adjustment layer.
We have increased the contrast in the water without affecting the saturation or the colour.
Now you can practise this method on all those bad sea pictures you put away!

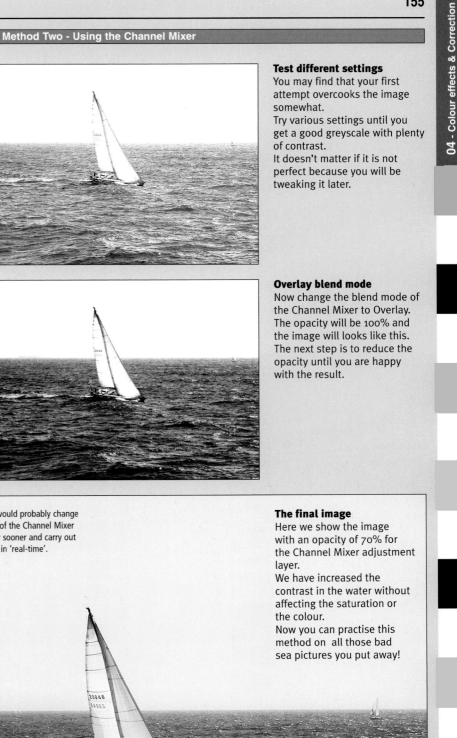

5
Light & Shadow

Difficulty: Easy	Colin Wood

Reparing digital photographs

Pictures from digital cameras can come with problems waiting to ruin your day. If you don't fix 'noisy' images early in the editing process, you will pay a high price later on. Here is a quick way to overcome a common problem found in pictures taken in dim light. The dreaded noise; a silent killer.

Some digital pictures may look OK at first glance, but there can be trouble lurking in every pixel for the unwary. It is always best to fix problems as early as possible because image enhancements often enhance the problems as well.

Here we have a typical digital picture. It was taken indoors under less than ideal artificial light.

The problem

If we examine the individual channels we can see that the Red and Green channels are fine. But the Blue channel is full of noise. When we sharpen this image, the problem will become evident.

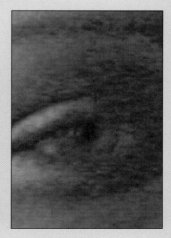

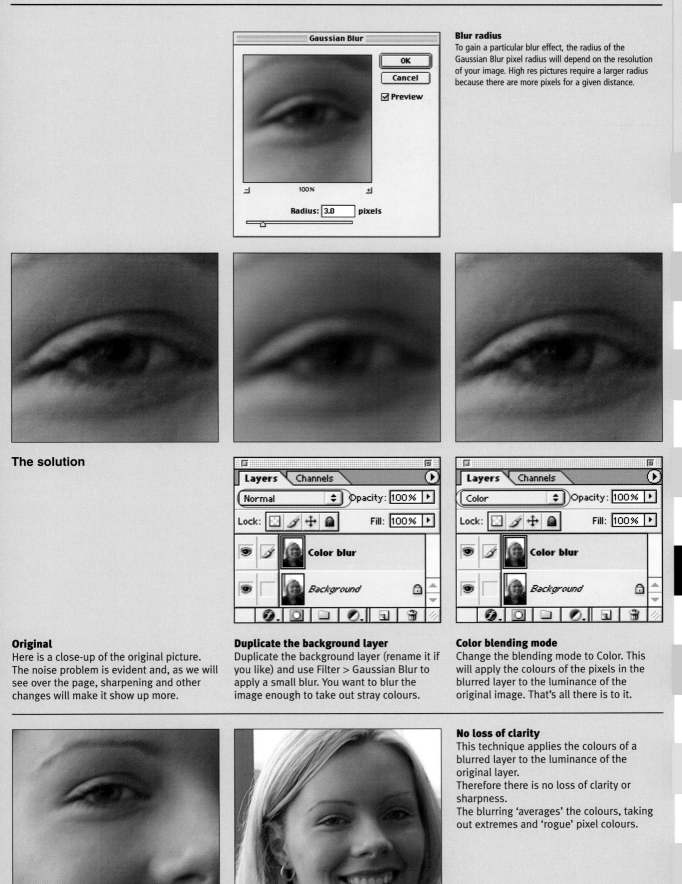

Blur radius
To gain a particular blur effect, the radius of the Gaussian Blur pixel radius will depend on the resolution of your image. High res pictures require a larger radius because there are more pixels for a given distance.

The solution

Original
Here is a close-up of the original picture. The noise problem is evident and, as we will see over the page, sharpening and other changes will make it show up more.

Duplicate the background layer
Duplicate the background layer (rename it if you like) and use Filter > Gaussian Blur to apply a small blur. You want to blur the image enough to take out stray colours.

Color blending mode
Change the blending mode to Color. This will apply the colours of the pixels in the blurred layer to the luminance of the original image. That's all there is to it.

No loss of clarity
This technique applies the colours of a blurred layer to the luminance of the original layer.
Therefore there is no loss of clarity or sharpness.
The blurring 'averages' the colours, taking out extremes and 'rogue' pixel colours.

Show and tell
Turn the page to see the process in more detail.

Seeing is believing

There are several ways to identify problems in Photoshop. You can use Levels to distort the tonal range or you can use Hue/Saturation to exaggerate the colours. We will use the latter as we have a colour problem.

To exaggerate the problem of RGB noise, we applied +50 saturation to the original file (without the extra layer) and then again to the file using the extra blurred layer.

Original picture

No blurred layer
This series of pictures shows the effects of Hue/Saturation, Unsharp Mask and Find Edges on the original file without the extra blurred layer.

'Fixed' picture

Using an extra blurred layer
This series of pictures shows the effects of Hue/Saturation, Unsharp Mask and Find Edges on the file with the extra blurred layer in Color blending mode.

Unsharp Mask
We applied a slightly excessive Unsharp Mask using an amount of 200, a radius of 2, and a threshold of 5.

Find edges
To demonstrate how this technique smoothes out the rough patches, we used Filter > render > Find Edges.
The underlying pattern is plain to see.

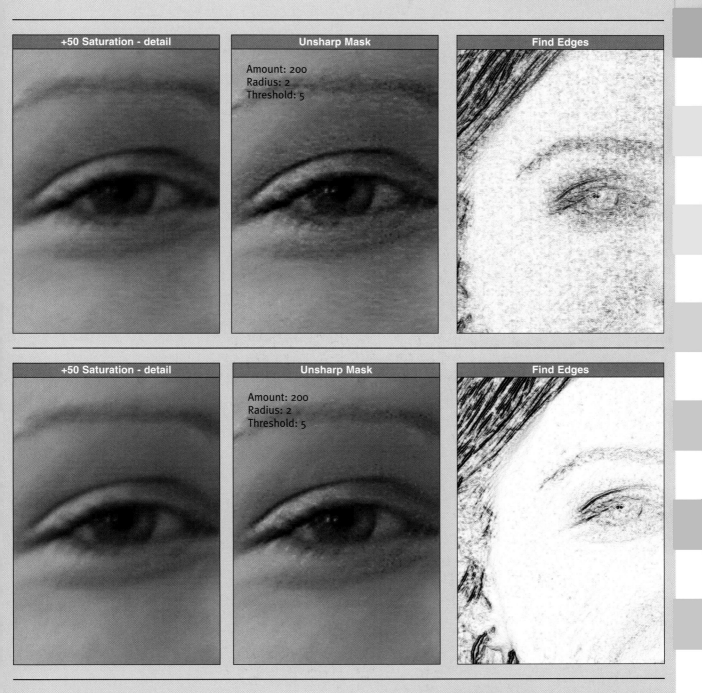

Simple but good
This quick and easy technique will enhance your difficult digital pictures in double-quick time and help you get the most out of every digital camera.

Difficulty: Intermediate	Colin Wood

More realistic drop shadows

Shadows didn't suddenly appear with the advent of the desktop computer. When we add artificial ones, they can appear unrealistic. A flat picture often needs that extra 'lift' to make the image seem to be sitting in the background; not floating in mid-air. Here's how to add that extra touch of realism.

There's something about a photographic print: it's tactile and is actually three dimensional.
Let's start with a flat picture and turn it into a printed photograph sitting on a surface.

Long days of summer
Here is our picture; a lovely summer's day on an English canal. The water's flat, and so is the picture.

Room to move

We're going to need some room around our picture so we should enlarge the canvas size. Double-click on your background layer to turn it into a layer.

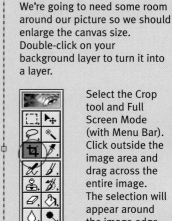

Select the Crop tool and Full Screen Mode (with Menu Bar). Click outside the image area and drag across the entire image. The selection will appear around the image edge. Drag out the side or corner handles to enlarge the selection.

Transparency rules

If you don't turn your background layer into a layer that can contain transparency, your picture will be a part of the larger background and hard to isolate later. You want your picture (surrounded by transparency) to be sitting on a larger background.

Keeping it in the middle

For many reasons it is a good idea when using the Crop tool in this way to hold down the Shift key to maintain the aspect ratio and the Option/Alt key to drag out from the centre (using any of the handles). In that way your picture stays in the middle of the image.

Nicely framed

If you enlarged your canvas size symmetrically, your image will now look like this.

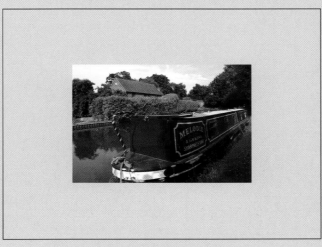

Curving with Shear

Now to work on the picture. Photographs rarely lay flat, so let's start by giving the picture a curve.

Use Filter >Distort >Shear to bring up the Shear dialogue. This is a very flexible filter that can be used to make extreme distortions. However, in this case we wish to make a subtle change.

In the dialogue box, click in the centre of the shear line to fix the centre and then drag the top and bottom handles to the left. Not too much now!

Tip
Add handles by clicking on the shear line.

Distorting the picture

Distorting the picture

Now for the fun part.
Make the canal image the active layer and use Edit >Free Transform (Command/Ctrl-T) to bring up the Transform selection with handles at corners and sides.
You can swap between the various transform functions before committing the transformation.

1 When any one of the transform functions are selected, the marquee surrounds the pixels on the layer and handles appear.
2 Perspective
Top and bottom corner handles work together.
3 Rotate anticlockwise.
4 Perspective (again)
5 Distort: to tweak the nearest corner.
6 Rotate: a final touch.

The available distortions

Edit > Transform > Distort
Scale
Rotate
Skew
Distort
Perspective

Free Transform (Command/Ctrl-T)
The default is for corner handles to change size of the shape within a rectangular marquee (distorting the image) while maintaining a rectangular shape. The Shift key will maintain the aspect ratio.
The side handles move the sides in or out and distort the image to fit. Using key modifiers, the Free Transform function can be changed into any of the five specialised distort functions.

The distorted picture

There is no formula or 'scientific' method to arrive at a convincing perspective view.
The eye of the designer must guide the process.
The desired result is one in which the picture still looks 'square'.
In some images, subtle bends in elements of the picture will fool the eye into believing that the picture is square but seen in perspective.

Now for more 'reality'

Now that we have a shape that can exist in a 3D world, it's time to add another subtle element that will assist in fooling the eye.

Edge selection

Giving it an edge

In order to give our picture some substance, we want it to look as if it is printed on a light card.
To do this we will add a highlight to the top and left-hand edges, and a shadow line along the bottom and right-hand edges.
We will do this using two Levels Adjustment Layers.
But first we need to make a mask for the edge.

Marching ants

First, Command-click on the Layer 1 (the distorted picture) layer icon to make a selection. The 'marching ants' will appear around the edge.

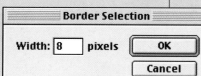

Modify border

Use Select >Modify >Border to bring up the Border Selection dialogue box.
The width of the border will depend on the output resolution of the image.
As this is a high resolution image (originally 3000 x 2000 pixels) we need to increase the width of the border to 8 pixels.

Save border as channel

Note that the border selection now extends to both sides of the original border.
With the selection active, click on the Channels palette and save it by clicking on the Save Selection as Channel icon.

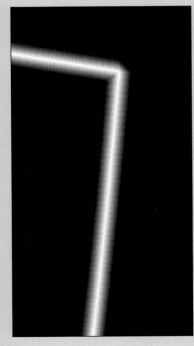

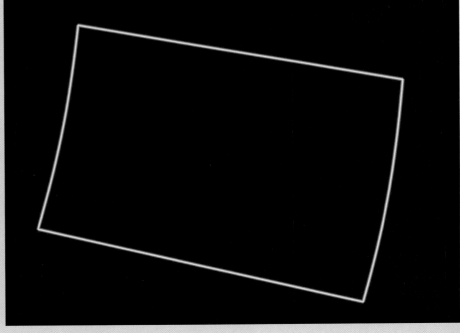

Highlights and shadow lines

Clipping groups

All types of layers can form clipping groups.
In a clipping group, the base layer acts as a mask for the entire group. All layers take on the shape, opacity and mode of the base layer. Several layers can be included in a single group.

Create adjustment layer
You can include Layers or Adjustment Layers in a clipping group. Here we wish to group Layer 1 and the Levels layer.

Creating an adjustment layer
With the cursor placed between the layers you wish to group, hold down the Option (Alt) key and click.

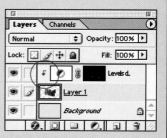

Indented layer icons
The overlying layer icon is indented and has the downward pointing arrow added.

How to add the highlight and shadow edges

Create a Levels adjustment
Using the New Adjustment Layer pull-down menu in the Layers palette, create a new Levels Adjustment layer. The Levels dialogue box will appear. Set the shadow slider to 128.

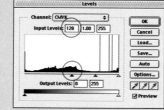

Now, that's dark!
The Levels adjustment will affect the entire image. We now need to mask the darker area so that it affects only the edge of the picture.

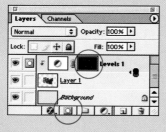

Mask ...
Load the selection from the saved alpha channel (the enlarged border), discard the Levels layer mask and then click on the Add Vector Mask icon to create a new mask.

... and clip
Then hold down the Option key and place the cursor between the layers. Click and layers will form a Clipping Group.

Another way to group
You can make the upper layer the active layer and use Command-G to group the layer with the previous (lower) layer.

Another way to add a mask
You can also load the selection before creating the Levels Adjustment layer. Using this technique, the Adjustment Layer mask is automatically attached.

Duplicate Levels adjustment
Drag the Levels Adjustment Layer to the Create New Layer icon to make a duplicate. Notice that the duplicate is automatically grouped with the previous layers.

At this stage it is a good idea to name your Levels Adjustment Layers 'Light' and 'Dark' as you will now need to identify them easily.

Highlight levels
Double click on the new Levels layer to bring up the Levels dialogue box.
Use Option Reset (the Cancel button becomes 'Reset' when the Option key is down) to reset the sliders.
This time set the highlight slider to 128.
Because the highlight Levels layer is on top, it will appear to affect the entire edge of the picture.

Complete mask

Highlight mask

Shadow mask

Highlight and shadow edges
Our next job is be to paint black in the layer masks so that the Levels adjustments apply to the correct edges.
Option-click in the layer mask icons to make the masks visible. Option-click again or click on another layer to return.

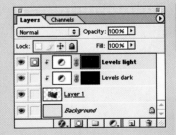

Edges complete
This is how your picture should look with the highlight and shadow edges.

The next job will be to add a shadow beneath the picture and to make it look realistic.

Creating a realistic drop shadow

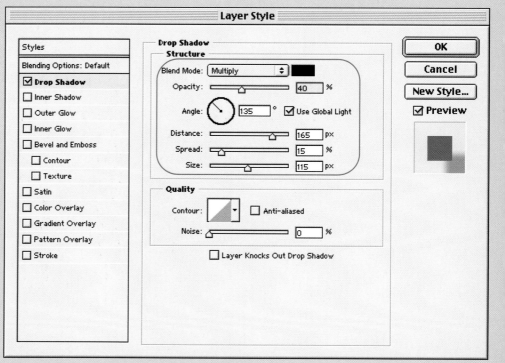

Making a layer style
Double click in the layer to bring up the Layer Style dialogue box. Click in the Drop Shadow and use the settings shown here as a starting point (for a high res image). Then experiment or tweak the settings to suit.

Shadow into a separate layer
For our final touch we need to have the shadow on its own layer.
Use Layer >Layer Style >Create Layer and the shadow will be placed on its own layer. It will be complete and will include the complete shape, including those areas which are currently hidden.

The final touch
Shadows are rarely square-on to the object.
Make the (new) shadow layer active.
Use Command-T to bring up the Free Transform marquee and rotate it clockwise.
You will be surprised how such subtle and unobtrusive effects can enhance your images and bring them to life.

Happy snaps
So there you have it; a much more realistic photograph.

05 - Light & Shadow

Difficulty: Intermediate	Carl Stevens

Realistic shadows

Creating a realistic drop shadow can be a tricky task. There are also situations where you'd like to replace an existing shadow when placing an object in a scene with a different shadow direction. Carl Stevens shows you how to create better shadows in Adobe Photoshop.

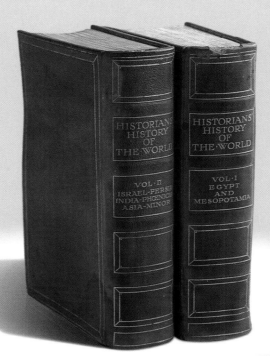

The problem

There is a trap waiting in the wings for those trying to create a perspective shadow that diminishes in strength while becoming less distinct as it recedes.

The problem is demonstrated here. You use a Gaussian Blur through a gradient selection, in order to have progressively greater blur in the distance. The result is a combination of the original sharp image and a blurred version.

What to do?

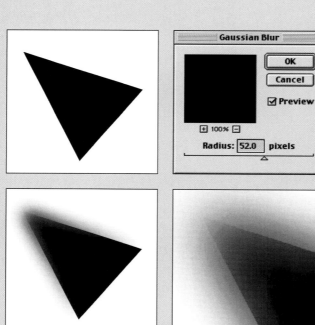

Image courtesy of **PhotoEssentials** (number 79 - old books): **'Colorful Objects'**.

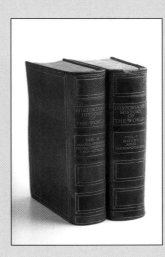

Let's begin
Start with the picture of the object you wish to create a shadow for.

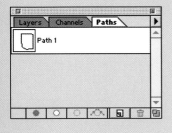

Object trace
Create a clipping path around the object using the Pen tool.

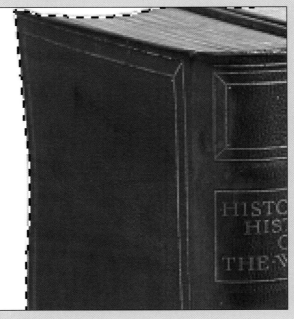

Select and layer
Turn the path into a selection by Command/Ctrl-clicking the path in the Paths palette.

Create a new layer called Books by copying the selection (Command/Ctrl-C).
Paste the selection into the new layer (Command/Ctrl-V). Name the new layer 'Books'.

Increase your canvas
Extend the image using Image > Canvas Size. Select the gray anchor point and select the middle-right of anchor block. Increase width and height of your canvas accordingly.

Canvas Size

Current Size: 7.7M
Width: 11.34 cm
Height: 17 cm

OK
Cancel

New Size: 10.9M
Width: 16 cm
Height: 17 cm
Anchor:

Room to shine
We now have space for our improved shadow to cast.

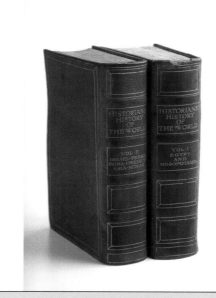

A new layer
Create a new layer (called 'White background') between the Background layer and the Books layer.
Fill the White background layer with white (Edit > Fill > White).

Layers | Channels | Paths

Normal   Opacity: 100 %

☐ Preserve Transparency

👁 Books
👁 ✏ **White background**
👁 Background

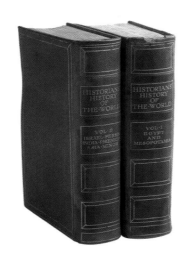

Shadow in progress
Create a new layer called Shadow 1 between the Books and White Background layers. Keep the Shadow 1 layer active and load a selection of the books by Command/Ctrl-clicking the Books layer. Then fill the selection on the Shadow 1 layer with black (Edit > Fill > Black).

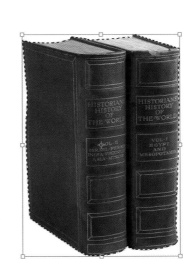

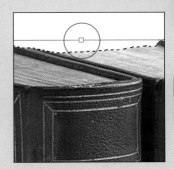

Tweak and distort
Keep the Shadow 1 layer active and select Distort (Edit > Transform > Distort).
Note: If Edit > Transform Path appears instead of Transform, and it's dimmed, go back to the paths palette and deselect the path by clicking under the path.

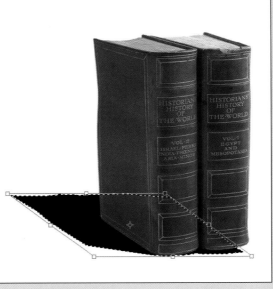

Cast shadow simulation
Use the top centre handle of the Transform selection and drag it to the left to simulate a cast shadow.
Double click on the Transform selection (or hit Return) to commit the transform when you are satisfied with its position.

Almost there
You now have the solid outline of your new shadow.

Channel work
Create an alpha channel (Alpha 1) by saving the selection (Select > Save Selection). Deselect the selection (Command/Ctrl-D).
Duplicate the alpha channel (Alpha 1) by dragging it onto the Create New Channel button. The new channel will automatically be named Alpha 2.

Gradual gradient
Click on the Gradient tool in the tool palette and select the black and white linear pattern from the Options Bar. (Ensure that the mode is normal.)
Using the Gradient tool, draw a diagonal line from the top left to the bottom right of the selection.

Click the Gradient tool to bring up the Linear Gradient options in the Options Bar.

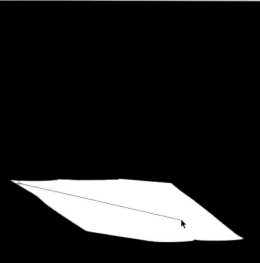

Mode: Normal | Opacity: 100% | ☐ Reverse ☑ Dither ☑ Transparency

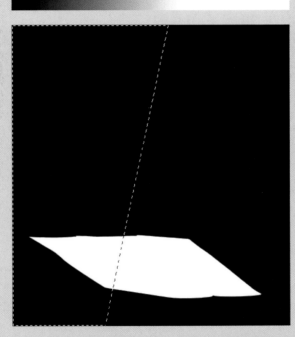

White light

Alpha 2 now looks like this. If it looks exactly like this, with white on the left and black on the right, you will need to invert the selection in the next step.

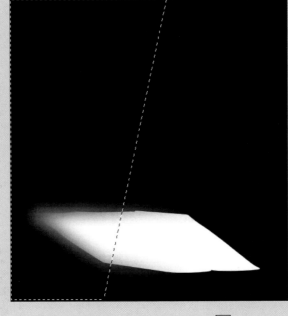

Mix , match and blur

Now we wish to load our new gradient channel into our cast shadow channel (Alpha 1) to make a selection that will create a shadow that fades with distance.

Select the Alpha 1 channel. Command/Ctrl-click on Alpha 2 in the Channels palette to load that selection into Alpha 1. Invert the selection (Select > Inverse or Shift-Command/ Ctrl-I).

Blur the new selection using Gaussian Blur (Filter > Blur > Gaussian Blur). The radius depends on the resolution of your file.

This is the **result**.

Fine tuning

Deselect the selection (Command/Ctrl-D), then blur the whole channel (Filter > Blur > Gaussian Blur) with a smaller radius (below).

This is the **result** after the second blur.

A smooth transition
Tweak the channel using Curves
(Image > Adjustments > Curves)
to eliminate the double-imaging
and to give the selection a
smooth transition between the
sharper area and the
soft/blurred area.

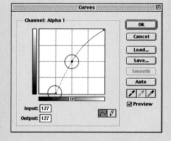

In the Curves dialogue box, drag the
shadow handle in about one quarter
(Input 25%, Output 0%).
Click and drag the curve to bump out
the mid-point to restore the highlights.

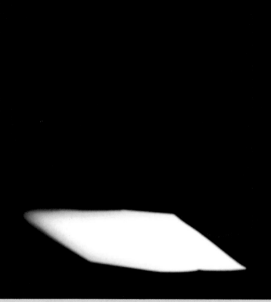

Now here's the cool part.
We can use our **new shadow
channel** in conjunction with the
Gradient tool to create a smooth
fading, blurred, perspective
shadow.

A little more involved
Turn off the Shadow 1 layer in
the Layers palette by clicking
the eye button. Create a new
layer called Shadow 2.
Load the Alpha 1 channel
(Select > Load Selection).
Select the Gradient tool, then
draw a gradient across the
selection.
Be careful to ensure that your
foreground/background colours
(in the Tools palette) are black
and white and that you will
draw the gradient in the correct
direction.

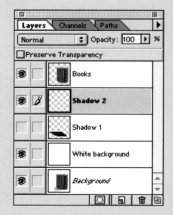

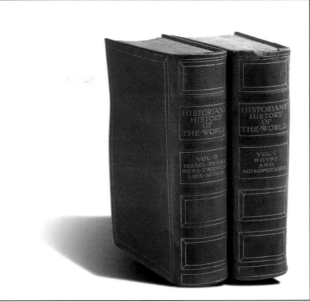

Don't forget that shadows should usually be in Multiply mode to combine with the background.

Too much shadow?

OK. So now we have a wonderful shadow but it extends in front of the books. So we must remove this part.

We will use a Layer mask to clean up the shadow which will leave our books looking stark against the white ground.
To add a touch of realism, we will add a small shadow under the books.

Clever solutions

1. To clean up the shadow, add a Layer mask to the Shadow 2 layer and carefully paint out the offending shadow.
2. The shadow itself will then look something like this.
3. Clean, but not realistic.
4. Add a new layer under the books, select the books, and fill the selection with black.

5. Deselect the selection. Give the new shadow a small Gaussian blur until you see it creeping from under the books. The books now look more solid and appear to be sitting on a surface.

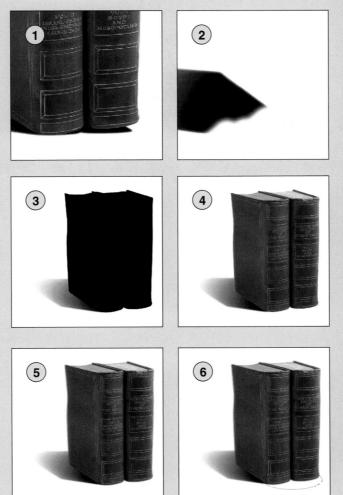

6. Finally, we need to use another Layer mask to have the new shadow appear only at the front of the books.
Experienced users may like to include a surface reflection of the books as shown in the introductory picture at the beginning of this article.

05 - Light & Shadow

Relighting An Image	**Difficulty: Easy**	**Carl Stevens**
	Photoshop's Lighting Effects filter gives you a wide range of possibilities for lighting your images. Carl Stevens shows you how to use Lighting Effects to relight a scene, adding light to dark images, changing the focus and adding warmth. You can even exaggerate the original texture with lighting effects.	

Starting image
This shop window is somewhat flat and too dark, so the eye is attracted by the lighter exterior. Much of the interesting detail is in shadow.
We wish to create a subtle focus inside and brighten the whole interior a little, adding warmth.

Lighting Effects

The Lighting Effects dialogue can appear daunting at first.
The main areas of interest are the preview window and the Light Type pull-down.
You can start lighting an image with these two areas before experimenting with the other controls.

Preview window

Expand or reduce the light's depth

Expand or reduce the light's width

Light centre point: reposition light by dragging point

Direction of light

Add new lights by dragging them into the preview window

Lighting Styles can be saved and reused

Three light types are available: Direction light, Omni light and Spotlight.

Lighting properties for each light can be adjusted here along with the colour of the light.

Grayscale images (including alpha channels) can be used as Texture Channels to give a 3D effect to your scene lighting.

Tip
Lighting Effects works only in RGB, not CMYK.

Tip
During a single session, Photoshop remembers the Lighting Effects settings you choose. So the next time you open Lighting Effects, the last used settings are there.

Tip
If you want to return to the default settings without quitting Photoshop, choose a style other than Default from the Style pull-down, then select Default to reset the default settings.

Tip
With 'Preview' selected, you will get instant feedback on the appearance of the light.

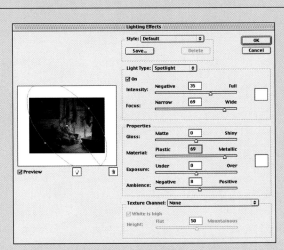

Default settings

This is how the Lighting Effects dialogue box looks when you first open it.
The light ellipse has sympathetic handles to control the effect.
Note that there is no lighting effect outside the ellipse and this shadow will show in the final result.

Adjusting the lighting

The light ellipse can be expanded or reduced using the handles at its top and sides. To move the position of the light, select its white centre point and drag it over your picture. To remove a light and start again, select the trash icon at the bottom of the preview window. To create another light, or to add additional lights, drag the lightbulb into the preview window. Expanding the default light ellipse's depth and width gives us a light which lights the lower half of our image.

Colouring the light

Click on the colour swatch in the Light Type Controls to change the colour of the light to a pale yellow (Y10) to resemble sunlight. Choose your preferred colour with the Color Picker, then click OK. Click OK again to apply the lighting effect.

The original
This is what we started with.

Duplicate the background
Our first step is to duplicate
the background layer.
The copy will be the layer on
which we perform the Lighting
Effects filter.
With the Background Copy layer
active, select the Lighting
Effects filter (Filter > Render >
Lighting Effects).

Normal blending mode
Using a Normal blending mode
for our 'Lighting' layer, the
shadows in the corners act
like a radiosity drop-off.
The yellow light source has
added warmth to the room
and created a suggestion
of reflected sunlight.

Lighten blending mode
Using the Lighten blending
mode for the 'Lighting' layer,
nothing is darker than it was
before.
We are left with only the
warming effects, making the
shop window seem more
inviting.

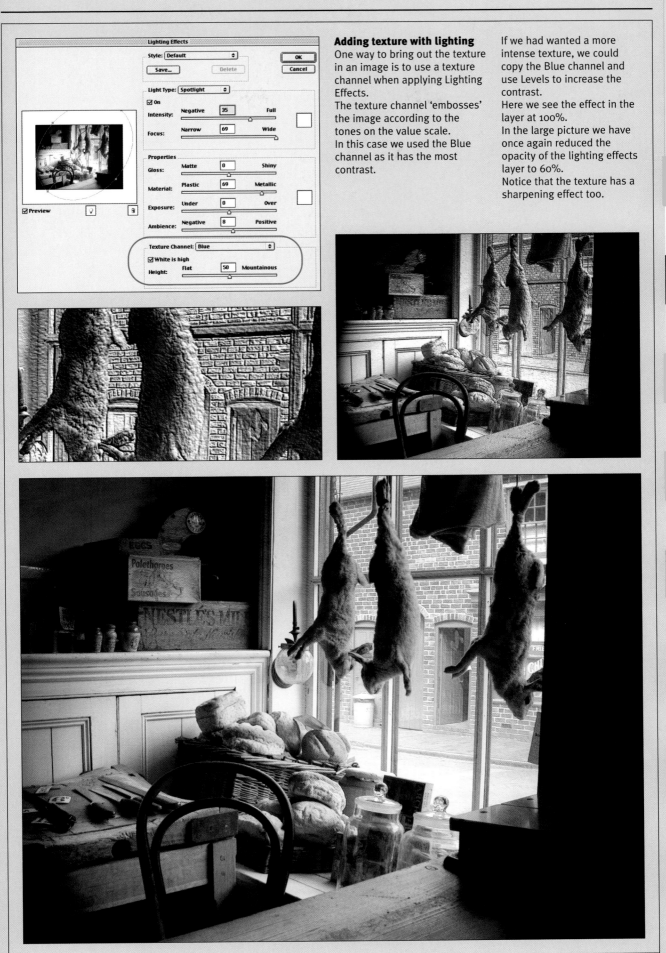

Adding texture with lighting

One way to bring out the texture in an image is to use a texture channel when applying Lighting Effects.

The texture channel 'embosses' the image according to the tones on the value scale.

In this case we used the Blue channel as it has the most contrast.

If we had wanted a more intense texture, we could copy the Blue channel and use Levels to increase the contrast.

Here we see the effect in the layer at 100%.

In the large picture we have once again reduced the opacity of the lighting effects layer to 60%.

Notice that the texture has a sharpening effect too.

	Difficulty: Intermediate	Colin Wood
Advanced levels	The first (and sometimes only) thing you have to fix in a picture is the levels. A picture may not have actual black and white points, but a narrow dynamic range makes for a 'thin' image. Photoshop's Levels adjustment does a great all-over job, but that's the problem; it's all over. Here's a new way with Levels.	

In this tip we will improve the levels of our picture by employing Photoshop's powerful blend modes. Then we will use Levels to tweak the results.

Ancient monument; old problem

This picture of Stonehenge was taken with a digital camera on a typically overcast day. It is generally dull and flat, but the sky is interesting and the clouds definitely add to the scene. The subject (the stones) is more or less in silhouette and sits as part of the middle distance rather than being the main subject of the picture. We can improve this.

Ideally we would like to enhance all three elements of this picture: the sky; the stones; and the grass. The contrast is bad and the detail is hard to see.

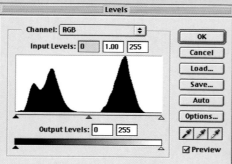

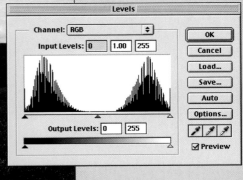

Auto Levels

In difficult cases like these, Auto Levels rarely does a very good job.
As you can see from the histogram, the two bunches of shades have expanded to cover a greater range, but the picture looks worse. The subject is even darker than when we started.

This is not the answer to our problem.

Manual Levels

Let's look at a manual Levels adjustment.
Here we have adjusted the black and white points and bumped out the midtones. The 'before' and 'after' Levels dialogue boxes are shown below.
The result is that the subject is a lot lighter but we have lost the sky detail. So while we have a picture that will print better than the original, it is still flat and a little uninteresting. If you examine the histograms you will see that we have stretched the tones over the full range, but the basic structure has remained the same. Ideally we would like to bring the sky down the scale and take the stones and grass up the scale.
We can do this by treating each of these areas in a different way.

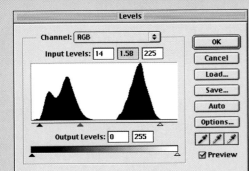

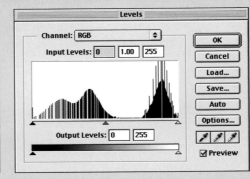

Before and after Levels

The Levels dialogue box on the left shows the original histogram and the settings that were used for the adjustment. The dialogue box on the right shows the histogram after the adjustment. The tones of the stones and the grass are distributed over a wider range but we have made the same adjustment to the entire picture.

Our solution involves using the Screen blend mode to lighten the stones and grass in conjunction with the Multiply blend mode for the sky. Both will interact with the original Background layer

The best map
Quite often it is advisable to use a duplicate of the image itself to make adjustments. After all, it contains a perfect 'index' of the tonal range and colours, and all in the right places!

Examine the original

Examine the original picture and its histogram and you will notice that the tones of the stones and grass are bunched towards the shadow end of the scale. We want to open out the shades and move them up the scale. The Screen mode will do that.

 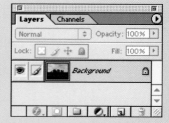

One Screen layer

Make a duplicate of the Background layer and use the Screen blend mode. The new layer will interact with the Background layer, as if we are shining light through the new layer. Notice how the tones in the histogram have opened up.

 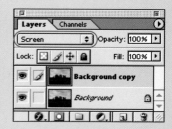

Two Screen layers

If you stack copies of the Screen mode layer, the image will get progressively lighter, moving the entire picture up the histogram scale.
For our purposes we will use just the one Screen layer.

 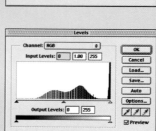 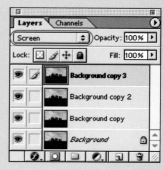

Make a mask from a channel

So that we can apply the blend mode layers to different sections of the picture, we need to create two masks (alpha channels), each the inverse of the other.
Select the RGB channel with the most contrast (in this case the Blue channel).

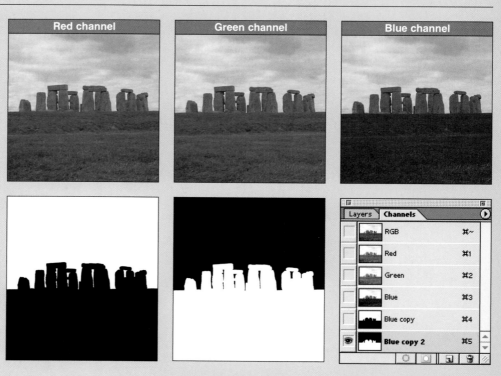

Red channel | Green channel | Blue channel

Duplicate and invert

Use Levels to turn the channel into solid black and white. Paint in difficult areas. Duplicate the channel and invert it (Command/Ctrl-I). This gives you two channels that can be used to create layer masks on the Screen and Multiply layers.

Multiplying the sky

Now we want to emphasise the clouds.

Duplicate the Background layer again and use the Multiply blend mode.

Here we have shown the new Multiply layer with the Screen layer turned off.

This has given the clouds a lot of body but has turned our monument into a silhouette.

Next we will use masks to separate the image areas affected by the Screen and Multiply layers.

Original	Image with Screen & Multiply layers

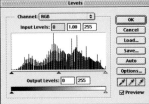

Overlapping tones

We have succeeded in moving the dark tones up the scale and the light tones down the scale. In fact they now overlap in the histogram.

The image is much better, but the Levels histogram of the complete image shows that we are not using the full dynamic tonal range.

So the final step will be the carry out another manual Levels adjustment.

Final layers

Opacity

Multiply layer	30%
Screen layer	100%
White glow	70%

There, that's better!

Now we have a much more dynamic picture. Our final tweaks were to blur the foreground grass a little (as it had become a little too prominent) and to add some white to the sky to help the monument stand out better.

Once you have grasped the fundamentals of this tip you will find it second nature (and very quick) to use a Screen and a Multiply layer to get a better balance of levels across your entire image area.

	Difficulty: Medium	Daniel Wade
Curves without colour shift	Photoshop's Curves command is a powerful correction tool that can save the day depending on your knowledge of how it works. It does have a tendency to create colour shifts, so we show you how to restrict adjustments using the Luminosity blend mode.	

Curves for better contrast

Photoshop's Curves command is a powerful correction tool that can save the day depending on your knowledge of how it works. Though the Curves dialogue can appear intimidating, there are a couple of easy adjustments you can make to most images which will improve the contrast or just make the image punchier.

The downside to Curves is that you can make a mess of an image quicker than with any other correction tool (except maybe Brightness/Contrast). Let's try a couple of adjustments and limit them to just the areas we want.

Go for an adjustment layer

The best method of making a Curves adjustment is to create a Curves adjustment layer (Layer > New Adjustment Layer > Curves). This means that we can re-edit the Curves without permanently affecting our original.

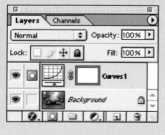

S-Curve

A common Curves adjustment, known as the 'S-Curve', increases the contrast.

Add a point towards the bottom of the curve and pull down. Do the same again at the top of the curve, but this time drag up. What this does is make the curve steeper through the middle of the curve which increases the contrast through the midtones.

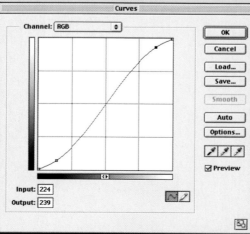

Curves?

Why use Curves when you can use Levels to adjust contrast and set black/white points? Levels lets you make adjustments that shift the tone values of an image or stretch them across a larger tonal range.

Curves also allow you to shift the tone values of an image and stretch or compress them to suit. The advantage that you have with Curves is that you can lock points on the curve which restricts your adjustments to either the shadows, midtones or highlights.

Original | Curves adjustment | Luminance mode

Maintaining skin colour

Our Curves adjustment shifts the colours in the image. This is especially obvious with skin colour.

The solution is to restrict the correction to the luminance so that the skin colour is unaffected.

Of course, Curves can also be used to increase the saturation of the colour. Experiment with blend modes and opacity of the Curves layer.

Unwanted colour shift

In some cases, the colour shift that you create by making an S-Curve adjustment will make the colours in your image more vibrant. Sometimes the colour shift can be quite marked.

No shifting

Blend modes are one of the really great features of Photoshop. You can restrict the Curves adjustment to a particular range of values simply by selecting the right blend mode.

Here we use Luminosity which restricts our adjustment to only brightness values which won't affect the colours in the image. An equivalent adjustment would be to change to LAB Color Mode and run the Curves adjustment on the Lightness channel. Experiment with different curves and the opacity slider to get the right correction.

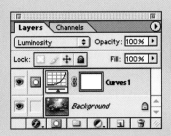

6
Helpful Hints

Difficulty: Easy	Carl Stevens

Make better line drawings

An artist expects to see the same fine lines of his drawing converted to his digital file. Most flatbed scanners have only a small preview area which makes it difficult to see the final result, and time consuming to get the desired quality. Carl Stevens demonstrates how to obtain the best result from your lineart scan.

Too light: details are lost
When scanning lineart you can use the scanner's lineart settings, but it can be difficult to find a setting that allows for the fine lines in the light areas, (left), and still shows all of the detail in the darker areas (right).

Too dark: areas fill in
Carl Stevens suggests that you start by scanning the lineart as greyscale and then make the necessary adjustments in Photoshop.

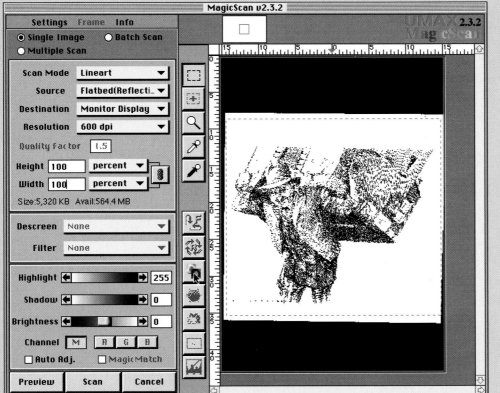

Small preview
With most scanners the preview window is only small making it difficult to see exactly what you will get.

Using the built-in scanner settings

Lineart scan: light setting
This scan uses the scanner's lineart setting. It does a good job in the shadow areas, but some of the finer lines are lost.

Lineart scan: darker setting
The second scan uses a darker lineart setting. It holds the fine lines but fills in a bit too much on the shadow areas.

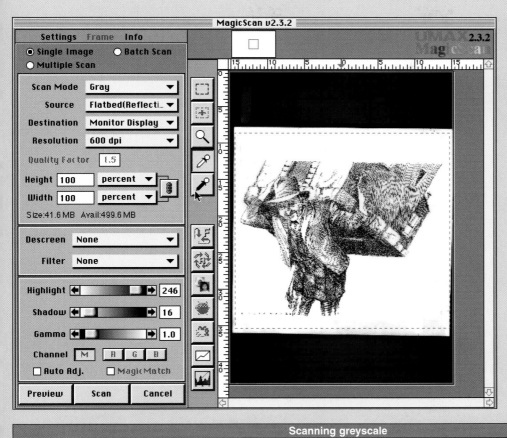

Scanning greyscale

Greyscale scans – the answer
The way I like to do these types of scans is to scan the image as a greyscale, giving it a higher resolution than is usual with a tiff image. Here I have used 600dpi. This will take more time to scan, but the results are worth it.

Tweak in greyscale mode
Once you have the greyscale scan, you can make the necessary fine adjustments in Photoshop.
Another advantage with this method is that you can take your artwork out of the scanner and have it as a reference as you are manipulating the job.

Brightness and contrast!

It is common opinion among imaging professionals that you should never use Photoshop's Brightness/Contrast control (Image >Adjustments > Brightness/Contrast). All proficient practitioners are supposed to use Levels and Curves. Well, Carl Stevens has found a use for the forbidden control.

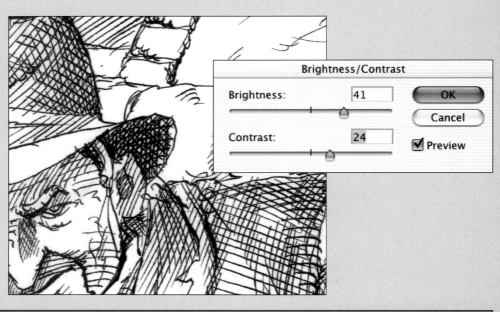

Adjusting the greyscale scan

Down to details

We first pick the areas that will be a problem—dark areas and thin lines.
Select an area that has both if possible and then adjust the Brightness and Contrast. Brightness acts on the white and Contrast darkens the lines. Be careful to check more than one area. Take it gradually doing a little bit at a time.

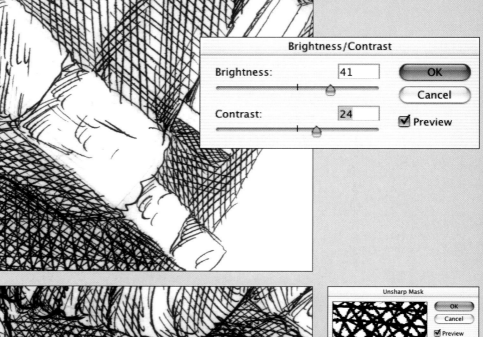

Increasing definition

When we've done as much as we can with the Brightness and Contrast settings, use Filter > Sharpen > Unsharp Mask which helps bring out the definition in the darker areas.
You can also use the Burn tool in any problem areas.

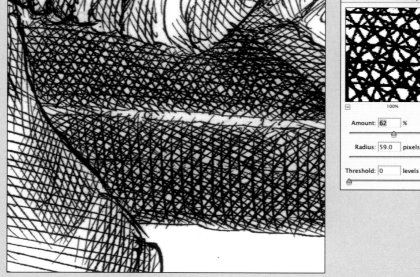

Image	**Mode** ▶	Bitmap...

Image menu:
- Mode ▶
- Adjustments ▶
- Duplicate...
- Apply Image...
- Calculations...
- Image Size...
- Canvas Size...
- Rotate Canvas ▶
- Crop
- Trim...
- Reveal All
- Histogram...
- Trap...

Mode submenu:
- Bitmap...
- ✓ Grayscale
- Duotone...
- Indexed Color
- RGB Color
- CMYK Color
- Lab Color
- Multichannel
- ✓ 8 Bits/Channel
- 16 Bits/Channel
- Color Table...
- Assign Profile...
- Convert to Profile...

Bitmap

Resolution
Input: 600 pixels/inch
Output: 600   pixels/inch

OK
Cancel

Method
Use: 50% Threshold
Custom Pattern:

Greyscale to Bitmap Mode

Finally, change the Mode from greyscale to bitmap by going to Image > Mode > Bitmap.

As you can see, by scanning the artwork as greyscale it allows you to work on any problem areas in Photoshop.
If you start out with lineart there is very little you can do with it in Photoshop so what you scan is what you get.

Final bitmap image

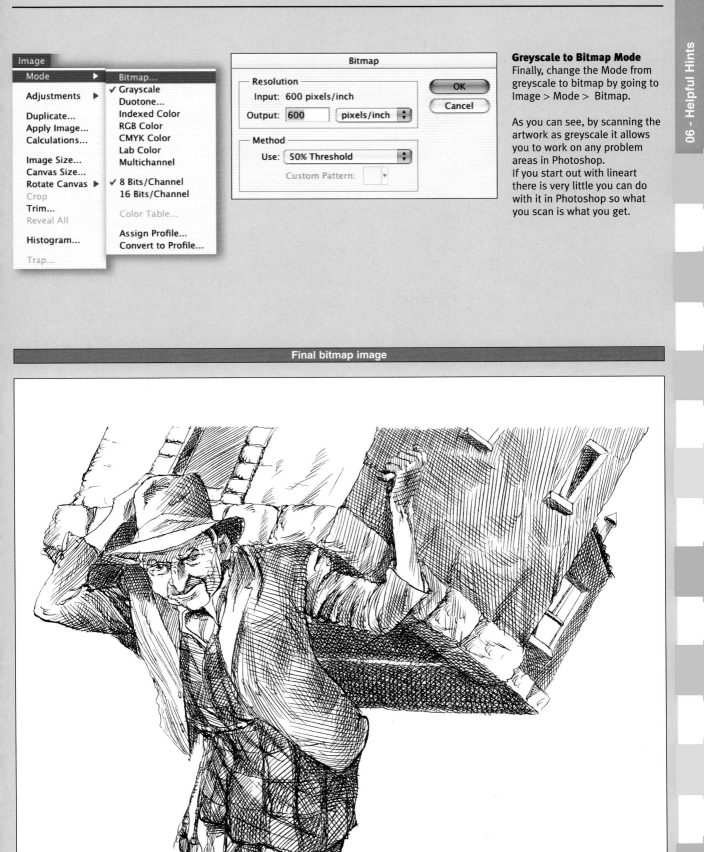

ROCCO·FAZZARI

Preparing scanned cartoons

Reproducing colour cartoons in print can be a nightmare, especially when there are fine black lines. If the print registration is not accurate, you will see all four CMYK colours instead of a solid black line. Carl Stevens explains how to reduce the colours under the black using CMYK Setup.

This cartoon was an RGB file that was sent to production to be printed. We need to ensure that there is as little CMY colour as possible under the black so that if the print is out of register, it won't be obvious.
All of this tip is concerned with the Adobe Photoshop CMYK Setup and the conversion from RGB to CMYK.
We show how the cartoon would look using Photoshop's default setting and then how to achieve superior results.

Note: An alternative way of doing this tip is to write an Action to change over all print set ups so that one Action button will fix the problem!

Image courtesy of Ken Emmerson

Medium Black Generation
Photoshop will convert from RGB to CMYK according to how the preferences have been specified.
Here is what happens if the Photoshop default setting of Medium Black Generation is used.

Out of registration
Without changing any of the default settings, simply change the mode from RGB to CMYK. Look carefully at each of the channels and you will probably find that cyan, magenta and yellow can be seen in addition to the black linework.
This is exactly what is needed for normal picture reproduction, but is not so good for linework. Unless the printer is spot on with registration, you may see all four CMYK colours.

Now let's look at Photoshop's CMYK setup and see what can be done to minimise the colour underneath the black lines.

If registration is not spot on, you may end up with results like this example.

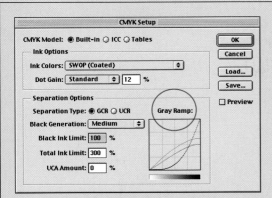

This example is concerned with only the Separation Options, which control how CMYK plates are generated.

Separation options

When converting RGB values to CMYK, Photoshop uses the information in the CMYK Setup dialogue boxes.

It is possible to modify Black Generation method, Ink Limits and change Separation Type when necessary. If you have already converted the image to CMYK, you must reconvert the image after adjusting Separation Options, and don't forget to revert to your previous settings once you have finished. Photoshop's default Separation Type is GCR (Gray Component Replacement), but you can also use UCR (Undercolour Removal). The choice on which to use is based on paper type and print requirements, so you should check with your printer. With GCR, black ink is used to replace portions of Cyan, Magenta and Yellow in coloured areas as well as in neutral areas.

You can choose the degree of Black Generation from the drop-down menu. The effect on the relative amounts of Cyan, Magenta, Yellow and Black are shown in the graph on the right (Gray Ramp).

In the example below, we have shown the difference between each of the CMYK plates when the Black Generation setting is changed from the default Medium to Maximum.

No black, just grey!
The illustrations on this page
have been changed from RGB
to CMYK using Medium Black
Generation.

The yellow plane is reproduced
without the black channel to
demonstrate that grey can be
created from cyan, magenta and
yellow alone.

The final illustration may look
the same as the one on the
opposite page but may be more
difficult to print.

Medium Black Generation
To test the effect of changing
Black Generation, select File >
Color Settings > CMYK Setup.
(In Photoshop 4, go to File >
Color Settings > Separation
Setup.)

The CMYK Setup dialogue box
shows the Photoshop default
settings.
Note that the Black Generation
is set on Medium, and see the
effect this has on CMYK values
in the Gray Ramp.

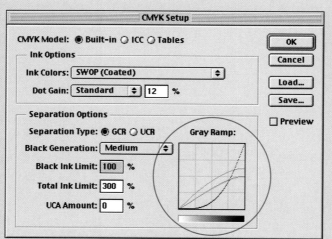

In the Gray Ramp, the horizontal axis
represents the neutral colour value,
from 0% (white) to 100% (black).
The vertical axis represents the amount
of each ink that will be generated
for the given value.

With this setting, neutral
colours have equal amounts of
Magenta and Yellow with the
Cyan curve extending slightly
beyond as a small extra amount
of cyan is required to produce a
true neutral.
However, as the example here
shows, if registration
is slightly off, all four of the
colour plates will be seen.
The answer is to reduce the
amounts of Cyan, Magenta
and Yellow and replace them
with Black.

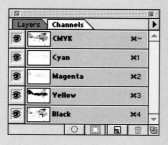

Clean me up!
The illustrations on this page have been changed from RGB to CMYK using Maximum Black Generation.

The yellow plane is reproduced without the black channel to show the areas from which we have removed Cyan, Magenta and Yellow and replaced them with black.

The final illustration may look the same as the one on the opposite page but will be easier to print.

Maximum Black Generation
Try each of the Black Generation settings and watch the Gray Ramp to see how the individual colours are affected.

When Black Generation is on Maximum, the Cyan, Magenta and Yellow curves are almost flat, resulting in minimal dot in the three colours. If printed slightly out of register, it will be very hard to notice.

Although this is a good answer for this cartoon, adjustments to the separation settings should be done with caution, and you should always speak to your printer about the best settings for the job you are working on.

And remember to change your settings back once you have finished the job!

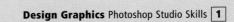

Design Graphics Photoshop Studio Skills 1

06 - Helpful Hints

Difficulty: Easy	Colin Wood

Bringing out detail without grain

Unsharp masking is the usually the first, and sometimes the only method we use to sharpen images for print or web. But sometimes you want to 'sharpen softly', without bringing out the grain or emphasising certain details or patterns. The High Pass filter is the answer.

Soft as a petal
This picture is a little soft to go straight to print. It needs to be sharpened slightly but we don't want to make it too harsh.

Close-up
The image has a resolution of 300dpi and is seen here at a magnification of 200% (thus you are seeing it at 150dpi. The larger picture (above) is reproduced at 54%.

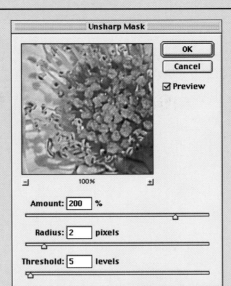

Unsharp Mask

For the purposes of this exercise, we will use settings slightly higher than normal for a digital picture like this.
Use Filter > Sharpen > Unsharp Mask to bring up the Unsharp Mask dialogue box.
Here we have used the following settings:
Amount : 200%
Radius : 2
Threshold : 5

Sharp and edgy

The sharpening has gone a little too far and lost the softness that was so appealing.

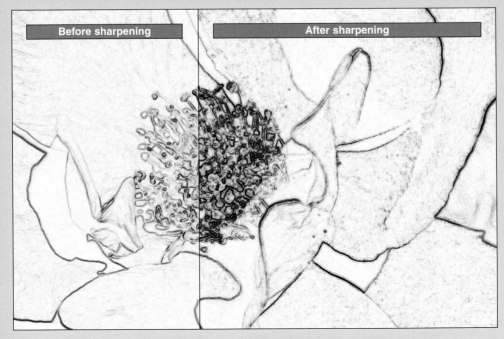

Before sharpening

After sharpening

How bad?

Sharpening works on edges. To see the extent to which you have introduced noise and edges, use Filter > Stylize > Find Edges. This is a very useful way to analyse your image.
Here you can see why the softness has been taken away.

Over the page we show how to avoid this problem.

High Pass layer

In order to use the High Pass filter instead of Unsharp Mask, duplicate the background layer.

Use Filter > Other > High Pass to bring up the High Pass dialogue box.

Use a small radius of between 3 and 5 pixels.

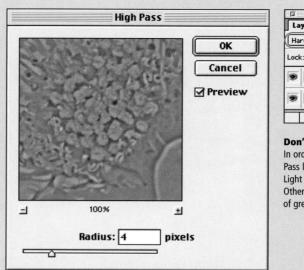

Don't forget

In order to sharpen the image, the High Pass layer must be changed to the Hard Light mode.

Otherwise you will be looking at a sea of grey!

Grey edges

Your image will now look like this. The High Pass filter turns the entire image into a 50% grey at a zero setting.

As the radius is increased, the edges come into view. It is the dark/light edges that sharpen the image when the layer is turned into Hard Light mode.

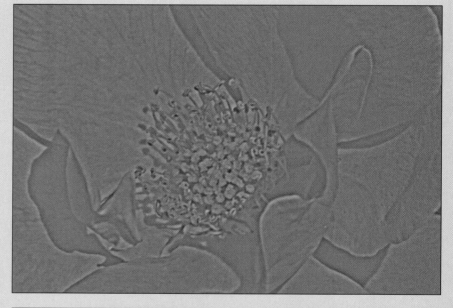

Comparison

Here is a comparison of our image in three forms:

1. The original image.

2. The image after an Unsharp Mask is applied (Amount 200%, Radius 2.0 pixels, Threshold 5).

3. The image using a Hard Light blend mode after the High Pass filter has been applied.

Original

Unsharp mask

High Pass

Old problem, new solution
Here is another example for which the High Pass sharpening technique is very useful.

Resolution and size
Image has a resolution of 300dpi and is shown here at 65% of actual size.

Detail
The details are shown at 200% of actual size.

Find Edges
Once again the Find Edges filter shows up the differences between the techniques.

Unsharp Mask

Amount 200%, Radius 2, Threshold 5

High Pass

Radius 3

High Pass filter test
This test file demonstrates the effect of the High Pass filter. Greater pixel radius settings are required for bigger files to have the same effect.

The High Pass filter
The High Pass filter is applied to the duplicate layer.

Blend mode: Normal
The original layer is underneath this but cannot be seen.

High Pass filter
Not used.

This is our starting point.

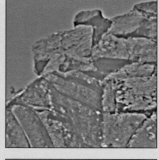

High Pass filter
Pixel radius: **4**

This radius enables the image to come through quite significantly and will create quite a difference once the blend mode is changed to Hard Light.

High Pass filter
Pixel radius: **0.1**

The minimum setting.
An all-over grey with slight detail is produced.

High Pass filter
Pixel radius: **10**

This is towards the top of the usable scale as a substitute for unsharp masking.

High Pass filter
Pixel radius: **1**

Notice how edges between light and dark areas are becoming visible. The greater the difference in adjacent tones, the sooner you begin to see something.

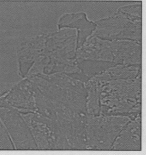

High Pass filter
Pixel radius: **25**

Notice how it becomes more difficult to discern the difference between settings as you go further up the scale.

High Pass filter
Pixel radius: **2**

Changes are quite marked at low radius settings. It is worth testing the final effect at this setting.

High Pass filter
Pixel radius: **50**

High Pass filter
Pixel radius: **3**

At this radius, the filter is quite effective in extracting detail.

High Pass filter
Pixel radius: **250**

This is the maximum pixel radius setting.

The High Pass filter
The High Pass filter is applied to the duplicate layer and the blend mode changed to Hard Light.

Blend mode: Hard Light
The High Pass layer interacts with the original layer, which is underneath.

High Pass filter
Not used

High Pass filter
Pixel radius: **4**

High Pass filter
Pixel radius: **0.1**

High Pass filter
Pixel radius: **10**

High Pass filter
Pixel radius: **1**

High Pass filter
Pixel radius: **25**

High Pass filter
Pixel radius: **2**

High Pass filter
Pixel radius: **50**

High Pass filter
Pixel radius: **3**

High Pass filter
Pixel radius: **250**

Don't forget
You will need greater pixel radius settings for higher resolution images.

	Difficulty: Intermediate	Julieanne Kost
RGB soft proofing	Photoshop 6.0 offers the ability to 'soft proof' your document directly on the monitor. This displays an on-screen preview of the document's colours as reproduced on a specific device. Julieanne Kost shows you how to set up Photoshop to print to a profiled printer that you have an ICC profile for.	

In past versions of Photoshop, you were only able to 'proof' what your image was going to look like on press. By selecting View > Preview, Photoshop previewed the image based on CMYK Setup settings. Photoshop 6.0 and later includes the same functionality for RGB images allowing you to preview how an RGB document's colours will look when reproduced on a variety of specific output devices.

Choose View > Proof Setup > Custom
Like Photoshop 5.5 you can preview the working CMYK, or the individual inks (working plates: C, M, Y, K), or the composite CMY inks (working plates). For on-screen work, you can still proof Macintosh RGB, Windows RGB or Monitor (Uncompensated) RGB.

View

Proof Setup	▶
Proof Colors	⌘Y
Gamut Warning	⇧⌘Y
Zoom In	⌘+
Zoom Out	⌘-
Fit on Screen	⌘0
Actual Pixels	⌥⌘0
Print Size	
Extras	⌘H
Show	▶
Rulers	⌘R
Snap	⇧⌘;
Snap To	▶
Lock Guides	⌥⌘;
Clear Guides	
New Guide...	
Lock Slices	
Clear Slices	

Custom...

✓ **Working CMYK**
Working Cyan Plate
Working Magenta Plate
Working Yellow Plate
Working Black Plate
Working CMY Plates

Macintosh RGB
Windows RGB
Monitor RGB

Simulate Paper White
Simulate Ink Black

Note
Uncheck Preserve Color Numbers to maintain the relationship between colours when soft proofing. This option is only available when the working space and profile space are in the same colour mode.

Create a custom profile setup
For Profile, select the profile for your output device that was supplied by the manufacturer or that you have created. If you can't locate a profile, check the manufacturer's web site.

Note
If you do not like the results of the Perceptual conversion, Colorimetric is also well-suited for photographs.

Specify a rendering intent for the conversion
Choosing Perceptual for the rendering intent typically results in the best conversion for photographic images.

Note
Not all profiles support these options.

Save the custom profile
Choosing Save, will save the settings as a group and add them to the bottom of the Proof Setup menu. If you're printing to more than one output device, saving custom settings can be more efficient and precise than constantly going back into the setup dialogue.

Tip
If you want the custom proof setup to be the default proof setup for documents, close all document windows before choosing the View > Proof Setup > Custom. Whatever you choose as the custom profile will then be selected when you select View > Proof Colours.

Additional options
Check the box to the left of 'Paper White' (Simulate > Paper White). This will enable you to preview—in the monitor space—the colour of the paper (or other print media) described by the profile. Selecting this option automatically selects the Simulate Ink Black option. Check Ink Black to preview—in the monitor space—the printable black on the specific paper (or other print media) as defined by the profile.

Friendly reminder
Remember that soft proofing is only as good as the profile for that device. Some manufacturers ship better profiles than others. To achieve the best results, it might be necessary to create a custom profile for your specific output device.

	Difficulty: Easy	Colin Wood
The big descreen	Outdoor events like this Formula One Grand Prix frequently have giant video screens which are difficult to photograph and which create moiré patterns when viewed on a monitor or when printed. Here's the fix.	

The day is sunny and yet the giant screen is easy to see when you are at the event. But they photograph a little dull and have a very pronounced dot grid which can give moiré patterns when viewed on a monitor or when printed. Here is a quick and easy way to make the most of a bad thing.

Two steps and we're done
What we have here is a two-stage process.
We will work only on the big screen, so the first thing to do is make a selection of the screen. First we will blur the image to get rid of the screen pattern. Then we will increase the colour saturation to brighten the image.

Cool tip
The screen will have perspective and so will be out of square. Make a rough selection, turn it into a QuickMask and then use Edit > Transform > Distort to tweak the selection.

This picture was taken with a Nikon CoolPix 990 digital camera. The image is 2,048 x 1,536 pixels, giving a 9Mb file.

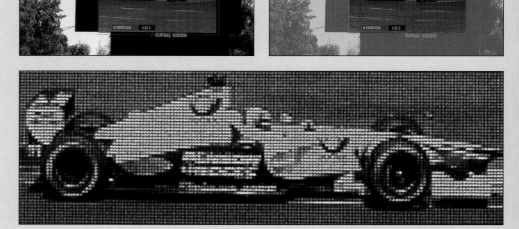

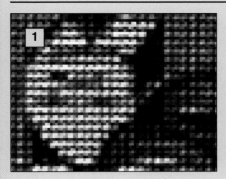

This is the problem
The screen image is formed from large pixels which are viewed against a black ground. The pattern will interact with any other pattern such as a monitor or when printed with a traditional screen.

Smooth but soft and dull
To this 9Mb file we applied a Gaussian Blur with a radius of 5. The blurring does eradicate the annoying screen pattern, but it also mixes the colours with the black between. This dulls the overall image.

Colour me bright
The image becomes soft which may be difficult to sharpen. But you can improve the dullness by increasing the colour saturation via the Hue/Saturation dialogue box. Increase it by +20 to +30.

What you think you see
So there you have it. Depending on the size of the screen in your image, it will probably look much better than it did despite the softness. People don't expect too much from outdoor screens. The best part is that you will not get an unsightly moiré pattern.

No edges
To see why this works so well, try Find Edges (Filter > Stylize > Find Edges) before and after the Gaussian Blur. That pesky pattern has completely disappeared, and so will your moiré pattern.

A touch of summer	Difficulty: Easy	Colin Wood
	Sometimes your memory of a scene is coloured by the weather; you remember the day as warm and sunny but your pictures look cool and overcast. Here's how to add a little sunshine easily using some colour and a layer blend mode.	

Cool

Warmer

This picture was taken on a summer's day but the weather was overcast and it looks a little cold. We would like to add some warmth, perhaps for a travel brochure to make it a little more inviting.
To make this a sunnier day we will add some yellow on another layer. The secret to success lies in selecting the best blending mode for the job.

Selecting a blending mode

Likely modes
It's often a good idea to try out various blending modes to see the effect they have. When you can see what they do you have a better idea of which may suit your purpose best.

Multiply mode adds colour everywhere and combines it with the background. This will give us a yellow sky and other highlights which is not what we want.

Screen mode is nearly what we want, for it does not affect the highlights. But it will leave a 'residue' of the light yellow colour over our background in the darker areas, thus reducing the dynamic range of the image.

Overlay mode combines the best of Multiply and Screen modes, lightening the highlights (note the sky) and combining the yellow with the darker tones. This is the mode we will use.

1

Original image

This is the image we wish to enhance with a little golden glow of summer.
Even though the sun is not casting hard shadows it is still possible to warm it up.

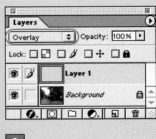
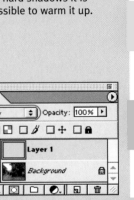

2

New yellow layer

Create a new layer and fill it with 100% yellow.
The layer blend mode will be the default of Normal. Change the blending mode to Overlay. At 100% opacity, the effect is far too harsh so we will need to reduce it.

3

Change opacity

Change the opacity of the new yellow layer to 10%.
Note that the highlights are clean (as with Screen mode) as the yellow mainly affects the darker areas and shadows. Worth a visit?

| Difficulty: Intermediate | Colin Wood |

Fixing sky problems

In your haste to catch the moment on film or CCD, sometimes you get more in your picture than you wanted — like the edge of a building in this case. If you don't want to crop off the offending intrusion, then you must fix the problem where it exists. Here are some tips for skies.

You can't pick the weather, especially if you're travelling, and you have to take the photograph come what may. Here we have a cloudy day in Paris, a sky that is very grainy and the edge of a building is intruding into the frame.

We will show you how to repair the sky, keeping the grain intact.

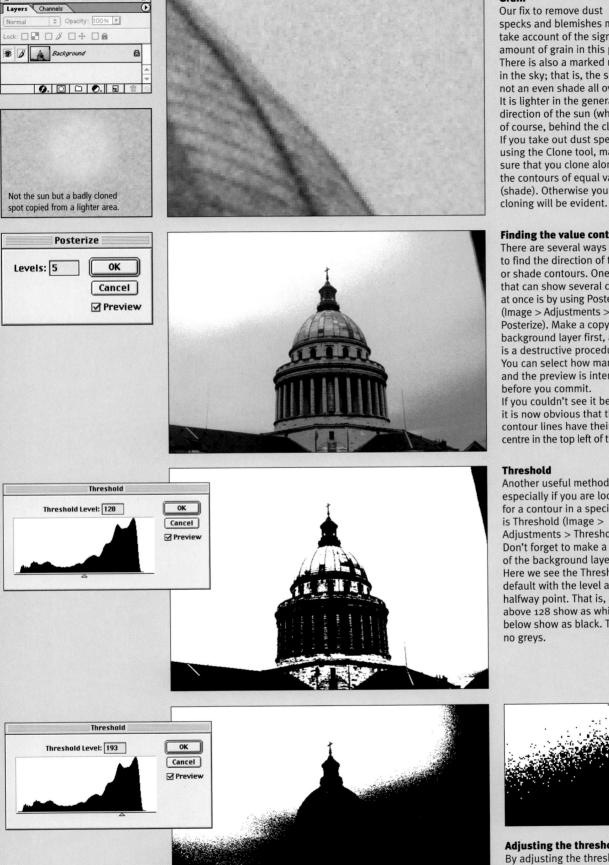

Not the sun but a badly cloned spot copied from a lighter area.

Grain

Our fix to remove dust specks and blemishes must take account of the significant amount of grain in this picture. There is also a marked radiosity in the sky; that is, the sky is not an even shade all over. It is lighter in the general direction of the sun (which is, of course, behind the clouds). If you take out dust specks using the Clone tool, make sure that you clone along the contours of equal value (shade). Otherwise your cloning will be evident.

Finding the value contours

There are several ways in which to find the direction of the value or shade contours. One method that can show several contours at once is by using Posterize (Image > Adjustments > Posterize). Make a copy of your background layer first, as this is a destructive procedure. You can select how many levels and the preview is interactive before you commit.
If you couldn't see it before, it is now obvious that the contour lines have their bright centre in the top left of the image.

Threshold

Another useful method, especially if you are looking for a contour in a specific area, is Threshold (Image > Adjustments > Threshold). Don't forget to make a copy of the background layer first. Here we see the Threshold default with the level at the halfway point. That is, all values above 128 show as white, all below show as black. There are no greys.

Adjusting the threshold

By adjusting the threshold slider you can move the point where black turns to white. Once again the preview is interactive so you can view the result before you commit.

Removing big things

Cloning is only good for small blemishes in the sky. When it comes to large ones we must replace the sky itself. We will copy a section of sky and move it over the blemish. Start by duplicating the background layer.
Then make a selection with the Lasso tool. To get straight lines, hold down the Option/Alt- key and click where you want a change of direction. Click and hold to draw freehand. Release the mouse and the ends will join up.

Save and blur

Save an alpha channel of the selection and then blur the channel. This will make for a smooth transition between the two sections of sky.

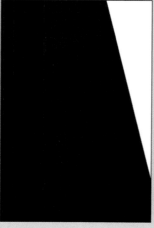

Looks the same

Load the selection and create a layer mask. The channel, Alpha 1, will automatically appear in the layer mask. At this stage the image will not have changed.

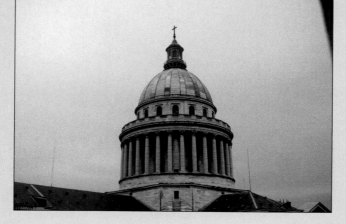

Unlink mask from layer

If we view just the new layer we can see that we have sectioned off the area of the sky that contains the blemish.
We wish to move the sky over but keep the mask where it is. So click in the layer palette between the two icons to unlink the mask from the layer.

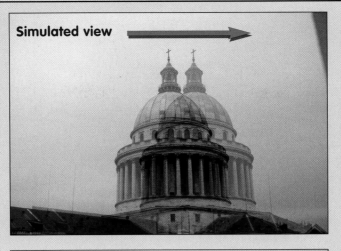

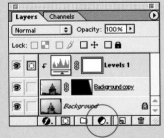

Here we have lowered the opacity of the upper layer in order to see through to the background layer. In practice you would not do this as you would want to see the final result as you move the upper layer.

Simulated view

Move the sky

Click on the Layer Mask. Select the Move tool and move the sky to the right. You will see the blemish disappear. If you wish to constrain movement to horizontal, hold down the Shift key. Depending on the position of the value contours, you may be able to move the sky to match the shades exactly without further adjustment.

New sky

The blur helps to disguise the edge of the moved sky. In this example the result is quite good as it is. But that is not always the case.

To create a grouped Levels adjustment, hold down the Option/Alt key while selecting the adjustment layer menu. This will bring up the New Layer dialogue box and you can then select 'Group with Previous Layer'.

Darker or lighter

You may find that the result shows lighter or darker than the original sky.

In this case you can use a grouped Levels adjustment. In the image below we have darkened the new sky which extends the darkening of the radiosity, thus aiding believability.

The finished result can be a perfect match, especially because you have used the original grain, colour and texture.

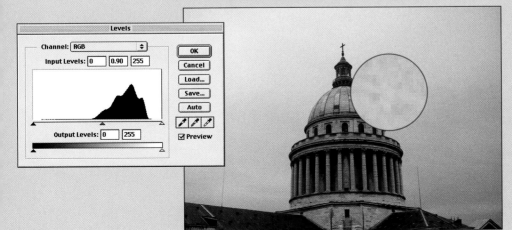

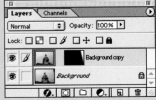

The final touch

In this case we darkened the new sky a little by moving the mid-point slider to 0.90.

This technique works well because it retains the original grain and follows the original value contour lines.

Simulating gingham fabric	Difficulty: Intermediate / advanced	Colin Wood
	It is sometimes easier to create exactly what you want rather than hunt around only to find that you still don't have what you need. This tip to simulate gingham fabric incorporates several hot tips that will save you hours and enhance your proficiency in Photoshop.	

In this tip you will learn how to use Calculations and Displacement maps to produce a realistic piece of woven fabric.

New empty file

Create a new empty RGB file. For this example our file is 1500 x 1,500 pixels. You will need the Layers and Channels palettes to be available.

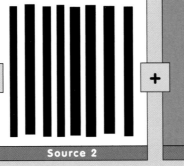

Create 3 alpha channels

In order to make the basic gingham fabric pattern, you will need to create three alpha channels. One channel will have solid black horizontal stripes, the second will have solid black vertical stripes and the third will be filled with 50% grey (Edit > Fill > 50% grey).

Source 1 + **Source 2** + **50% grey** **Mask**

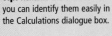
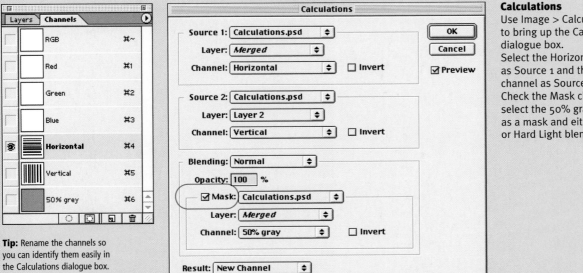

Tip: Rename the channels so you can identify them easily in the Calculations dialogue box.

Calculations

Use Image > Calculations to bring up the Calculations dialogue box. Select the Horizontal channel as Source 1 and the Vertical channel as Source 2. Check the Mask checkbox and select the 50% gray channel as a mask and either Normal or Hard Light blend mode.

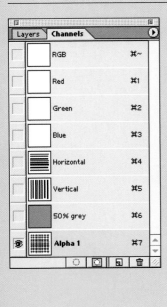
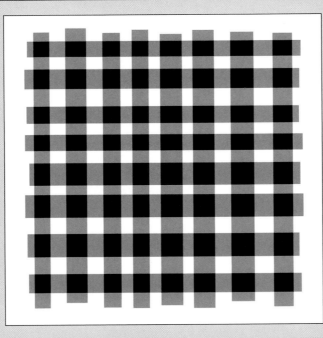

Gingham pattern

Hey presto! A gingham pattern appears in the new channel created by Calculations. Because the mask works as a positive mask on one channel, and a negative mask on the other, mask values of exactly 50% act the same on both. Where they overlap they combine to give a value of 100%.

R: 208
G: 77
B: 79

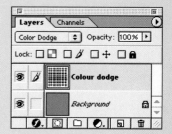

Just like magic!
This is the core of the tip.
Create a suitable foreground
colour and fill the background
layer with it (Option/Alt-Delete).
Copy the new (gingham pattern)
channel and paste it into a
new layer (it will change from
greyscale to RGB automatically).
Change the blend mode to
Color Dodge and the pattern
will take on colour.

Wow, that's really cool!
Now we need to add some
fabric texture.

Creating a weave texture
Create a new black channel
and fill with noise
(we used Uniform noise).
Make 2 copies of the channel.
In one copy, use Filter > Blur >
Motion Blur to stretch the
noise vertically, in the other,
stretch it horizontally.
Use Levels on both to
increase the contrast.

Use Calculations to combine the
vertical and horizontal stretched
noise into a new channel.
Use Overlay or Hard Light blend
mode (each will give a different
horizontal to vertical bias but
the effect is basically the same).

New channel
Add noise

Copy 1
Motion blur vertical

Copy 2
Motion blur horizontal

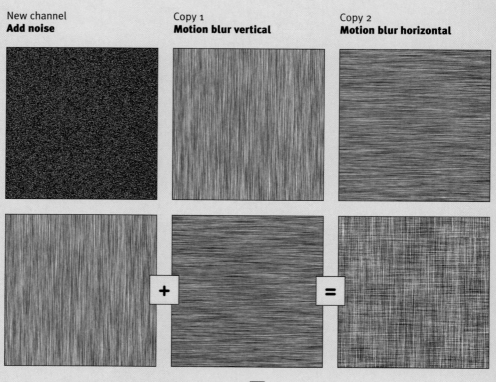

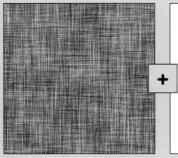

+

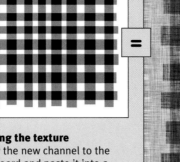

=

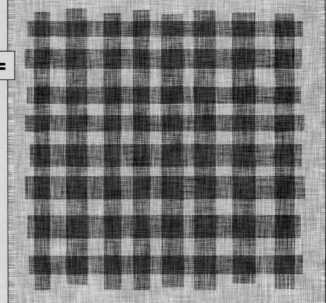

Adding the texture
Now use Calculations again to combine the weave texture with the gingham pattern. This time use the Subtract blend mode and create a new channel.

Adding the texture
Copy the new channel to the clipboard and paste it into a new layer. Duplicate this new layer twice and change the blending modes to Luminosity and Overlay.
Both of these layers will need to be at about 35% opacity.

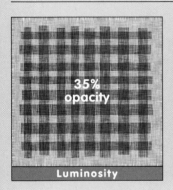

35% opacity

Luminosity

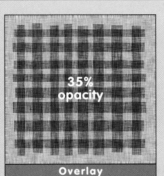

35% opacity

Overlay

Colour Dodge

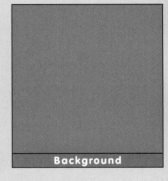

Background

The layer stack
The final effect is gained with just 4 layers: two copies of the texture layer. one copy of the gingham pattern, and the base colour layer.

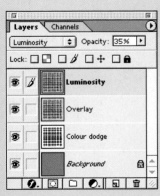

The layer stack in the palette
Texture: Luminosity, 35% opacity
Texture: Overlay, 35% opacity
Gingham pattern: Color Dodge
Background colour

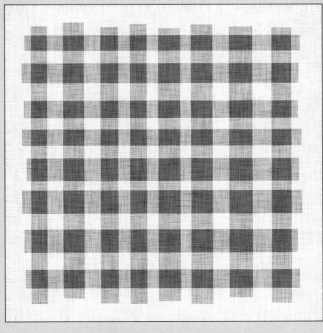

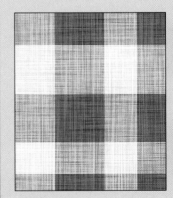

A flat sheet
We're almost there. Now we have a convincing but flat piece of fabric. Notice the edges have a fringe effect which is caused by Photoshop's inability to motion blur the noise right to the edge. In this case it is a fringe benefit! The next steps will add some 3D realism.

Creating wrinkles

Fabric is rarely absolutely flat, so we will add some wrinkles. We will do this by moving the pixels using a displacement map.

Click on the default colour icon in the Tool palette to return the colours to black and white. Create a new channel and use Filter > Render > Clouds to fill the channel with a cloud pattern.

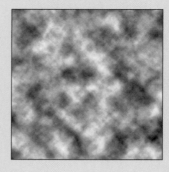

Select all and copy the channel to the clipboard. Create a new file which, by default, will be the same size as whatever is on the clipboard. It will also be a greyscale file. Paste the channel into the new file as a layer. Name and save the file as a Photoshop file (not a tiff image). This will be your displacement map.

What displacement maps do

A displacement map moves the pixels according to the light and dark areas of the displacement map. Light areas go up and to the left; dark areas go down and to the right.

How much they move is controlled by the horizontal and vertical scales in the Displace dialogue box. Minus values move the pixels the other way.

A simple example

Here is the result of displacing diagonal lines with a simple half black/half white displacement map with horizontal and vertical scales of 50%.

Here we have used the cloud pattern we made to displace some diagonal lines. Shades of grey move pixels proportional to their greyscale value.

This is a detail of the same clouds displacement map applied to a regular grid.

The Displace dialogue box allows you to specify the amount of displacement.

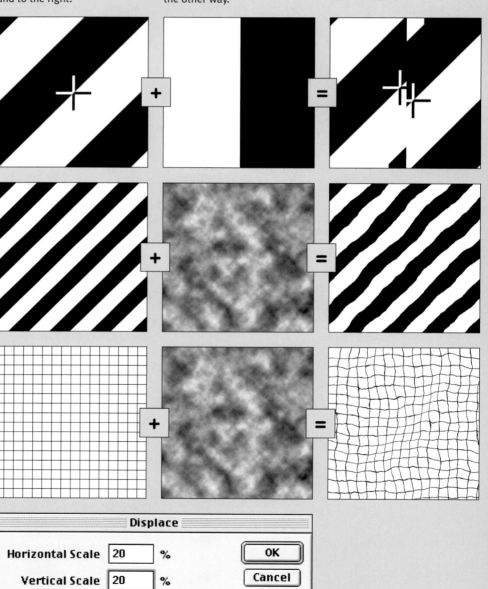

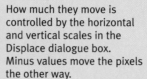

Displacing the fabric

Merge your four layers into one layer and have that layer selected.

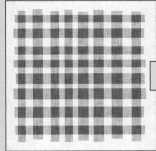 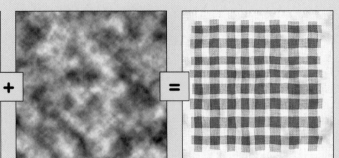 

Use Filter > Distort > Displace to bring up the Displace dialogue box.
Choose your horizontal and vertical scales (we used 20%) and click OK.
Then select the displacement map you wish to use (in this it is our clouds file).
Click OK and the displacement map will be applied.

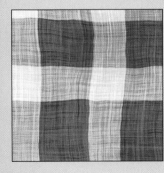

Final touch

To add that additional touch of realism, copy your clouds channel into a layer (it will convert from greyscale to RGB automatically) and use it at a reduced opacity for shadows.

06 - Helpful Hints

Difficulty: Intermediate +	Colin Wood

Transform Again

Changing the size and shape of an element is a breeze using the Transform function. By mastering the Transform Again function, either in multiple or single layers, you will be able to create hypnotic patterns or dazzling multiple images in minutes.

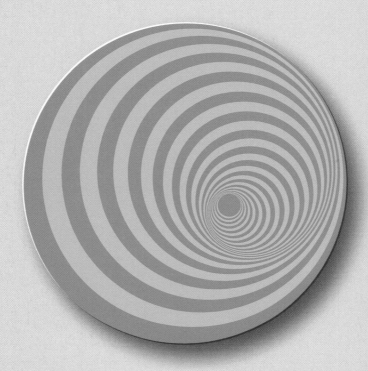

The Transform function

| ⊞ ⊞⊞⊞ | X: 1138.0 px △ Y: 833.5 px | ▣ W: 100.0% ⧉ H: 100.0% | ∠ 0.0 ° | ⟋ H: 0.0 ° V: 0.0 ° | ☒ ✓ |

Reference point · Relative position · Scale · Rotation · Skew · Cancel/Commit

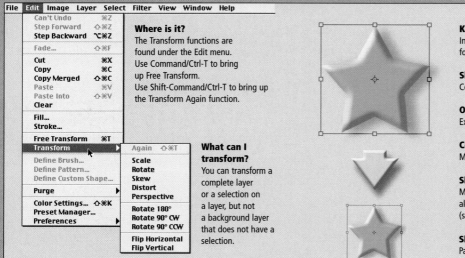

File Edit Image Layer Select Filter View Window Help

Can't Undo	⌘Z
Step Forward	⇧⌘Z
Step Backward	⌥⌘Z
Fade...	⇧⌘F
Cut	⌘X
Copy	⌘C
Copy Merged	⇧⌘C
Paste	⌘V
Paste Into	⇧⌘V
Clear	
Fill...	
Stroke...	
Free Transform	⌘T
Transform	▶
Define Brush...	
Define Pattern...	
Define Custom Shape...	
Purge	▶
Color Settings...	⇧⌘K
Preset Manager...	
Preferences	▶

Again	⇧⌘T
Scale	
Rotate	
Skew	
Distort	
Perspective	
Rotate 180°	
Rotate 90° CW	
Rotate 90° CCW	
Flip Horizontal	
Flip Vertical	

Where is it?
The Transform functions are found under the Edit menu. Use Command/Ctrl-T to bring up Free Transform. Use Shift-Command/Ctrl-T to bring up the Transform Again function.

What can I transform?
You can transform a complete layer or a selection on a layer, but not a background layer that does not have a selection.

Keyboard modifiers
In the Transform function you'll find the following keyboard modifiers very useful.

Shift
Constrains proportions.

Option/Alt
Expands/contracts from the centre.

Command/Ctrl
Moves one point at a time.

Shift-Command/Ctrl
Moves one point but constrains movement along one side of the bounding box (starting with vertical or horizontal).

Shift-Option/Alt-Command/Ctrl
Parallelogram.

What can I transform?
You can transform any layer, even type and shape layers. The layer can have a picture or solid colours.

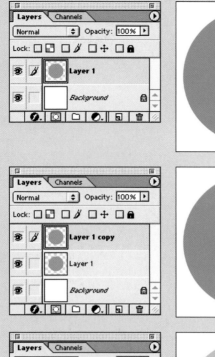

Create a shape in a new layer
As the Transform function does not work on a background layer, the first thing to do is create a new layer.
Create a selection and fill it with a colour.

Duplicate the layer
Duplicate the layer (otherwise the original will not be available as you will have transformed it).

Change the colour
Fill the image with a new colour (Shift-Option/Alt-Delete will fill with the foreground colour while preserving the transparency, effectively changing the colour of the existing image).

Important
In order to use the Transform Again function, you must first use the Transform function.
Photoshop then remembers what you have done (the settings), and is then ready to do it all over again.

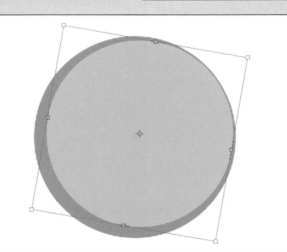

Transform
Use Command/Ctrl-T to bring up the Transform marquee and handles.
Rotate, reposition, reshape and resize to taste. Note that the Transform function uses percentages to calculate the changes you have made, so distances are relative, not absolute.

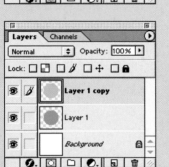

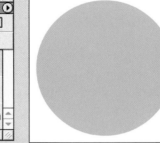

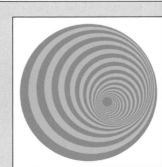

Repeat the Transform
Use Shift-Command/Ctrl-T to repeat the Transform. You can keep duplicating your current shape to a new layer, transforming your image to create a progression of altered images all following a perfect path, repeating the initial settings you have used. Next we'll show how to get the same effect without repeatedly duplicating the layers.

Apart from simply repeating a transform, the function can be used to create repeating patterns.
These can be executed using a stack of layers, one for each transform, or by keeping all the progressive transforms on one layer.

Colours first
In order to create a repeating pattern as shown here, first prepare the foreground and background colours you wish to use.

Transform Again - into multiple layers

Transform Again: multiple layers
In this example we start with two coloured layers; the same colours as our foreground and background colours.

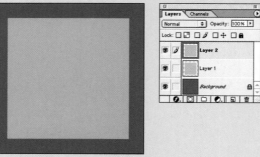

Layer stack
Using this technique you will end up with a layer stack that gives the opportunity to make alterations later on, but which is a little unwieldy.

Transform
Make Layer 1 the active layer. Use Command/Ctrl-T to bring up the Transform handles. Use Shift-Option/Alt-drag (from a corner) to make the square smaller, keeping the centres in line.

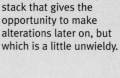

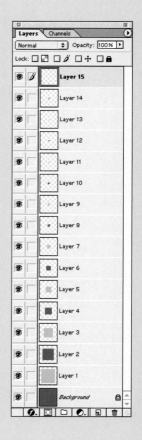

Duplicate Layer 1
With Layer 1 still selected, use Command/Ctrl-J to duplicate the layer. Photoshop will name this as Layer 2.

Transform Again
With Layer 2 selected, use Shift-Command/Ctrl-T to Transform Again.
Note that the selection is still active.
Then use Option/Alt-Delete to fill the selection with the foreground colour.

Continue with the sequence:
- Command/Ctrl-J to duplicate the layer.
- Shift-Command/Ctrl-T to Transform Again.
- Fill with alternating foreground and background colours.

Your Transform choices

Transform	Transform 2	Transform again	Transform again 2
• **Command/Ctrl-T** simply transforms the image once according to the changes you make.	• **Command/Ctrl-T** used for a second time will give you the Transform handles ready to make another (different) Transformation.	• **Shift-Command/Ctrl-T** (Transform Again) will take the entire layer, or a selection within it, and re-apply the same settings, replacing the image with a transformed one. To have a repeated image it is necessary to duplicate layers.	• **Shift-Option/Alt-Command/Ctrl-T** transforms the selection again according to the previous settings and puts it on the same layer. Note: If you started with a selection it will still be active.

A perspective illusion

Perspective
Because Photoshop's Transform Again function treats size changes as relative (as a percentage of the original), repeated objects can easily be placed in perspective.

Prepare your colours
In this part of the tip we will be filling selections with alternating foreground and background colours.
Prepare your colours in advance.

Transform Again - into the same layer

Create a new layer
As the Transform function does not work on a background layer, start by creating a new layer. In the new layer we have placed a triangle which we will transform repeatedly to form the design shown above.

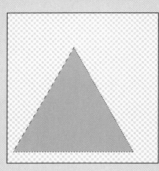

There are two reasons why you need a selection before using Transform Again:

• Without a selection, Shift-Option/Alt-Command/Ctrl-T will simply change the entire layer according to the previous transform and not leave a copy behind.

• With a selection, it will leave a copy AND give you a selection for the next Transform Again. Otherwise the entire layer will be transformed again (you are working in a single layer).

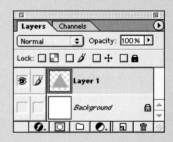

Duplicate and Transform
To use Transform Again you must complete an initial Transform. To preserve the triangle in its starting position, duplicate Layer 1.
On Layer 2, use Edit > Free Transform (Command/Ctrl-T) and resize, reposition and rotate the image.
Press Enter to commit and complete the transform.

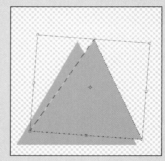

Transform Again
After the initial transform, the selection will remain active. Shift-Command/Ctrl-T will activate the Transform Again function, but will transform the selection to a new position. However, if you add the Option key (Shift-Option/Alt-Command/Ctrl-T) to Transform Again, the transformed selection is added to the same layer, with the original selection unchanged.

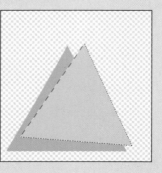
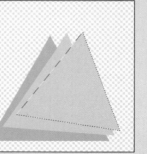
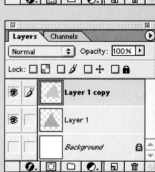

And again, and again ...
Alternate between Option/Alt-Delete and Command/Ctrl-Delete to fill with foreground and background colours.
Get into a rhythm: Transform Again; fill with foreground colour; Transform Again; fill with background colour and so on. Stop when you're finished or dizzy!

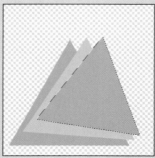
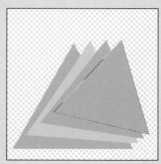

Patterns from nature

Great effects

The Transform Again function can be used to create some wonderful effects.

Natural scenes can become entrancing patterns, adding action while retaining elements of the original.

If you go too far and wish to back up to a previous state, the History palette will take you back – it remembers earlier transforms so that you can pick up from where you left off and head off in a new direction.

Try some yourself. This is an effect that is worth the effort.

Repairing JPEG artifacts

Difficulty: Intermediate

Carl Stevens

JPEG has formed the backbone of photographic image delivery on the web and digital camera storage for several years. One of the drawbacks of the format is that at lower quality levels, JPEG artifacts can reduce reproduction quality. Carl Stevens helps out with JPEG repair techniques.

The problem with digital photography

Most digital images are converted to JPEG in-camera to keep file sizes down and image capacities high. Depending on the quality level chosen (the JPEG quality), you may see the tell-tale signs of JPEG compression. Let's take a look at some techniques to reverse the JPEG effects.

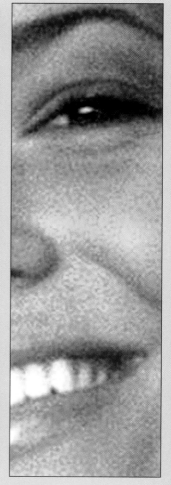

Mandy Moore
Photographed by William Mottram while Mandy Moore was in Sydney promoting her film 'A Walk to Remember'.

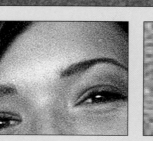

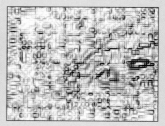

What's that pattern?
The JPEG compression algorithm reduces file size by discarding image information that the human eye doesn't see. It does this in 8 x 8 pixel squares, and if the compression is too harsh, you'll see the tell-tale square pattern in your image.

Sharpening
Sharpening for print only makes the problem worse as the JPEG artefact squares are seen as edges to sharpen by the Unsharp Mask filter.

Up close and artefacted
Zooming in shows us the magnitude of the problem with a very obvious square JPEG artefact pattern.

Find Edges
Taking it a step further, Adobe Photoshop's Find Edges filter shows us the underlying JPEG pattern.

Must-have photos

Even with a high-end camera, you can still be at the mercy of JPEG compression. Here we have a great shot except for the JPEG artefacts, which will become more pronounced when we sharpen the image for print.

Method 1 - LAB Color

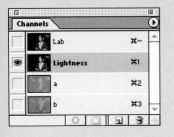

LAB Color

A technique to remove noise, or in this case JPEG artefacts is to take advantage of the way the LAB Color mode represents image information.

Rather than R, G, and B channels, LAB Color consists of Lightness (Luminance), a and b channels. The Lightness channel holds much of the JPEG artefacts, so we'll concentrate our efforts on this channel.

Choose Image > Mode > Lab Color.

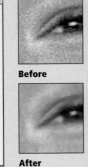

Before

After

Dust & Scratches

Choose Dust & Scratches (Filter > Noise > Dust & Scratches) with a Radius of 2 pixels and a Threshold of 5 levels.

This blurs the JPEG artefacts to the point where they are no longer visible.

To return to RGB Color choose Image > Mode > RGB Color.

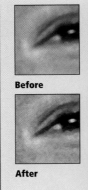

Before

After

Sharpen for print

Finally, we want to sharpen our image for print reproduction. Choose Unsharp Mask (Filter Sharpen > Unsharp Mask) with an Amount of 130%, a Radius of 1.3 pixels and a Threshold of 0 levels.

Normally a Threshold of 0 levels would be too harsh and introduce too much grain.

In this example, it brings back some of the detail that is lost with the Dust & Scratches filter.

Dust & Scratches in RGB

If you want to remain in RGB, you can still take advantage of the Dust & Scratches technique. Rather than targeting a single channel, we'll use the filter on all channels to varying degrees.

Blue channel

The Blue channel is likely to contain the greatest amount of noise, so we'll start there. In the Channels palette, select the Blue channel.

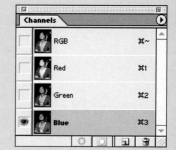

Dust & Scratches

Choose Dust & Scratches (Filter > Noise > Dust & Scratches). The Blue channel is noisy, so we'll use a Radius of 1 pixel and a Threshold of 5 levels. Click OK. Next, select the Green Channel from the Channels palette. This channel is not as noisy, so we'll choose Dust & Scratches again with a Radius of 1 pixel and a Threshold of 4 levels. Finally, select the Red Channel, then choose the Dust & Scratches filter with a Radius of 1 pixel and a Threshold of 3 levels.

Red channel   Green channel   Blue channel

Sharpen for print

We then want to sharpen our image for print reproduction. Select the composite RGB channel in the Channels palette, then choose Unsharp Mask (Filter Sharpen > Unsharp Mask) with an Amount of 130%, a Radius of 1.3 pixels and a Threshold of 5 levels.
In this example, a Threshold of 5 levels brings back enough of the detail where a Threshold of 0 creates too much noise.

Before

After

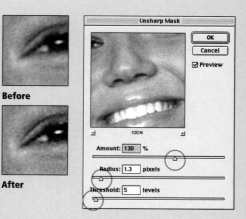

Somebody call a doctor

Alien Skin's Image Doctor suite of plug-ins automate image repair including a very effective JPEG Repair tool.
The one-step filter shortens the time required to get rid of JPEG artefacts, and gives you live feedback for fine tuning.
A demo of Image Doctor is available from the Alien Skin web site which gives you a fully functional, though time-limited version to test.
Visit: www.alienskin.com

Image Doctor JPEG Repair

The all-in-one JPEG Repair filter can be found at the bottom of the Photoshop Filter menu.
Select Filter > Alien Skin Image Doctor > JPEG Repair.
The interface is very simple with Remove Artefacts, Blur Edges, and Add Grain sliders and a large zoomable preview window. Experiment with each slider while your image is zoomed in to get the best result.

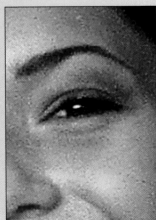

Quick and effective

JPEG Repair turns a several step process into one handy dialogue which will save you a great deal of time if you are in the business of cleaning up digitally photographed images. You can also use the plug-in to take low quality JPEGs from the web and clean them up for print reproduction.

	Difficulty: Easy	Colin Wood
Making pattern grids	You may not think of a chequerboard or a line grid as being repeating patterns, but they are. By reducing them to their basic shapes you can simply repeat the patterns to produce chequerboards and grids of any dimensions. You have tried the long, laborious way; here's the shortcut.	

Start with a small file

We will make a chequerboard grid, making each square 80 x 80 pixels. To do this we will need to make up a pattern of 2 x 2 squares which will repeat to produce a grid of any size. Start by creating a new file 160 x 160 pixels. Use Command/Ctrl-R to bring up the rulers.

In the Layers palette, double-click on 'Background' to convert it into an editable layer. Use Command/Ctrl-T to bring up the Transform function. Note that this brings up handles (that are magnetic) in the corners, half way along each side and (most importantly) in the middle.

Drag out guides from the rulers as shown. Press the Return key. This will divide your image into four identical squares. You are now ready to make a selection.

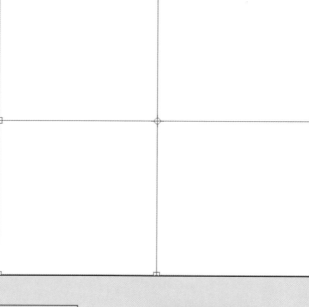

Tip
This technique of calling up the Transform function is useful to find the centre of any image.
Once you have dragged out the guides you simply hit Escape to exit the Transform function leaving the guides in place.

Select two squares

Select the rectangular marquee tool. Drag out a selection in the top left square. Hold down the Shift key and add another square in the bottom right. Check that your foreground and background colours are set to default (black and white). Fill the selection with black (press Option/Alt-Delete or go to Edit > Fill and choose 'Foreground Color'). Use Command/Ctrl-D or click outside the selection to deselect. You now have the basis of your chequerboard.

Tip
Hold down the Shift key to add to any click-and-drag selection.

Tip
Option/Alt-Delete will fill with the foreground colour; Command/Ctrl-Delete will fill with the background colour.

Define your pattern

Use Edit > Define Pattern to bring up the Pattern Name dialogue box. Because you have no selection, your entire image is used as the pattern. Name your pattern and click OK. You can now use this pattern to create grids of any dimensions.

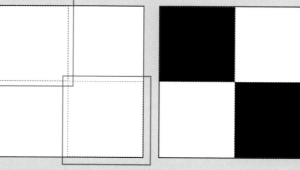

Tip
Once you have created the pattern, the pixel dimensions are fixed.
A pattern is not a vector shape.

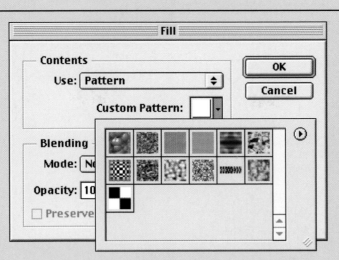

File size formula
Create a new file. Ideally, your file size should be a multiple of the pattern size. Our file is 1,600 pixels wide so that the pattern will fit exactly ten times. Photoshop always begins to fill with a pattern from the top left-hand corner.

Fill with your pattern
Use Edit > Fill to bring up the Fill dialogue box.
For the contents, select Pattern from the drop down list and then click the small arrow to bring up the Custom Pattern palette. Your new pattern will be the last one.

Ok to go
Click OK and the image will magically fill with your chequerboard.
Photoshop will fill using the pattern regardless of whether the pattern fits the image size exactly.

Once you have mastered this technique you will be able to produce all manner of patterns.

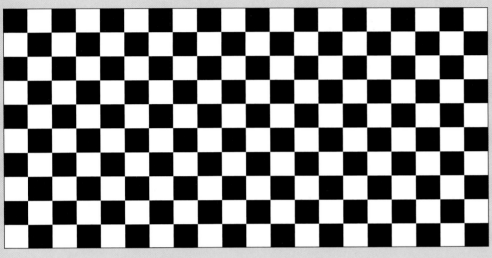

Making a grid

A grid of lines is just a repeating pattern of two lines in a reverse 'L' shape.

Tip
If your ruler units are set to pixels (Edit > Preferences > Units & rulers) you can use the Info palette to create accurate selections.

Start with a small file
We will make a chequerboard grid with each square 80 x 80 pixels. Hold down the Shift key (to constrain the selection to a square) and drag out a selection from the top left-hand corner but stop short of the edges. Use Command/Ctrl Shift-I (or Select > Inverse) to invert the selection, leaving an 'L' shape. Fill with black. Deselect.

Save your pattern
As before, use Edit > Define Pattern to save your pattern.

Fill with pattern
Use Edit > Fill and fill with your pattern.
Hey, presto! A grid in seconds. You can duplicate one of the RGB channels as an alpha channel, and invert the channel (Command/Ctrl-I) to produce white lines on a black ground. This can then be used as a selection to create a grid in a layer.

Difficulty: Easy	Daniel Wade

Align & Distribute

Photoshop's Align and Distribute tools found in the Options bar give you twelve options for aligning or distributing elements on linked layers. A few minutes experimenting with the buttons should translate into speed improvements when laying out your next composition.

Align

The Align options are the first six buttons in the Options Bar when you have the Move tool selected and at least two layers linked.

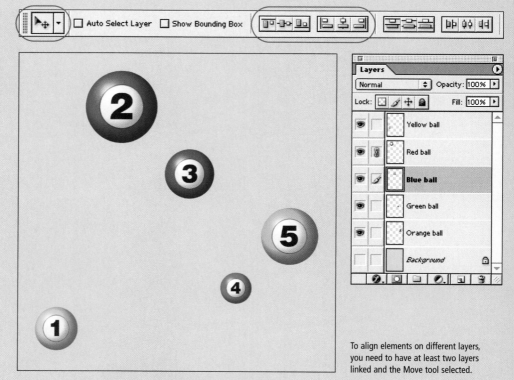

To align elements on different layers, you need to have at least two layers linked and the Move tool selected.

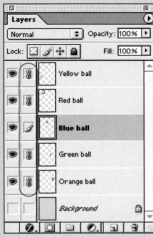

All layers are linked except the Background layer.

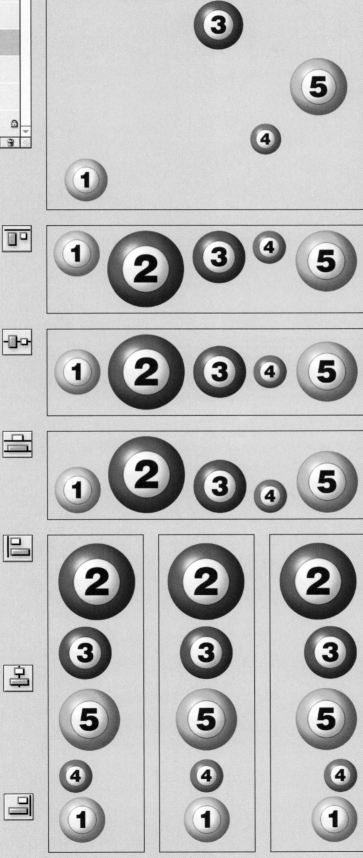

Linked layers

To use the align and distribute buttons, you need to link the layers you want to align.

In this case, we want to align all of the layers except the background, so we click in the link well to the right of the view layer icon in the Layers palette.

Note:

1. It's important to remember that you will be aligning the other layers to the object on the active layer. In this case we are aligning to the 'Blue ball' layer.

2. If you want to change from horizontal to vertical alignment as you experiment, you will need to return to this initial state.

Align Top Edges

Aligns the tops of all elements on linked layers, to the top of the element on the selected layer.

Align Vertical Centres

Aligns the vertical centre of all elements on linked layers, to the vertical centre of the element on the selected layer.

Align Bottom Edges

Aligns the bottom of all elements on linked layers, to the bottom of the element on the selected layer.

Align Left Edges

Aligns the left edge of all elements on linked layers, to the left edge of the element on the selected layer.

Align Horizontal Centres

Aligns the horizontal centre of all elements on linked layers, to the horizontal centre of the element on the selected layer.

Align Right Edges

Aligns the right edge of all elements on linked layers, to the right edge of the element on the selected layer.

06 - Helpful Hints

Distribute

The Distribute options are the second group of six buttons in the Options Bar when you have the Move tool selected and at least three layers linked.

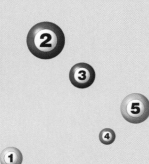

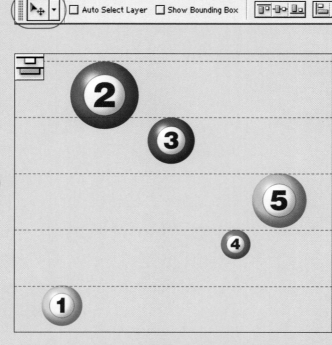

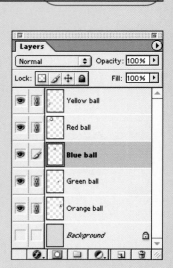

To distribute elements on different layers, you need to have at least three layers linked and the Move tool selected.

Distribute Top Edges

Equally distributes elements based on their top edges across the linked layers.

Distribute Vertical Centres

Equally distributes elements based on their vertical centres across the linked layers.

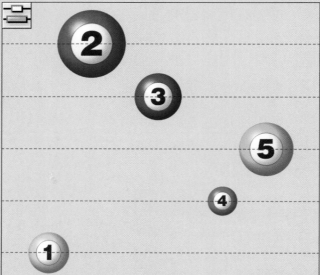

Distribute Bottom Edges

Equally distributes elements based on their bottom edges across the linked layers.

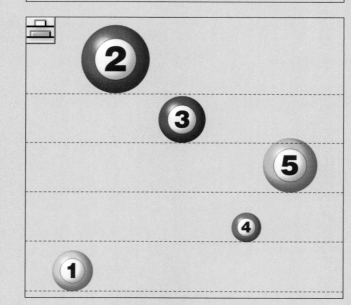

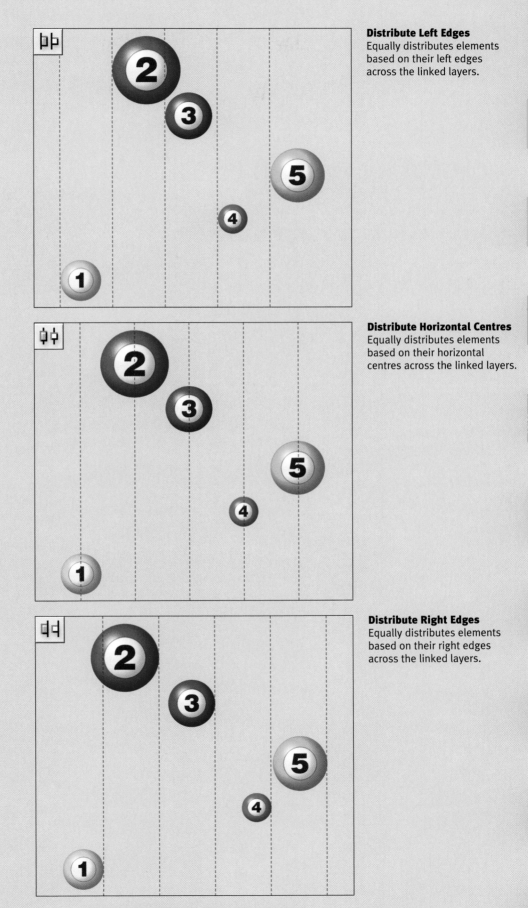

Distribute Left Edges
Equally distributes elements based on their left edges across the linked layers.

Distribute Horizontal Centres
Equally distributes elements based on their horizontal centres across the linked layers.

Distribute Right Edges
Equally distributes elements based on their right edges across the linked layers.

Difficulty: Easy	Carl Stevens

Combining two scans for a better final image

Photoshop is excellent for improving and manipulating images, but you can assist the process by capturing as much correct information as possible at the time of the scan; even if different areas need different settings. Carl Stevens shows how to get the desired result by combining two scans of the same image.

Scan once for the sky

This image presents a bit of a problem.
Scanning to retain the sky detail leaves the foreground quite dark, but scanning to lighten the foreground will lighten the sky too much, losing the detail.

Scan again for the foreground

And then combine them for a great image!

Manual Scan Range

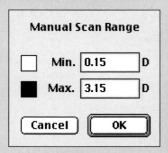

| | Min. | 0.15 | D |
| | Max. | 3.15 | D |

Cancel   OK

As we want the best result in the highlights with the first scan, we use the lower end of the Dynamic Range. The D-Min (Minimum Density) is set at 0.15, and then the scanner's dynamic range (3.0) is added to get the D-Max (Maximum Density) setting of 3.15.

Manual Scan Range

| | Min. | 0.350 | D |
| | Max. | 3.350 | D |

Cancel   OK

With the second scan, we want as much detail as possible in the shadows, so we use the upper end of the Dynamic Range. The Minimum Density is set at 0.35, and the Maximum Density at 3.35.

D-Min In both scans the Dynamic range **D-Max**
0.15 is 3.0. The difference is the **3.15**
range of tones that is captured.

Scan 1 - expose for sky

Scan 2 - expose for foreground

0   1.0   2.0   3.0   4.0

D-Min   **D-Max**
0.35   **3.35**

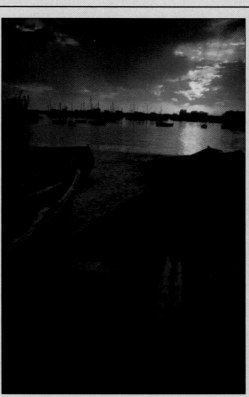

Sky first
The image is scanned using a setting that captures all of the detail in the sky, but without worrying too much about the foreground.

To adjust the outcome of the scan, many flatbed scanners will let you manually set the Density Range of the scan.
To do this you need to know your scanner's Dynamic Range; ie. the maximum density range that the scanner can capture (look in the literature that came with the scanner).
This Dynamic Range floats between a D-Min (Minimum Density) and a D-Max (Maximum Density).

Foreground second
The image is scanned a second time, concentrating on the foreground.

With the second scan, the settings are changed to capture the detail in the shadows in the foreground. We don't need to worry about what happens to the sky—we already have a good scan of that.

Important:
Make sure both scans are made with exactly the same crop and scale settings.

Tip:
Hold down the Shift key after you have started dragging the image, and it will be placed in the centre of the target layer.

Layers | Channels

Normal ⇕ Opacity: 100 ► %

☐ Preserve Transparency

👁 ✏ Layer 1

👁 Background

Combine the two scans
We now want to combine the sky of Sunset1 and the foreground of Sunset2
Open both files in Photoshop, and Click on Sunset2 to make it the active window.
Select All (Command/Ctrl-A) and, using the Move tool, drag Sunset2 into Sunset1. Because the image area is the same in both files, they align exactly.

Design Graphics Photoshop Studio Skills 1

Measure the angle

Measure the angle where the two layers will be joined. Select the Measure tool (it is located with the Eyedropper and Color Sampler tools). In this image, the best place to join the two layers is at the water line where the sky and the foreground meet. Measure the angle of the water line, so that you can make an accurate gradient mask.

Measure the angle using the Measure tool (Shortcut: I/Shift-I).
In Photoshop 4, use the Line Tool with a line width of 0.

Check the angle in the Info palette. Here it is 3.5 degrees.

Make a Gradient Mask

One way to do this is to make a gradient on a channel. You can do this on a new channel, but an easier way is to duplicate an existing channel that shows clearly the area where the gradient will be made. In this case we have duplicated the Cyan channel.

Duplicate a channel by dragging it over the New Channel icon at the bottom of the Channelsl palette.

Angular measures

Click on the new channel to make it active. Select the Gradient tool. Set the default colours (foreground: white, background: black) by hitting the D key, then select Linear Gradient from the Options Bar. Bring up the Info palette (Window > Info) .
Place your cursor above the water line and drag downwards until the info palette projects – 93.4 °. This is the same angle as measured for the shoreline. (90° being a vertical line.)

Load the Channel
Make Layer 1 the active layer in the Layers palette, then Command/Ctrl-click the Alpha 1 channel in the Channels palette to load the channel as a selection.
Depending on how you made the channel you may need to invert your selection so that the foreground is the area selected.

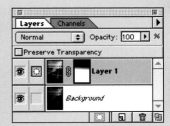

Making a Layer Mask
Making a Layer Mask instead of deleting parts of the Layer, means you are able to keep the unwanted parts of the image in case you need to make changes.

Layer Mask
Click on the Layer Mask icon at the bottom of the layers palette to create a layer mask.

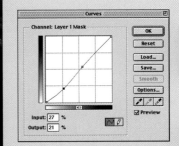

A layer mask will appear next to the Layer 1 icon and a mask icon will appear in the palette well.

Refining the gradient
The Layer Mask can be adjusted if necessary using Curves to refine the gradient.

The final step is to flatten the image.

And there it is, the final image is made up of a combination of the two scans without any visible join.

7
Special F/X

Difficulty: Intermediate	Michael Ninness

Distorting text

The Displace filter is an undervalued tool in the Photoshop toolbox. Michael Ninness showed attendees at a Thunder Lizard Productions Photoshop Conference how to use it in combination with 'Blend If' in Layer Styles to combine text with textures to great effect.

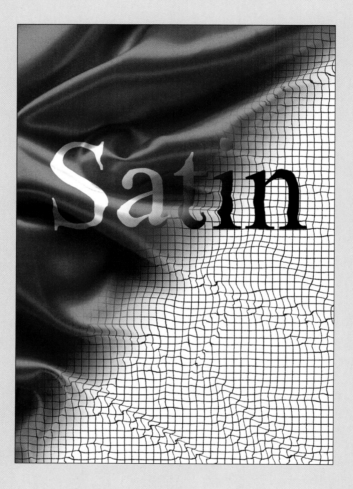

Make type follow the folds
In this tip Michael Ninness shows how to distort type using a displacement map to make it follow the folds in a satin background. Displacement maps are not as hard to understand and use as you may think. Just follow along and you will see how easy it is.

Shadows are easy too
Learn how to blend the type into the background by letting the background show through in the shadows.

Duplicate a channel

We want to make a new displacement map which we will apply to our text layer. To do this we will select a channel with maximum contrast and save it as a separate file.

View each channel in the Channels palette separately and select which channel has the most contrast (in this case, the Red channel). Duplicate the selected channel to a new file, and save it as a separate document. Be sure to flatten the file and save it as a Photoshop file (.psd) as this is the format the Displace filter is expecting.

Note: The Displace filter will only work with greyscale images. Copying a channel (which is greyscale) and pasting it into a new document will automatically change the Color Mode to Grayscale.

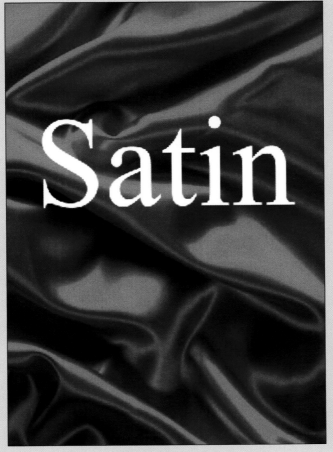

Create a type layer

It's now time to add the type that we want to blend into our satin. Create your type, and colour it white. When placing your type, look at the background image to ensure that there is a good mix of light and dark areas which will bend the type.

Rasterize?

Choose Filter > Distort > Displace. Because you are applying the Displace filter on a Type layer, a dialogue will appear asking if you want to rasterize the Type layer first. Click OK.

Adobe Photoshop

This type layer must be rasterized before proceeding. Its text will no longer be editable. Rasterize the type?

Cancel   OK

Layers Channels

Normal   Opacity: 100%

Lock: Fill: 100%

Satin

Background

The Displace filter

Once the Displace filter is open, set the Horizontal and Vertical Scale values to 7%. (You might need to undo this step and try it again with different values because there is no preview before you apply this filter.) Click OK.

Displace

Horizontal Scale   7   %   OK

Vertical Scale   7   %   Cancel

Displacement Map:
- ⦿ Stretch To Fit
- ○ Tile

Undefined Areas:
- ○ Wrap Around
- ⦿ Repeat Edge Pixels

Find a map

An Open file dialogue will appear asking you to choose a displacement map. Locate and select the file you saved previously.

Choose a displacement map.

From: 📁 Satin

📁 Satin   ▷   🖼 Red channel.psd

Distorted type

Our type has now been distorted based on the contrast of the red channel giving the effect of it following the folds of the material.

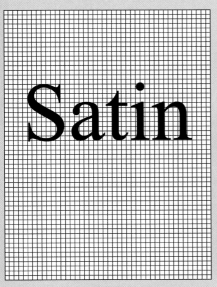

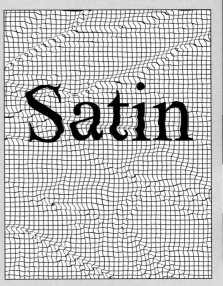

What's really happening?

The Displace filter can take a little time to fully grasp. The theory behind the filter is that it will displace pixels in one image based on the greyscale information of another image. The filter uses the luminosity values (lights and darks) of the greyscale image to do this. White, or light values, will distort an image up and to the left. Black, or dark values, will distort an image down and to the right. A 50% grey value will have no displacement (distortion). Above we have created a grid to show the effect of the red channel of the satin when used as a displacement map on the grid. The whiter areas of the image have moved the grid up and to the left while the darker areas have moved the grid down and to the right. This gives us the effect of the grid following the contour of the satin.

Duplicate the background
Select the Background layer
and duplicate it (Command/
Ctrl-J). Move the duplicate layer
above the 'Satin' type layer
in the Layers palette.

Blending Options
Double-click on the duplicate
layer (not on the name) in the
Layers palette to bring up the
Blending Options for the layer.
At the bottom of the Advanced
Blending options section,
change the Blend If option
from Gray to Red.
Because this image
is predominantly red,
we will blend out the red
of the top image to reveal
the underlying type layer.
Drag the white triangle slider
in This Layer section to the left
until you see the white type
appear at the strength you
would like. Hold down the
Option/Alt key to split the
triangle into two parts, and drag
the right half back to the right
to create a smooth transition.

Layer Style

Styles

Blending Options: Custom

☐ Drop Shadow
☐ Inner Shadow
☐ Outer Glow
☐ Inner Glow
☐ Bevel and Emboss
   ☐ Contour
   ☐ Texture
☐ Satin
☐ Color Overlay
☐ Gradient Overlay
☐ Pattern Overlay
☐ Stroke

Blending Options
General Blending
Blend Mode: Normal
Opacity: ———————— 100 %

Advanced Blending
Fill Opacity: ———————— 100 %
Channels: ☑ R ☑ G ☑ B
Knockout: None
☐ Blend Interior Effects as Group
☑ Blend Clipped Layers as Group
☑ Transparency Shapes Layer
☐ Layer Mask Hides Effects
☐ Vector Mask Hides Effects

Blend If: Red
This Layer: 0   29 / 156

Underlying Layer: 0   255

OK
Cancel
New Style...
☑ Preview

Blend If

The Blend If function in the Layer Style dialogue allows you to blend pixels from the current layer or show through pixels from lower layers based on their brightness.

By selecting a colour channel (R, G, B, or C, M, Y, K depending on the colour space you're working in) and adjusting the sliders, you can determine which pixels from the channel will be blended. Dragging the right slider blends the colours from the selected channel with the layer beneath.

You'll notice that there is an abrupt transition between the blended colours by doing this. To soften this transition, hold down the Option/Alt key and drag the right slider which separates the slider to give you a softer transition. These examples show the results of blends from the various colour channels.

You can see where the colours have blended into the white background.

Note: When working in CMYK, you must use the left slider to achieve the same blending effect as the right slider in RGB.

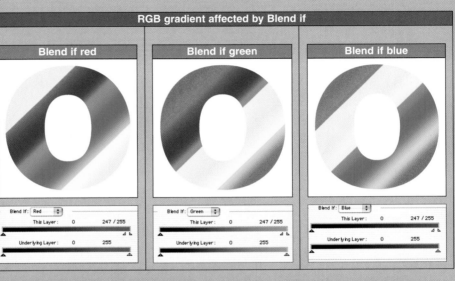

Original RGB image

Note: For reproduction purposes, these RGB images have been output as CMYK images.

RGB gradient affected by Blend if

Blend if red — Blend If: Red — This Layer: 0 247 / 255 — Underlying Layer: 0 255

Blend if green — Blend If: Green — This Layer: 0 247 / 255 — Underlying Layer: 0 255

Blend if blue — Blend If: Blue — This Layer: 0 247 / 255 — Underlying Layer: 0 255

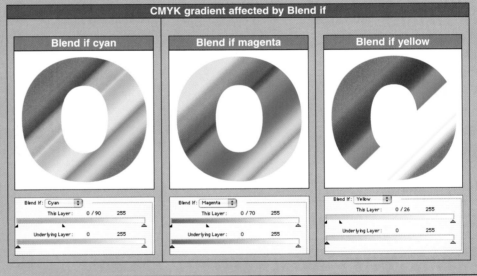

CMYK gradient affected by Blend if

Blend if cyan — Blend If: Cyan — This Layer: 0 / 90 255 — Underlying Layer: 0 255

Blend if magenta — Blend If: Magenta — This Layer: 0 / 70 255 — Underlying Layer: 0 255

Blend if yellow — Blend If: Yellow — This Layer: 0 / 26 255 — Underlying Layer: 0 255

The final result

As you can see, the text now follows the creases of the satin with highlights appearing whiter and shadows appearing grey.

Difficulty: Easy

Ben Willmore

Creating stone textures

Jazz up your page by creating some funky stone textures with the built-in capabilities of Photoshop and the expertise of Ben Willmore, author of the best-selling book, Adobe Photoshop 7.0 Studio Techniques.

Start by opening a new document in Photoshop. Make sure the background is white. This sample file is 10cm (4") square at 300dpi (1,181 x 1,181 pixels).

Clouds filter

To create a base for the texture, apply the Clouds filter.
Filter > Render > Clouds.

The Clouds filter works with the colours in the foreground and background swatches in the tool palette. We used the default colours, ie. foreground black and background white.

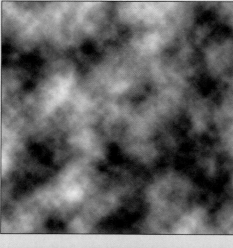

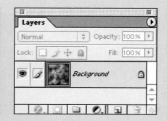

For more contrast when applying the Clouds filter, you can hold down the Option/Alt key.

Difference Clouds Filter

This time choose Filter > Render> Difference Clouds. This will apply the subtle ridges naturally found in stone.

The Difference Clouds filter is applied in the same manner as the regular Clouds filter, but it uses the same method as the Difference mode found in many of the Option palettes, blending with the existing image.

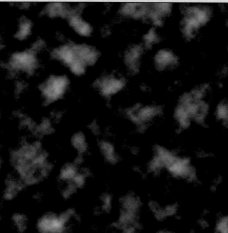

An alternative that achieves the same results is to add a second layer, apply the Clouds filter and change the mode to Difference.

Emboss

The stucco texture is achieved by applying the Emboss filter.
Choose Filter> Stylize > Emboss.
Use a moderate amount for the Height setting, and experiment with the Angle and Amount settings for varied results.

Levels

You can now use Levels to provide more contrast in the stone texture you have created. Open the Levels dialogue box (Command/Ctrl-L) and adjust the input sliders until you are happy with the result.

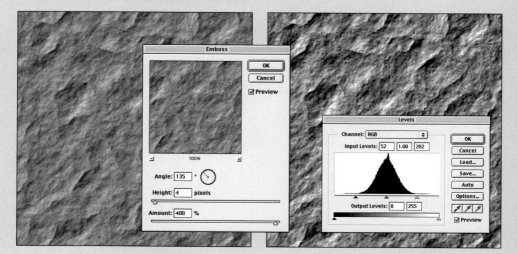

When resizing images, it is best to work in pixels to ensure that the new file is the exact size you want. As an alternative, you can use the Crop tool, select Fixed Target Size in the Options Bar and type in the exact dimensions you want the final file to be.

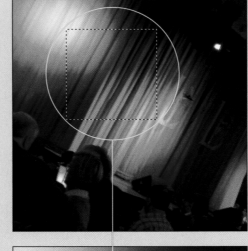

Adding colour
Once the texture is made, you will probably want to add some colour.
One way to do this is to blur an existing image so that the colours are still there, but the shapes are not identifiable. Here we have copied part of an image that has the colours we want. We then paste this into a new file and adjust the size of the file so that it matches the size of our stone texture file.

Blur
The next step is to apply a Gaussian Blur (Filter > Blur > Gaussian Blur) at a high amount. In this instance we used a radius of 50 pixels.

Copy and paste
Copy the blurred image and paste onto a new layer in your texture file.

(below) Use the different Layer Modes to achieve the result you want.

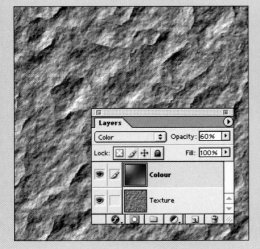

Layer modes
There are two easy ways to combine the colour layer with the texture layer.
You can either:
1. Place the colour layer above the texture layer and change its mode to Color. If you don't want lower layers to be affected, group these two layers,
or,
2. Move the colour layer beneath the texture layer and change the mode of the texture to Luminosity.
Whichever method you use, you can then adjust the Layer Opacity slider until you are happy with the result.

Image restoration	**Difficulty: Easy**	**Brian P. Lawler**

A great number of important images have been made over the years on photographic materials that are less than 'archival'. Thanks to Photoshop and its ability to bring back images to their former glory, Brian P. Lawler brings Gran back from obscurion.

Archiving

Though many photos have faded away to nothing, some retain an adequate amount of information to restore them to attractive appearance—even though they may not look as good as they looked when new. Thanks to Adobe Photoshop we can rebuild images close to their former glory, by painting-in the cracks and fixing the unpleasant effects of time and environmental damage.

Digital files are forever (maybe)

One of the distinctive advantages we have with digital tools for photo retouching is the advantage of digital storage. Once an image is repaired, it can be saved in one of the many digital file formats that should last forever.

Kodak suggests its writable CD media has a shelf-life of over 100 years, and in the archivist's terms this is very impressive. The irony of digital storage, however, is that the devices that read the disks, tapes or whatever may not last long enough to make the files readable when they are needed. A good example of this is the 5.25-inch floppy disk drive (or the eight-inch drive!). Just try to find one of those in working

condition today and you'll get a bonus for being a digital archivist.

The lesson here is to maintain your digital archives in formats that can be read by current media readers.

CD-ROM discs are legible to CD-ROM drives, and fortunately, to the newer DVD-drives.

But what will happen when DVD is supplanted by a newer technology? Will the newer technology read DVD? Will it read CD-ROM? If not, it will be important to copy your digital files on CD-ROM—a harmless event—to a more modern digital medium. Only then will the archive be archival.

The business of restoration

Photo studios and photo artists all over the world are discovering the benefits of restoration as a service to their clients. Restoring old or damaged images is a great addition to any imaging business, and adds value to rare photo and image collections. Some of my favourite images are one-of-a-kind photos of my parents and grandparents. I have been able to print them and give framed copies to my sisters and brothers. Schools, libraries and other institutions are also enjoying the benefits of restoration. Analysing the images as a part of the restoration process also adds to the value of the images as historical records. The opportunities are endless.

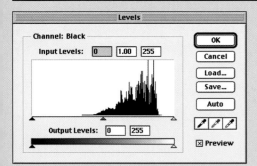

Compressed tonal range

Looking a the Levels histogram (Command/Ctrl-L), we can see that there are big spaces in the tonal range without image information.

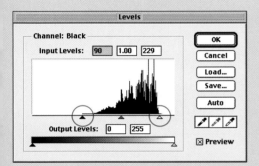

Adjusting the tonal range

When adjusting the histogram, it is important to discard the right information. When adjusting the shadow slider (black triangle), look for dark blemishes on the photo which are not part of the image.

These will give you a thin line of tonal information on the left hand side of the histogram. Bring the slider in to the right of this thin line. Similarly, bring the highlight slider (white triangle) in a little way past the rightmost tonal information.

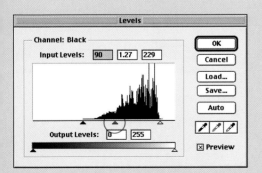

Adjusting the midpoint:

After bringing in the shadow and highlight sliders, you need to adjust the midpoint. Each image you restore will require a different midpoint, so adjust it until it looks good onscreen.

Fade to white

The photograph on the facing page was taken in 1937-38 on black and white film, and printed on colour paper. Over the years it faded to the colour of the paper, making it less recognisable.

When images fade, they usually fade to the paper stock (though not white, we could call it white), although some silver-based images do the opposite, fading to black. In either event, the restoration may be a relatively simple process of taking the remaining tonality and expanding it back to a full-tone image. Reducing the image to greyscale allows the picture to be restored better.

Starting with Levels

By working with Photoshop's Levels controls, it is relatively easy to restore a normal tonality to the image.

This histogram tells us the obvious—the photo is faded. By moving the shadow and highlight sliders under the histogram, the image can be restored to a better tonality—almost as good as the original.

Full tone

As you can see, there is a big improvement in the tonality of the image. Looking at the histogram, you can see that the image has expanded back to a full-tone image.

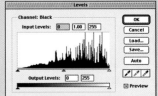

Difficulty: Intermediate	Julieanne Kost

Using Liquify

Photoshop 6.0 introduced a great new feature for creating custom distortions to images called 'Liquify' and it's even better in version 7. Julieanne Kost gives you a tour of this dynamic distortion and warping tool that allows you to push, pull, rotate, enlarge and shrink any area of an image.

Image courtesy of
Tim Whitehouse

Liquify tools
The Liquify window gives you access to eight different warping tools.

Warp

Twirl Clockwise

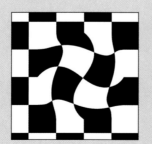

Pucker

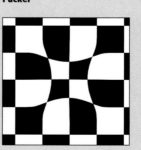

Bloat

Shift Pixels

Reflection

Freeze

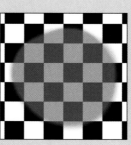

Thaw

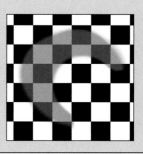

Open your image
In this case we open a file
of a friend on the phone that
we want to set on fire
(the phone, not the friend).

Separate the object
In this photo, we want to
distort only the phone,
not the background.
Select the phone with the
Lasso tool and then choose
Layer > New > Layer Via Copy
(Command/Ctrl-J) to place
a copy of the phone on
a new layer.

Remove the original phone
Turn off the 'phone copy' layer,
then make the Background layer
active. Select the Clone Stamp
tool and sample from areas of
similar colour and value areas
in the Background to cover
the phone.

Note
It would have been easier to take two
photographs—one with the phone and
one without—but since we only have
this image we use the Clone Stamp tool
to create missing information.

Select an area to Liquify

Make the 'phone copy' layer active, then select the rectangular Marquee tool and drag a rough selection around the area that you want to distort.

This will cause Photoshop to zoom into the desired area when displaying the image in the Liquify window.

Select Liquify

Select Filter > Liquify to bring up the Liquify window.

Select an appropriate brush size and pressure under 'Tool Options' and distort the phone as desired.

In this example, the Warp and Shift Pixels tools are used to give the phone its distorted appearance.

Warped and shifted

The phone takes on a heat-affected wobble after using the Liquify effects.

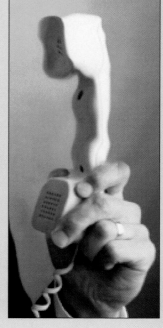

Adjust the colour of the phone

In order to make the phone look like it's on fire, select Layer > New Adjustment Layer > Hue/Saturation. Check the option to 'Group with Previous Layer' so that the adjustment only affects the phone and not the background. Check Colorize, then drag the Hue slider into the orange and increase the Saturation.

Add the flames

Create a new layer called 'Flames', and in order to create the illusion of the phone melting, add some flames from another image (extract using Filter > Extract and choose the Force Foreground option). Setting the blend mode to Screen reveals the lighter flames and hides the darker flames.

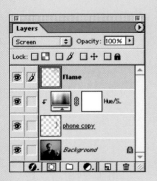

Add some smoke

To add smoke to the flames, select the 'Flame' layer. Go to Layer > Layer Styles > Drop Shadow.
Changing the colour to white and the Blend Mode to Screen colour to white creates the white smoke.
Note: we also use an Opacity of 67%, a lighting angle of -81˚, a Distance of 65 pixels and a size of 7 pixels

Adding more flames

To add more depth to the flames, duplicate the flame layer by dragging it down to the new layer icon. Changing the blend mode to Multiply creates the darker flames and add a slight blur by selecting Filter > Blur > Gaussian Blur.
Reposition the 'Flame copy' layer below the original 'Flame' layer. The keyboard shortcut to do this is Command/Ctrl-[(the left square bracket).

Back on the phone

To make the top of the phone appear burned, click the new layer icon to add a new layer called 'Blackened area'. Reposition the new layer below the 'Flame Copy' layer (Command/Ctrl-[ ).

Blackening the phone

Command-click on the 'Phone copy' layer to load it as a selection (so you don't paint outside of the phone). Select the 'Blackened area' layer and use the Brush tool with a lowered opacity to slowly paint in the black area.
If it looks too smooth, select Filter > Noise > Add Noise and increase the Amount until the textures match.

Distort the face

Finally, to make the face appear even more of a caricature, target the 'Background' layer, draw a marquee around the face and select Filter > Liquify. Use the Bloat tool on the eyes to make them appear larger and use the Pucker tool to shrink the mouth.

Pucker up

The Pucker and Bloat tools were just two of the options introduced with Photoshop 6.0's Liquify function. It's certainly one of the more fun features of Photoshop in the last few revisions.

The result

Using the new Liquify tool we have a caricature in minutes. All without leaving Photoshop.

Ageing metal textures	Difficulty: Intermediate	Bill Fleming
	Finding the perfect texture in the 'real world' can be a difficult process, particularly if you're trying to show a 500 year-old post-nuclear holocaust, windbeaten, chemical ravaged, heat-affected sheet of metal. Bill Fleming shows you how to combine multiple images to make a 'super texture'.	

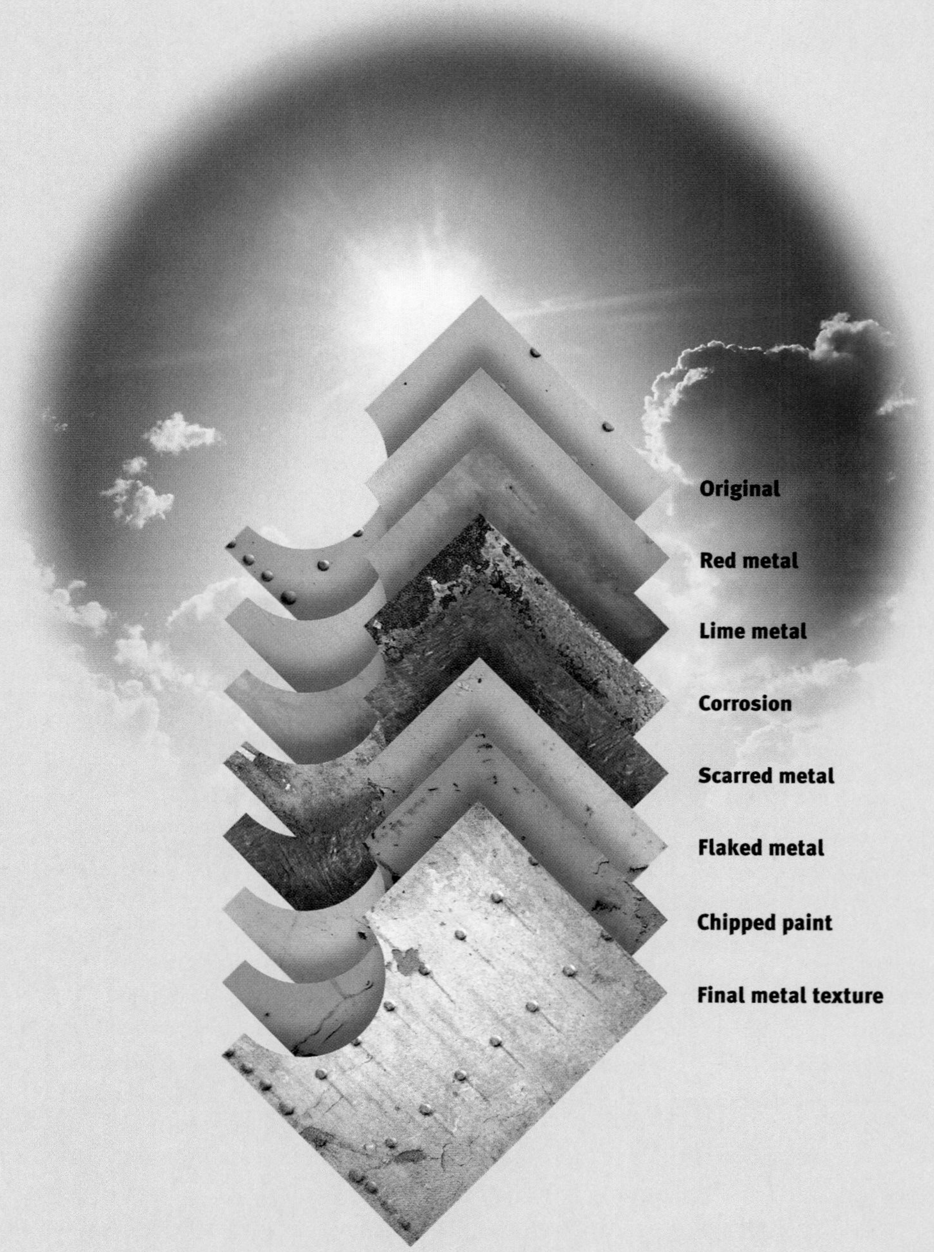

Original

Red metal

Lime metal

Corrosion

Scarred metal

Flaked metal

Chipped paint

Final metal texture

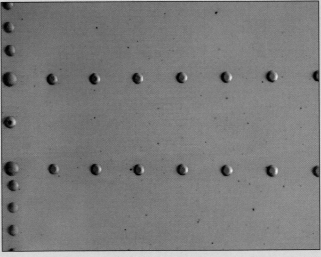

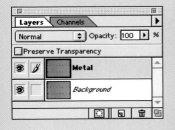

The original metal texture

We start by loading the original file: 'Metal'. Duplicate the Background layer and name the copy 'Metal'. We'll need this layer above the background so we can properly apply the blend modes.

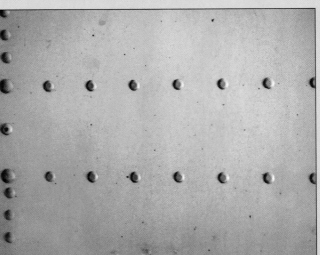

Adding texture detail

Load the 'Red metal' image, Select All (Command/Ctrl-A) and copy the image to the clipboard (Command/Ctrl-C). Click on the Background layer in the Metal file and Paste (Command/Ctrl-V) the image to create a new layer above the Background layer. Option/Alt-click on this layer and name it 'Red metal'. To combine the layers, we make the Metal layer blending mode Hard Light with an Opacity of 100%. Notice how the texture details of the 'Red metal' texture are now rendered onto our clean metal.

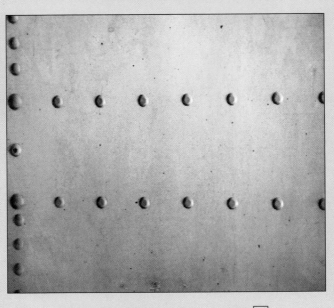

Changing colour and texture

Next we load the 'Lime metal' image, then copy it to a new layer above the 'Red metal' layer, naming it 'Lime metal'. This texture is actually a piece of cement that was under a water drain on an old building. The aging metal of the roof was bleeding a lovely green colour that stained the cement under the drain. Finally, we change the layer blend mode to Overlay. The metal texture now becomes a more natural yellow colour and gains a few more chaotic details, particularly some larger dark blotches and raised pimples.

Adding surface flaking

Load the 'Corrosion' image
and copy it to a new layer above
the 'Lime metal' layer and name
the new layer 'Corrosion'.
This is a picture of an old piece
of sheet metal found stacked
behind an abandoned building.
It was exposed to the elements
so it rusted quite a bit.
Next we change the layer
blend mode to Soft Light.
This blend mode adds the
nice detail of the metal
surface flaking away.
We now need several layers
of destruction on the metal
for it to be realistic.

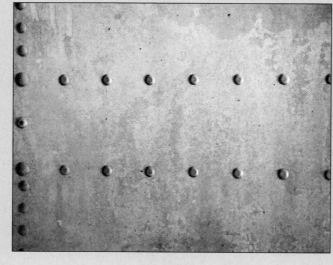

Adding additional scarring

Load the 'Scarred metal' image
then copy it to a new layer
above the 'Metal' layer, naming
it 'Scarred metal'.
This new layer is added above
the 'Metal' layer so the effects
are more prominent.
Now we change the layer blend
to Soft Light, which renders
a variety of scars on the metal
texture. It also adds richness
to the texture by saturating
its colours.
Next we can focus on the
final and most interesting
detail, which is the flaking.

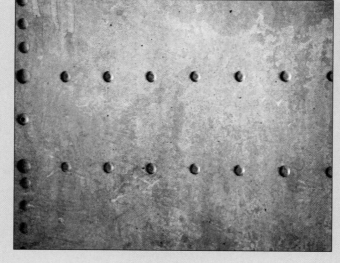

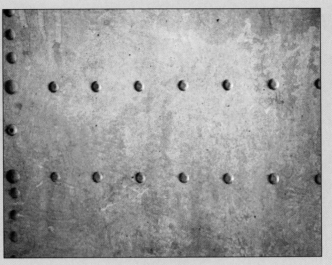

Adding a second layer of flaking

Load the 'Flaked metal' image then copy it to a new layer above the 'Scarred metal' layer naming the layer 'Flaked metal'. Finally, we change the layer blend mode to Soft Light, which renders a flaked area down the middle of the texture. This new flaked area looks great but we have one more layer of flaking to add—the most severe. We're going to add some large areas where the metal has completely flaked away revealing the metal beneath.

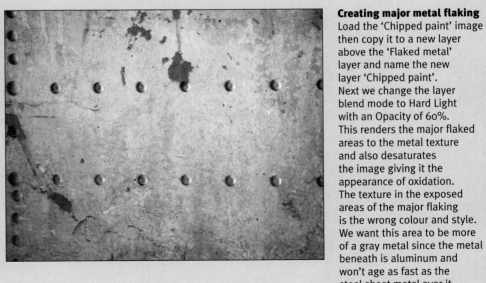

Creating major metal flaking

Load the 'Chipped paint' image then copy it to a new layer above the 'Flaked metal' layer and name the new layer 'Chipped paint'. Next we change the layer blend mode to Hard Light with an Opacity of 60%. This renders the major flaked areas to the metal texture and also desaturates the image giving it the appearance of oxidation. The texture in the exposed areas of the major flaking is the wrong colour and style. We want this area to be more of a gray metal since the metal beneath is aluminum and won't age as fast as the steel sheet metal over it. To change the metal in the exposed areas we'll be using another photo texture, but first we must define the exposed area to fill with the new metal.

Defining the exposed metal selection

Duplicate the 'Chipped paint' layer and call it 'Exposed metal'. Desaturate the layer (Image > Mode > Desaturate). Using Brightness/Contrast (Image > Mode > Brightness/Contrast), set the Brightness to 25 and the Contrast to 100.

Isolated

This isolates the exposed areas as black spots on a white background.

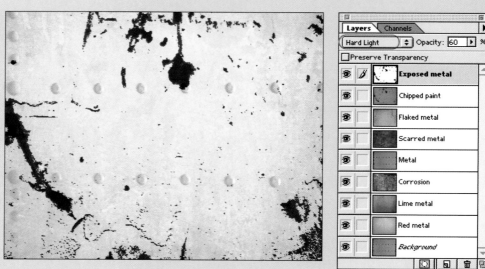

Exposed metal channel

Select All and Copy, then switch to the Channels tab and add a new channel called 'Exposed metal'. Paste the selection into this channel.
This is the selection we'll be using to fill the exposed areas.

Exposed Metal selection

Exposed Metal channel

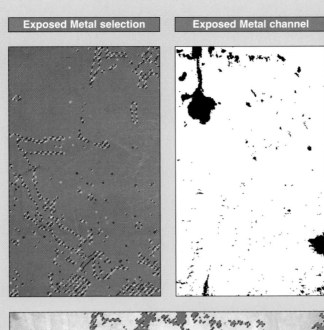

Adding the underlying metal

Load the 'Scratched metal' image then copy it to a new layer above the 'Chipped paint' layer, naming it 'Scratched metal'. To finish the underlying metal we load the 'Exposed metal' selection (Command/Ctrl-clicking the 'Exposed metal' channel) and then press Delete to remove the selected area. This leaves us with gray metal pieces over the exposed areas.

Colour blend mode

Now we set the layer blend mode to Color with an Opacity of 40%.

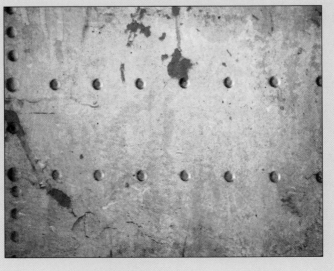

Exposed metal

This changes the exposed metal to a soft grey metal texture.

Adding drip stains

Adding dripping rust is simple. The foundation colour is already present. We just need to take advantage of it. For the rust to appear realistic it needs to have chaotic colour variations, which could take plenty of time to paint by hand but since the aged metal already has this chaos, we can use it for the rust. Save your file as 'Metal.psd', then flatten the image.

Flattened

Our aged metal is now ready for some drip stains.

Burn tool

Select the Burn tool, set the Brush Size to 13 pixels and the Exposure to 20%.

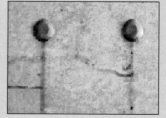

Vertical strokes

Paint vertical strokes underneath the rivets. With the dripping rust complete, we're ready to lift the foreground metal off the background in the exposed areas.

Notice how the colour becomes a rust tone. All we are doing is saturating the colour that is already present.

As we paint the strokes under the rivets on the left we see the colour is a darker shade of brown, which is the predominant colour in this region. Burning the rust using the actual image colours ensures the rust we create looks natural.

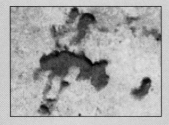

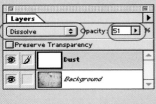

Raising the surface metal
To raise the surface metal, set the Brush Size to 5 pixels and paint strokes under the top edge of the exposed areas. Burning this area darkens it, creating a shadow that lifts the surface metal off the underlying metal.
Okay, we're now finished with the Burn tool.

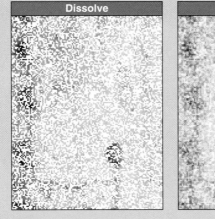

Creating the dust layer
Add a new layer called 'Dust', fill with white, then set the blend mode to Dissolve and the Opacity to 51%. We need to soften the dust speckles and also make the layer editable. We'll need to render the layer so the dissolved pixels but on a layer with a Normal blend mode. Add a new layer, switch off the background layer and Merge Visible to combine the visible layers. Apply a Gaussian Blur with a Radius of .4 to soften the dust speckles.

Blending the dust
Set the layer blend mode to Screen and the Opacity to 30% to blend the dust with the metal below. We now have a subtle dust layer covering the metal, though it covers it too completely.

Removing dust under rivets
The spots under the rivets should have less dust so we need to remove it in this area. Select the Eraser tool with a Brush Size of 13 pixels and a Pressure of 100%. Paint strokes directly under the rivets to remove the dust. It's a subtle effect, but we are striving for photorealism.

| Difficulty: Intermediate | Rita Amladi |

Adding depth of field

Sometimes you can make a subject stand out by making it appear in sharp focus against an unfocused background. Rita Amladi shows you how to create the illusion of depth by changing the depth of field of an image with some simple techniques.

The basis of this tip is that if you take a sharp image and create a copy on another (higher) layer …

… and then blur the new copy layer …

… you can control the opacity of that layer by creating a greyscale ramp like this …

… and use it as a layer mask so that the black section completely masks the layer, the white lets it all show and the greys allow a partial view. So this is what you would expect to see.

But in practice you also allow the original sharp image to show through, so you get to see both. This gives the effect of a soft halo which, if done with restraint, does not affect the overall effect.

Adobe Photoshop Special F/X
This tip is based on the VTC CD-ROM
Adobe Photoshop Special F/X by
Rita Amladi.

(USA) VTC USA
Phone: 888 872 4623
www.vtco.com
(Aust) VTC Australia
Phone: 07 3367 8451
www.vtco.com

The illusion of depth

In this image we'd like to add the illusion of depth by creating a blur that makes the architecture behind this gondola appear to recede into the background.
In other words, we want the objects closer to the gondola appear to have a stronger focus than the objects towards the back of the image or towards the vanishing point in the picture.
To begin, select the Background layer, go to the Layers palette menu and select 'Duplicate Layer'. (Or choose the icon to create a new layer in the Layers palette.)

Start with a blur

Apply the Gaussian Blur filter to the layer 'Background copy', keeping in mind how you'd like the very end of the vanishing point to look.
Here we use a radius of 4.5 to achieve the desired blur.

An all-over blur

Our image now has an all-over blur. To bring some of the objects in the scene back into full or partial focus, we'll user layer and selection masks.

Layer mask

Add a layer mask to the Background copy layer by selecting the 'Add a mask' icon from the Layers palette.
We now need to add a gradient to the layer mask to determine which areas of the image will be completely defocused, which will be partly defocused and then the areas that will remain unaffected.

Gradient

To bring some focus back to the foreground, we'll create a black and white gradient that blocks out the blur effect in the foreground.
Select the Gradient tool, then set the default colours (foreground: white, background: black) by hitting the D key.
Select Linear Gradient from the Options Bar.
With the layer mask active, drag the gradient from the bottom of the image to the top.

Option/Alt-clicking the layer mask icon shows us how our gradient looks. Option/Alt-clicking the icon returns us to the original view.

What about the gondola?

The gradient still leaves part of the gondola unfocused. We'll rectify this by filling in a selection of the gondola with black in the layer mask.

Quick Mask Mode
Painting black into an image in Quick Mask mode allows you to build up a selection.

Quick Mask
Using Photoshop's Quick Mask feature, create a selection around the gondola by painting black into the background (select the original sharp background layer to work on to ensure an accurate fit). Note that the colour of the mask you will be painting is dependent on your colour selection in Quick Mask options.
When you're happy with the result, return to the Standard Editing mode.

Standard Mode
Returning to Standard mode gives you a selection which can then be used to create a mask.

Gondola selection
With your gondola selected, you're now ready to reverse the effects of the blur on the central object in the image.

Options
Use Edit > Fill > Black or Option/Alt-Delete with your foreground colour set to black to fill the gondola selection with black.

Unblurring the gondola
Making sure that the layer mask is active, fill the gondola selection with black.
This blocks the gondola from being affected by the blur we have applied.

Onwards to the bridge
With the gondola safely unblurred, we're ready to tackle the bridge.

Quick Mask
Still working in your layer mask, create a selection around the bridge (using Photoshop's Quick Mask feature again) by painting black into the background. When you're happy, return to Standard Editing mode.

The middle ground
We now want to partially affect the overhead bridge by the blurring it to create a middle-distance effect. To do this we'll fill the bridge selection with a mid-grey.

Going grey
Fill the selection with mid-gray using Edit > Fill > 50% Gray. Alternatively, select a mid-grey using the Color Picker and Option/Alt-Delete to fill the selection with mid-gray.

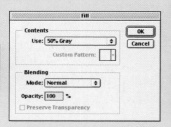

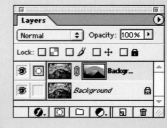

Partially blurred
The bridge is now partially blurred which creates the illusion of it being in between our sharply focused gondola and the blurred background. Deselect the bridge (Select > Deselect or Command/Ctrl-D).

Calculations

More experienced users will find it easier to make individual channels for all of the selections and then combine them using the Image > Calculations command.

Final adjustments

The final differences we are making to the image can be seen on the one layer. However, the final image will be an amalgam of both this and the original image.

Final result

Here we can see a the dramatic effect of the gondola appearing sharply in focus while the bridge is partially focused and the background is blurred.

Difficulty: Intermediate	Katrin Eismann

Restoration & Retouching

In her book, 'Photoshop Restoration & Retouching', Katrin Eismann explains techniques for saving and improving images. Here she shows us a number of alternative techniques for dustbusting and removing mould from an image.

Remove airborne grit without the dust and scratches filter.

Dry clean mouldy old clothes.

Sweep the streets clean.

Making A Mask

An effective technique for cleaning up areas of an image that have minimal detail, such as a sky or background, is to float and move the difficult area and use a Lighten blending mode to remove flaws. For even greater accuracy, you can use a mask to float the sky layer to the edge of the buildings.

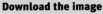

Download the image
To follow this tip, download the image from the Photoshop Restoration & Retouching web site at: www.digitalretouch.org/download/ch_04/cho4_large/ch4_berlin_lg.jpg

Dustbusting 101
An important concept to recognise is that there is no dust in a digital file. The dust was on or in the original. In the digital file all you really have is lighter or darker pixels in contrast to darker or lighter backgrounds. Taking advantage of this concept can speed up your dustbusting sessions. In this photograph, we have a lot of dust and mould distributed evenly over the whole image. Starting with the sky, we want to use the 'float and move' technique to reduce the noise while not affecting the buildings and trees.

Start with a mask
Change to the Quick Mask mode, then with a 10-pixel brush, with a Hardness of 85%, paint along the edge of the objects that meet the sky.

Paint it red
When you have completed the painting of the skyline, choose the Paintbucket tool from the Tool palette, and fill the foreground by clicking on it.

The mask
We are now halfway to having a mask that blocks out everything in the photograph except for the sky.

Standard Editing mode

Return to Standard Editing mode by selecting the button in the Tool palette.

This will produce a selection which contains only the sky. To make the selection a channel, choose Select > Save Selection and name it Sky. This will add the 'Sky' channel to the Channels palette which we will then refine.

Fine tuning the mask

Because we used a brush with a Hardness of 85%, there is a gap where the transparent pixels meet the area filled by the Paintbucket tool.

Fine tuning the mask

With the 'Sky' channel active, select the Paintbrush tool and paint over the white pixels with black.

Note:

if your channel looks different to this (black where it should be white and vice versa), Quick Mask Options was probably set to 'Selected areas' and not 'Masked areas' as it should have been. To rectify, go back to your original selection, choose Select > Inverse and resave your selection.

A snug selection and mask

Go back to the background layer and Command/Ctrl-click the 'Sky' channel to load a selection based on the channel.

Float & Move

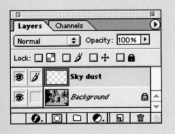

Float

Returning to the Background layer in the layers palette, select Layer > New > Layer Via Copy (Command/Ctrl-J) to float the sky selection to a new layer. Name the layer 'Sky dust' by selecting Layer properties from the Layers palette pop-up menu.

Lighten

The Lighten Blending mode hides dark spots by showing through the lighter pixels from the Background layer.

Float and move

With the 'Sky dust' layer active, select the Move tool (v) and use the arrow keys to nudge the layer down and over to the right 2-3 pixels. Set the Blending mode to Lighten. Notice how we've lost some building pixels.

Layer Mask

The layer mask based on the Sky channel protects the buildings from the Lighten adjustment.

Layer mask

To avoid the problem of damaging the building, we'll use our sky channel to create a layer mask.
With the 'Sky dust' layer active, load the 'Sky' channel (Command/Ctrl-click the channel), then choose the Layer mask icon in the Layers palette. Set the blending mode to Lighten again. This time, you'll notice that the sky has been cleaned up without interfering with the buildings.

Clear skies

As you can see, the majority of dust and mould in the sky has been removed.
The remaining problem areas would be best cleaned up using the Clone Stamp tool.

Dust & Scratches filter

The 'float and move' technique works very well on image areas such as sky or studio backgrounds. When you want to maintain texture or film grain, the Dust & Scratches filter provides more control.

Down on the street
With the sky treated using the 'float and move' technique, we'll now use the Dust & Scratches filter on the street scene. Start by creating a mask of the foreground using the Quick Mask mode. Be careful to paint over any objects that you don't want the Dust & Scratches filter to affect. Here, the pedestrians' shadows have edges that we don't want to affect, so we'll include them within our Quick Mask.

Street selection
Return to Standard Editing mode. This will produce a selection which contains only the street scene that you haven't painted over. To make the selection a channel, choose Select > Save Selection and name it Street. This will add the 'Street' channel to the Channels palette.

A snug selection and mask
Command/Ctrl-clicking the 'Street' channel will give us a selection based on the channel.

Street layer
Returning to the Background layer in the Layers palette, select Layer > New > Layer Via Copy (Command/Ctrl-J) to float the street selection to a new layer. Name the layer 'Street' by selecting Layer Properties in the Layers palette pop-up menu.

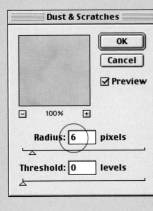

Dust & Scratches
With the Street layer selected and the Street selection active, select Filter > Noise > Dust & Scratches. Move the Radius setting up until the dust is obliterated.

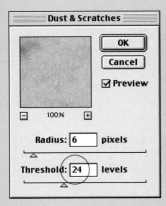

Threshold
Using only the Radius removes the dust and texture. Increase the Threshold value of the Dust & Scratches filter so that the texture is maintained while the dust remains hidden.

07 - Special F/X

Keeping your options open

With the sky and street treated, we now want to clean up the areas that are still showing dust and mould.

Create a new layer named 'Composite', then select Command-Shift-Option-E (Ctrl-Alt-Shift-E for Windows). This composites all of your visible layers into the new layer. We can now use the Clone Stamp tool to clean up the rest of the image.

Mould removal

Create a new layer above the 'Composite' layer and name it 'Mould removal'. Select the Clone Stamp tool and set the options to work in Normal mode at 100% Opacity and—most importantly—click Use All Layers. This tells the Clone Stamp tool to sample down through all the layers. Working on an empty layer with the Clone Stamp tool gives you the ability to add and erase repairs without affecting the original layer.

Using the Clone Stamp tool, target the remaining dust and mould and clone it out.

Tough to clone areas

With heavily affected images, you may find that areas of mould cover detailed areas while still showing some of that detail through the discolouration. Rather than using the Clone Stamp tool, it can be easier to change the colour of the mould to blend with the image.

Hue/Saturation

Go back to the Composite layer and using the Lasso tool, make a rough selection around the mould-affected area. Select Hue/Saturation (Image > Adjustments > Hue/Saturation), then adjust the Hue, Saturation and Lightness sliders until the mould blends into the image.

The 'float and move' technique, the Dust & Scratches filter, cloning with the Clone Stamp tool and adjusting problem areas with Hue/Saturation give us a much improved result over the original. With these techniques you can fight the ravages of time, and rescue emotionally valuable images for yourself, your family or your clients.

Photoshop Restoration & Retouching
features step-by-step examples and downloadable images allowing readers to work through each technique.

For more information, see www.digitalretouch.org

<table>
<tr><td rowspan="2">Quick textures from scratch</td><td>Difficulty: Easy</td><td>Michael Ninness</td></tr>
<tr><td colspan="2">The first port of call for many designers in need of a texture is a stock image library or a third-party plug-in. At Thunder Lizard Production's Photoshop 2001/DC conference, Michael Ninness showed some quick steps to create detailed textures using Photoshop's standard filters.</td></tr>
</table>

Stone & Slate

Clouds

The stone texture is very easy to create. First, reset your colours to default black and white by pressing the D key. Choose Filter > Render > Clouds.

Difference Clouds

Choose Filter > Render > Difference Clouds to create the detail that will be accentuated by the Emboss filter.

Emboss

Choose Filter > Stylize > Emboss (Angle: 135, Height: 3, Amount: 300) to produce the stone/slate effect.

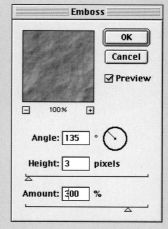

Hue/Saturation

Finally, select Image > Adjustments > Hue/Saturation (Command/Ctrl-U) to colorise the stone to your requirements. Note: Ensure you have the colorise option selected in this dialogue box.

Woven fabric

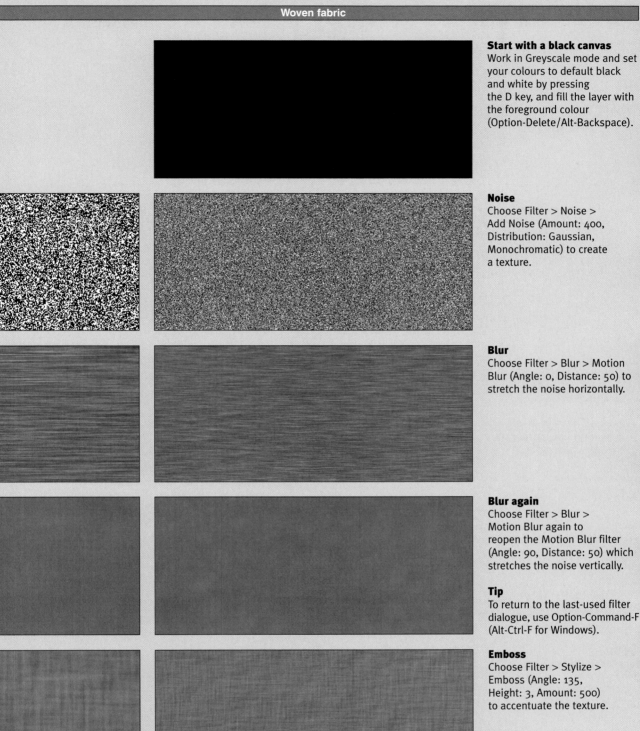

Start with a black canvas
Work in Greyscale mode and set
your colours to default black
and white by pressing
the D key, and fill the layer with
the foreground colour
(Option-Delete/Alt-Backspace).

Noise
Choose Filter > Noise >
Add Noise (Amount: 400,
Distribution: Gaussian,
Monochromatic) to create
a texture.

Blur
Choose Filter > Blur > Motion
Blur (Angle: 0, Distance: 50) to
stretch the noise horizontally.

Blur again
Choose Filter > Blur >
Motion Blur again to
reopen the Motion Blur filter
(Angle: 90, Distance: 50) which
stretches the noise vertically.

Tip
To return to the last-used filter
dialogue, use Option-Command-F
(Alt-Ctrl-F for Windows).

Emboss
Choose Filter > Stylize >
Emboss (Angle: 135,
Height: 3, Amount: 500)
to accentuate the texture.

Levels
Choose Image > Adjustments>
Levels (Input Levels: 85, 1.00, 170)
to improve the contrast and
bring out the detail in the
texture.

Recycled paper

Base colour
Fill a layer with the base colour for the paper.

Neutral colour
Create a new layer with an Opacity of 25% and a blend mode of Multiply. Fill the new layer with a neutral colour (in this case white).

Note: From Photoshop 6 onwards, you can set all of these properties in the New Layer dialogue (Layer > New > Layer).

Pointillize
Still working on the new layer, choose Filter > Pixelate > Pointillize (Cell Size: 10) to introduce the coloured noise effect.

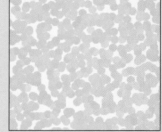

Find Edges
Choose Filter > Stylize > Find Edges to accentuate the texture.

Dry Brush
Choose Filter > Artistic > Dry Brush (Brush Size: 2, Brush Detail: 8, Texture: 1) to show more of the original paper colour.

Add noise to suit
Finally, merge the layers and then add a slight amount of noise (Filter > Noise > Add Noise) to add grain to the paper. In this example, we have specified an amount of 25%.

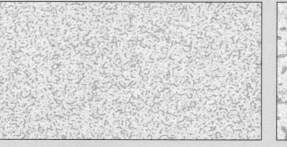
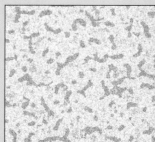

Rust

Clouds
Set the Foreground colour to (RGB: 33, 19, 5) and the Background colour to (RGB: 76, 56, 21), then choose Filter > Render > Clouds.

Add grain
Choose Filter > Texture > Grain (Intensity: 50, Contrast: 65, Type: Speckle) to add detail.

Unsharp Mask
Choose Filter > Sharpen > Unsharp Mask (Amount: 400, Radius: 5, Threshold: 25) to bring out the detail.

Dry Brush
Choose Filter > Artistic > Dry Brush (Brush Size: 2, Brush Detail: 2, Texture: 2) to create areas of grey simulating the underlying metal.

Add noise
For the final rust effect, choose Filter > Noise > Add Noise (Amount: 8, Distribution: Gaussian, Monochromatic).

07 - Special F/X

First a gradient
Create a linear gradient
from black to white.

Difference Clouds
Choose Filter > Render >
Difference clouds.

Invert
Choose Image > Adjustments >
Invert. The diagonal shape of
the lightning can be seen.

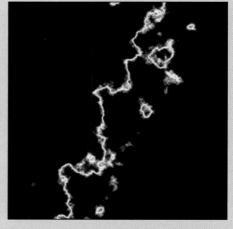

Levels
Choose Image > Adjustments >
Levels and adjust the three
Input Levels (highlights,
midtones and shadows)
until the lightning bolt(s)
appear to your liking.

Clean up
Use a black paintbrush to take
away the parts of the image
that you don't want.

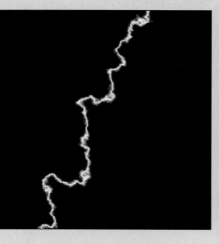

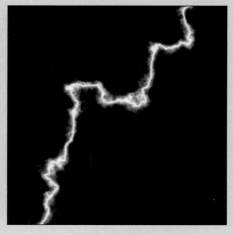

Final tweak
The complete image is probably
too much and needs simplifying.
Use the Transform function
(Command/Ctrl-T) to enlarge
and rotate the image until
the lightning looks right.
You can now transfer this layer
and use it in Screen mode to
add lightning to any scene.

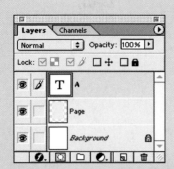

Set up the effect

Create a rectangular shape on a new layer named 'Page' and fill it with the page colour of your choice.

Create an additional type layer that has the text you want to appear on the page and align the text on the page.

Merge and Shear

Merge the type layer with the 'Page' layer and choose Filter > Distort > Shear. Create an 'S' shape on the distortion grid and click OK.

Rotate

Use the Free Transform mode (Command/Ctrl-T) to rotate the page to the desired orientation.

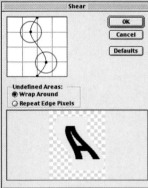

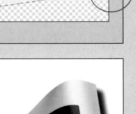

Lighting Effects

Create a layer above the merged 'Page' layer. Command/Ctrl-click on the 'Page' layer to load the page selection on the new layer and set the Airbrush to 10% pressure. (Note: The Airbrush tool is part of the Paintbrush tool in Photoshop 7. Select 'Airbrush Soft Round 50%' from the pull down menu in the Options Bar.) Paint in black for shadows and white for highlights on the page.

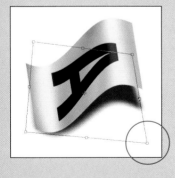

Drop Shadow

Add a Drop Shadow Layer Style to the 'Page' layer. Choose Layer > Layer Style > Create Layer to convert the Drop Shadow effect into its own layer. In this example we have used Normal blend mode with 41% Opacity, 120° Angle , 23% Distance, 6 % Spread and 21% Size.

Perspective Cast Shadow

Use the Free Transform mode to stretch, rotate and position the shadow to your liking.

Perspective distort

Hold down the Command/Ctrl key and drag a corner handle
to perform a perspective transformation on the shadow.

Curled paper

The final result is a curled sheet of paper that can be created in just a few minutes using a standard Photoshop filter.

	Difficulty: Intermediate	Colin Wood
Seeing the big pixel	Here we show you how to combine giant pixels in a layer mask with a high resolution image. The trick lies in creating a coarse pattern of pixels at a low resolution and then increasing the resolution of pixels while retaining the same pattern.	

Frog and **Tutenkhamun**
images courtesy of
Photo Essentials.

To understand how this technique works you must first understand the difference between greyscale and bitmap images. All pictures are made up of pixels (picture elements); a series of coloured squares butted against each other.

Greyscale
Greyscale images are made up from 256 shades of grey (including black and white). In a blend there is a smooth transition between shades.

Bitmap
Bitmap images have pixels that are either black or white. There are no shades of grey in a bitmap image.

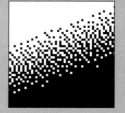

Greyscale images
Photoshop uses 8-bit channels to create greyscale (monochrome) images.

RGB colour images
Colour images are made up from three 8-bit channels, one each for red, green and blue. There are approximately 16,700,000 (256 x 256 x 256) possible colours.

Our sample is 300dpi
Here is our candidate for a large pixel blend.
The image is shown here at actual size with a resolution of 300dpi to allow for high quality printing.
For images intended for the web the process would be the same, as would relative size percentages, but the pixel count would be lower.
The size of our image is 1,075 x 717 pixels.

Copy a channel
We wish to position a blend so that it will not interfere with our frog's face, so we copy one of the channels (in this case we chose green, of course) to act as a guide.

Create a blend in the channel
Select the Gradient tool, set the default colours by hitting the D key, then select Linear Gradient from the Options Bar.
Make a gradient directly inside the copy of the green channel, positioning your mouse in the middle of the page and dragging from left to right diagonally.

Automatic size and mode
When you have copied the (greyscale) channel to the clipboard, Photoshop will automatically select the same pixel dimensions and mode (greyscale) for the new file..

Smaller file size
When you decrease the size of your file to 10% of the original, it will look quite small on your monitor at first.
Double-click the Zoom tool to bring it back to a usable size and you will see that the gradation is now very coarse.

Image Size

Pixel Dimensions: 23K (was 2.21M)

Width: 108 pixels
Height: 72 pixels

Document Size:

Width: 10 percent
Height: 0.61 cm
Resolution: 300 pixels/inch

☑ Constrain Proportions
☑ Resample Image: Bicubic

OK
Cancel
Auto...

New file
We must now work on the channel in a separate greyscale file so that our next few steps do not affect our image.
Copy the blend channel to the clipboard, create a new file (which will be greyscale by default) and paste the channel into it (as a layer). Our aim is to reduce the image size so that we can achieve a coarse pixel pattern and have less pixels.
In this case, we must reduce the file to one tenth of its size in both width and height. (File will be one hundredth of the original size.) At this stage we still have a smooth blend, albeit at a low resolution.

This effect is possible because of Photoshop's ability to resample using Nearest Neighbor, thus retaining the coarse pixel pattern.

Convert from greyscale to bitmap

Use Image > Mode > Bitmap to convert the image to the bitmap mode in which there are no shades of grey, only black or white pixels. Use the same input and output resolutions. Notice how coarse they look at this resolution.

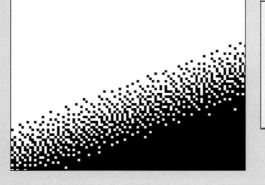

And then back to greyscale

Use Image > Mode > Grayscale to convert the image back to greyscale using the default size ratio (one).

So here's the first trick

The shades of grey do not return. You now have a greyscale version of the bitmap pattern.
It's just very small, that's all.

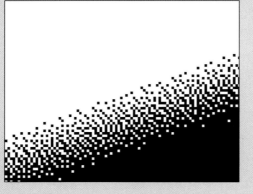

Increase the resolution

Now we must return the file to the original pixel count so that it can be used as an alpha channel in the original file. Use Image > Image size to return the image to the original resolution.
You can key in the original pixel dimensions to ensure an exact fit.

Here's the second trick

It is essential that you resample the image using 'Nearest Neighbor' to ensure that your image looks exactly the same as it did at the smaller file size.

Paste image as an alpha channel

Paste the greyscale image back into your original file as an alpha channel. Double-click on the background layer to turn it into a layer and use Command/Ctrl-Click on the new alpha channel to load it as a selection.

Note: If your gradient is not created from the middle of the image, the desired effect will not be achieved.

Make a layer mask

Click on the layer mask icon to create a layer mask. Now you have a combination of a high resolution image and a low resolution layer mask.

You can use the hard edges of the bitmap layer mask for various effects. Here we have included our page background colour and placed a shadow under the image to make the pattern stand out.

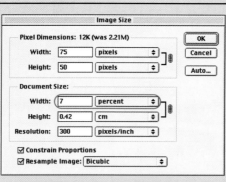

Include optical conundrums in your work by combining different resolutions in the same image

Small frog, big pixels
There are other ways to combine mixed pixel sizes for creative effect.
Here we have taken our original frog image and reduced the pixel count to 7 percent.
As you can see, the image is very coarse.

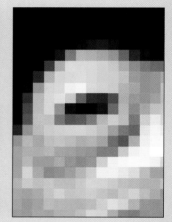

Upsample with Nearest Neighbor
As before, increase the pixel count to the same as the original image, using Nearest Neighbor to preserve the large pixels.

Layer swap
Now we need to place both images in the same file with the low res layer beneath the high res layer.

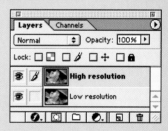

Make a selection
Select an area of the image to return to high resolution and save the selection as a channel.

Add a layer mask
With the original high resolution image on a layer above the low res version, add a layer mask to allow the lower layer to show through.
Here we have added a drop shadow and a highlight edge to make the high res section stand out. To increase the difference between the two parts of the image, we have placed a dark green layer above the background

The large pixel technique works with all types of blends. Try it with radial blends to create pixel dust. The size of the particles can be controlled through the pixel count. Experiment to get the effects you want.

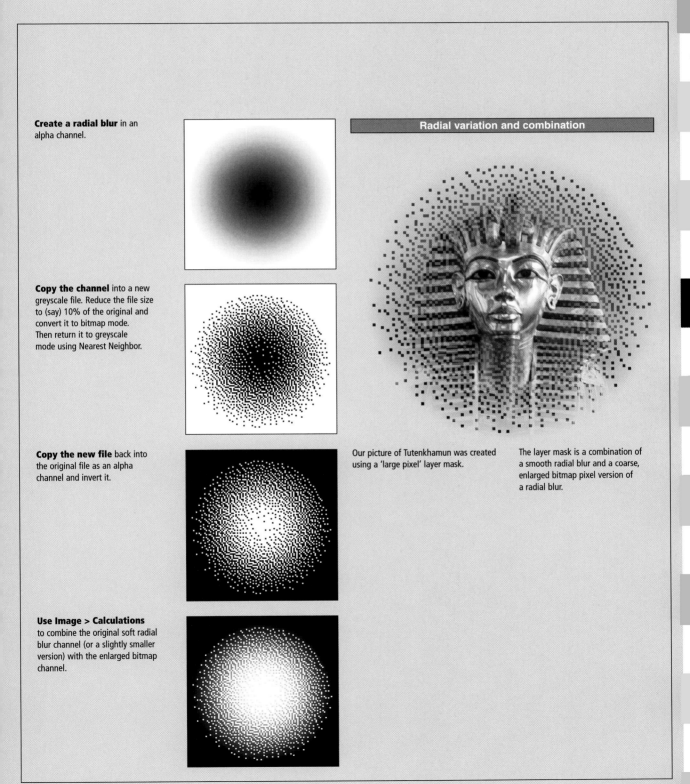

Create a radial blur in an alpha channel.

Copy the channel into a new greyscale file. Reduce the file size to (say) 10% of the original and convert it to bitmap mode. Then return it to greyscale mode using Nearest Neighbor.

Copy the new file back into the original file as an alpha channel and invert it.

Use Image > Calculations to combine the original soft radial blur channel (or a slightly smaller version) with the enlarged bitmap channel.

Radial variation and combination

Our picture of Tutenkhamun was created using a 'large pixel' layer mask.

The layer mask is a combination of a smooth radial blur and a coarse, enlarged bitmap pixel version of a radial blur.

Difficulty: Intermediate	Colin Wood

Fast and flexible knockouts

The knockout feature in Photoshop 6 is powerful and flexible, so flexible that many of the variables are interchangable. This can make your head spin trying to understand it. Here is a simple guide to show how it works together with some sample settings that will enable you to get fabulous effects fast.

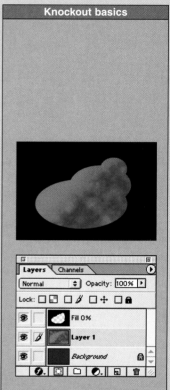

Drilling down through layers in transparent areas can create some awesome effects. And while you can impress your friends with your almost mythical powers, the feature is also a very powerful production tool.

Its power lies, in part, in its flexibility, because in some cases you can achieve the same result using different settings. Thus the knockout feature can appear confusing. This guide will give you all you need to know to put you on the road to a full understanding.

A knockout can be applied to any layer that contains some transparency. The knockout appears in the non-transparent areas. The knockout area can be type (as straight type or rasterised) or a shape. The opacity of the type or shape layer must be reduced (start with zero to become familiar with the feature). In the example above, a knockout applied to the black shape layer will expose the background layer (whether the knockout is shallow or deep).

In order to use the knockout feature, you must have a multi-layered file that includes some transparency on the layer to which the knockout will be applied.
A knockout can be applied using a rasterised layer with a shape in it, a type layer or a shape layer.
The full power of the knockout feature (for deep and shallow knockouts) is available only when you use a layer set.

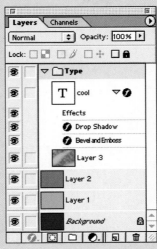

Layered file
Here is our layered Photoshop file. We have a type layer on top, a texture beneath, and the type on a layer within the same layer set as the type. Under that we have two layers filled with solid colours and finally a background layer, also containing a solid colour.

At the start
This is how the file will look with just the inner bevel and drop shadow active.

As it appears outside the type area, the drop shadow will be treated as part of the background by Photoshop when we apply a knockout.

Type layer
This is our type layer with transparency surrounding the type. The type has been given a drop shadow and an inner bevel in the Layer Styles palette.

Texture
This texture is in the Type layer set. The type will interact with this when:
• the Type layer has a Normal blend mode.
• there is no knockout.

Layer 2
This plain colour is in a layer directly beneath the Type layer set. The type will interact with this when:
• The type layer's knockout is set to shallow.

Layer Style dialogue box

The knockout feature controls can be found in the Layer Style dialogue box under Blending Options.

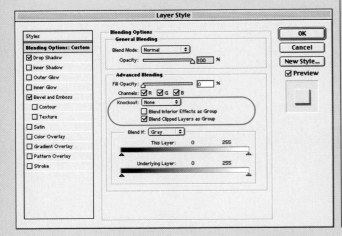

Layer 1
This plain colour is in the next layer down. The type will interact with this when:
• The type layer's knockout is set to shallow and Layer 2 is not visible.

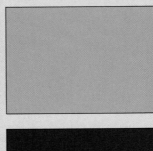

Background layer
A deep knockout drills right down to the background, bypassing all other layers in between. If there is no actual background layer (or background layer is switched off), transparency will fill the knockout area.

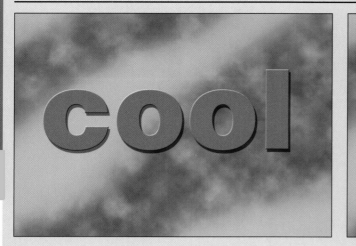

Control areas
To achieve and modify knockouts, there are two areas in which to make adjustments.

Layers palette
Any layer can have a (deep) knockout applied to it, but the shallow knockout is available only when using a layer set. Layer sets have an extra blending mode called Pass Through which is used to expose layers outside of the layer set.
(In other words, two or more layers are grouped into the same folder.)

When you have the basics of the knockout feature under control you can experiment with opacity settings and blend modes for some exciting results.

Layer styles
The Layer Styles dialogue box is brought up by double-clicking on the layer name in the Layers palette.
The Knockout feature is available in the Advanced Blending section.

The main controls are Fill Opacity and Knockout.

Fill opacity
This must be less than 100% for any knockout effect to be seen. It is best to start at 0% until you are familiar with this feature.

Knockout
The pull-down menu has three options: None, Shallow, Deep.

Our examples on the following pages show how these items interact.

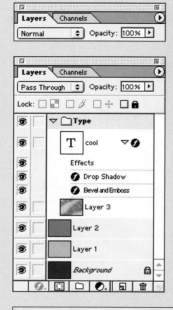

**Knockout:
an overview**

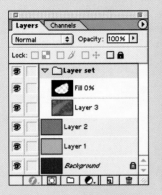

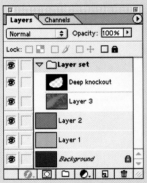

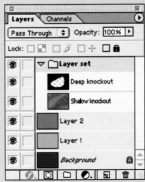

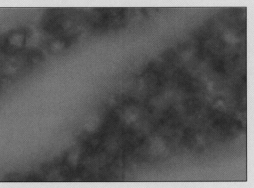

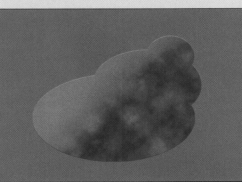

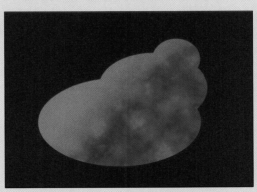

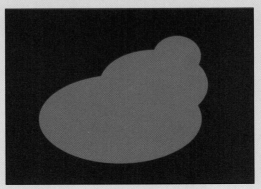

Preparing a knockout
The knockout feature can
be used with type layers,
shape layers or any layer
that contains transparency.
Here we have a layer with
a black fill and a transparent hole.
The blend mode of all layers
is Normal.
As you would expect, Layer 3
shows through the hole in
the black layer.

Reduce the fill opacity
With the fill opacity reduced to
zero in the Layer Style dialogue
box, the black disappears and
you can start to work with the
knockout feature.
Initially the layer will disappear
(but the shape is still there)
and the knockout feature works
on the shape, not the colour.

Creating a knockout
Here the Layer set blend
mode in the Layer Style
dialogue box is set to Normal.
So if a Shallow knockout is
applied to the black layer (with
the fill opacity still set to zero),
you will see through to Layer 2.
If the Knockout is set to Deep,
the background will disappear
altogether.

Deep knockouts
A Deep Knockout is activated
when (and only when) the
Layer set blend mode is
set to Pass Through.
Note that a Deep Knockout
drills all the way to the
background layer, bypassing
any layers in between.
Note: the background layer
must be a true background layer
(recognisable by its associated
padlock icon) and not merely a
regular layer.

Combination knockouts
You can use combination
knockouts too.
This state is the same as the
one above except that Layer 3
now has a fill opacity of 0%
and a Shallow Knockout.

Knockout - None

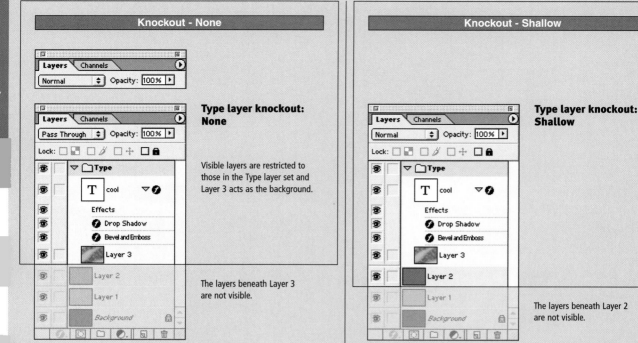

Type layer knockout: None

Visible layers are restricted to those in the Type layer set and Layer 3 acts as the background.

The layers beneath Layer 3 are not visible.

Knockout - Shallow

Type layer knockout: Shallow

The layers beneath Layer 2 are not visible.

Layers palette

▽ 📁	Type layer set	●	Normal
	or	●	Pass Through

Layer style: Blending options

T	Fill opacity	●	0%
			100%
T	Knockout	●	None
			Shallow
			Deep

Layers palette

▽ 📁	Type layer set	●	Normal
			Pass Through

Layer style: Blending options

T	Fill opacity	●	0%
			100%
T	Knockout		None
		●	Shallow
	or	●	Deep

Option
This state is available using:
Layer set blend mode
Normal
Knockout
Shallow or deep
or
Layer set blend mode
Pass Through
Knockout
Shallow only

Knockout - Shallow

Layers	Channels	▶
Normal	⬍ Opacity: 100% ▶	

Lock: ☐ ☐ ☐ ☐ ☐ ☐ 🔒

- 👁 ▽ 📁 Type
- 👁 T cool ▽ 🗇
- 👁 Effects
- 👁 🗇 Drop Shadow
- 👁 🗇 Bevel and Emboss
- 👁 Layer 3
- Layer 2
- 👁 Layer 1
- 👁 *Background* 🔒

Type layer knockout: Shallow

The background layer beneath Layer 1 is not visible.

Knockout - Deep

Layers	Channels	▶
Pass Through	⬍ Opacity: 100% ▶	

Lock: ☐ ☐ ☐ ☐ ☐ ☐ 🔒

- 👁 ▽ 📁 Type
- 👁 T cool ▽ 🗇
- 👁 Effects
- 👁 🗇 Drop Shadow
- 👁 🗇 Bevel and Emboss
- 👁 Layer 3
- 👁 Layer 2
- 👁 Layer 1
- 👁 *Background* 🔒

Type layer knockout: Deep

The background layer is visible.

Layers palette

▽ 📁	Type layer set	●	Normal
			Pass Through

Layer style: Blending options

T	Fill opacity	●	0%
			100%
T	Knockout		None
		●	Shallow
			Deep

Layers palette

▽ 📁	Type layer set		Normal
		●	Pass Through

Layer style: Blending options

T	Fill opacity	●	0%
			100%
T	Knockout		None
			Shallow
		●	Deep

Option
This state is available using:
Layer set blend mode
Normal
Knockout
Shallow or deep
or
Layer set blend mode
Pass Through
Knockout
Shallow only

Note
This is almost the same as the example at left, except that Layer 2 is not visible.

Note
To see through to the background the Type layer set must be set to Pass Through.

Difficulty: Intermediate	Colin wood

Gradient Map halos

The Gradient Map is a great way to create very cool brushes.
In fact, any greyscale art that contains a range of greys can be used
as the basis for a colourful image. You can even paint with crazy cool
brushes and create halos from heaven.

Mountains image courtesy of
Canon PhotoEssentials from the
Images of the World collection.

Start with your background.

Create a new empty layer and draw
something in black with a feathered edge.
In this way you can position your artwork
to suit the background. Save this shape as
a selection (Alpha Channel).

Create another new layer beneath the new
art you have just drawn. Either group or
flatten the two new layers so that you
have (in effect) a single layer with black,
white and greys.

New gradient map

Basic gradient map

Create a Gradient Map on top of all other
layers, and group it with the previous
layer. This will substitute colours according
to the various shades on the value scale.

At first the gradient map will interact
solely with the black & white layer.
In order to see through this layer to the
background we must create a layer mask.

First we copy our Alpha Channel, and ...

... paste it to a layer mask on the black
and white layer, disconnecting the layer
icon from its layer mask.

Use the Transform tool to reveal more (or
less) of the background. You can now
paint on the black and white layer with a
very fancy brush!

Halo candidate

Here we have a file with a background and a layer containing a contoured image. We will show how to give this statue a wonderful halo using a gradient map adjustment layer. Start by making the contoured lion (Layer 1) the active layer.

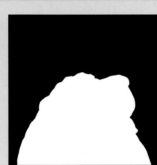

Make a selection

Command/Ctrl-click on the lion layer (Layer 1) to make a selection and save the selection as an alpha channel.

This is the alpha channel which follows the shape of our candidate exactly. Of course, this will not give us a halo so we must make it larger, keeping the general shape following the original.

You can make the white area larger in several ways. Here we have used Filter > Other > Maximum. You could also use Edit > Transform (Command/Ctrl-T) and hold down the Shift key to constrain proportions.

Here is our larger version.

Use Filter > Blur > Gaussian Blur to soften the selection significantly.

Basic halo

Copy the blurred alpha channel to the clipboard. Create a new layer immediately above the background layer and paste the alpha channel art into the new layer. It will automatically assume the mode of the file (RGB or CMYK, whichever you are working in). At this stage you will have covered up the background with a black ground and a white halo.

Creating a Gradient

When you create a Gradient Map adjustment layer, you invoke the Gradient Map dialogue box. The default gradient setting uses the current foreground and background colours from the Tool palette.
Click on the ramp itself to bring up the Gradient Editor in which you can select a preset or create a unique custom gradient.

Selecting colours

To change colours in the ramp, double-click on the colour patches to bring up the Color Picker.
Click beside the ramp to add additional colours; drag the patches away to delete them.

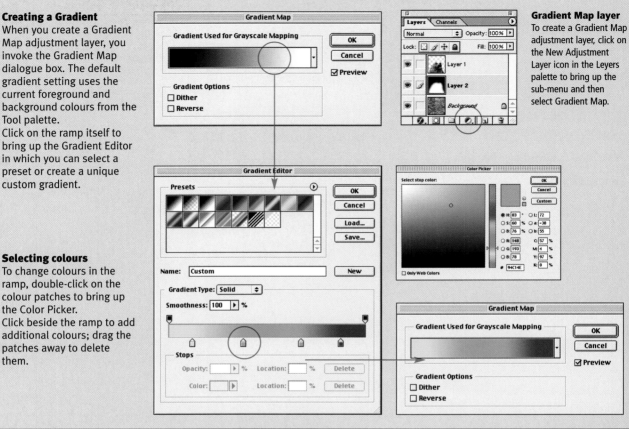

Gradient Map layer

To create a Gradient Map adjustment layer, click on the New Adjustment Layer icon in the Leyers palette to bring up the sub-menu and then select Gradient Map.

Before the Gradient Map

This is how the file looks before you add a gradient map to Layer 2.

Hold down the Option/Alt key and click the adjustment layer icon to bring up Layer sub-menu. This will allow you to select the option: 'Group with previous layer'. In this exercise, you will group the adjustment with Layer 2.

After the Gradient Map

This is how the file looks when the Gradient Map is applied using the settings shown above. Note that the background layer can't be seen.
We will need a layer mask on Layer 2 to fix that.

Once you have loaded the section onto Layer 2, click on this icon to turn it into a layer mask.

Click between the layer icon and the layer mask icon to disconnect them so that the mask can be enlarged without affecting the layer image.

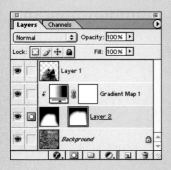

First halo

Load the blurred alpha channel you used to make the halo as a selection (Command/Ctrl-click on the channel).
Then use that to make a layer mask for the halo. At this point the background will be visible again, leaving a halo. But we might want to see more of the halo.

Growing the halo

Click between the layer and the layer mask to remove the link. You will now be able to make the layer mask bigger without affecting the size or position of the coloured halo.
Click on the layer mask icon to make it active.
Use Command/Ctrl-T to activate the Transform function.
Click and drag the corners of the Transform marquee; the halo will grow or shrink before your eyes.
When you are happy with the result, hit Return to commit the transformation.

Warm glow of success

So there you have it; a multi-coloured halo that follows the shape of the object. Using the Gradient Map you are able to change any or all of the colours later on. The shape of the halo can also be varied by repeating the Transform function.

07 - Special F/X

| Difficulty: Intermediate | Daniel Wade |

Photoshop Pattern Maker

Photoshop 7's Pattern Maker allows you to create random seamless patterns based on any area of an image with a wide range of controls. It's also a useful tool to make your own Pattern presets which can then be used to paint out unwanted elements in an image.

Too many sheep
Photoshop 7's Pattern Maker allows you to create seamless patterns from any selection.
It's also a useful tool for painting out unwanted elements in an image such as a group of sheep.
You might argue that the Clone Stamp tool would be just as effective at removing unwanted objects, but in combination with the Pattern Stamp tool, you can dramatically speed up the process.

Working with Pattern Maker

Pattern Maker

Select Filter > Pattern Maker (Shift-Option-Command-x/ Shift-Alt-Ctrl-x) to launch Pattern Maker.
You'll notice that the dialogue is quite similar to the Liquify and Extract interfaces with tools in the top left, a large preview in the centre, and controls on the right of the interface. Ensure that the Marquee tool is selected, then drag out a selection in your image that you want to create a pattern from and select generate.

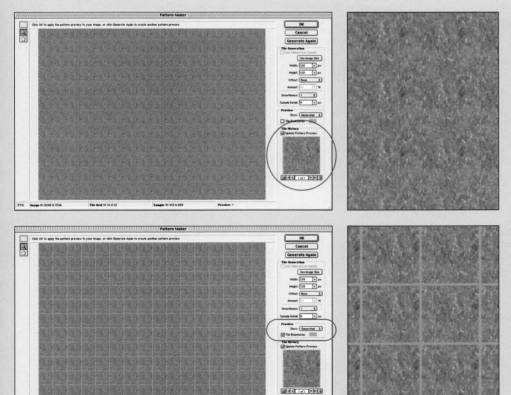

Seamless pattern

Pattern Maker will create a seamless pattern based on your selection at the default dimensions of 128 x 128 pixels. The tile will also appear in the Tile History window which you can use to navigate through patterns as you create variations.

Know your boundaries

To make things a little clearer, you can view the boundaries of your tiled pattern by checking the Tile Boundaries option in the Preview panel.
That's the basics of the Pattern Maker dialogue. We're now ready to start creating a new pattern. Cancel from the Pattern Maker dialogue.

Making a pattern preset

From the beginning
This time we want to change the dimensions of our pattern. Create a selection in the foreground, then select Filter > Pattern Maker (Shift-Option-Command-x/Shift-Alt-Ctrl-x) to launch Pattern Maker. Click on the Use Image Size button in the Tile Generation panel so that only one pattern tile will fill the size of your image. Click the Generate button to create a new pattern.

Really seamless
The new pattern will span the full dimensions of your image giving you a super-large tile. To check the size of the tile, check the Tile Boundaries option again in the Preview panel. This time, the boundary covers the whole preview window. You can keep clicking the Generate button to get variations of your pattern. When you're happy with your pattern, select the Save Preset Pattern button in the Tile History panel.
You'll then be asked to name your pattern preset which will then appear in your presets library. When you have done this, click Cancel.
Note: If you click Ok, your entire image will be replaced by the pattern.

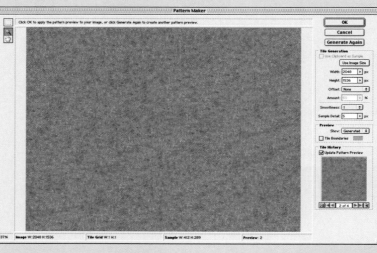

Tile History
Tile History allows you to choose from one of up to 20 generated patterns and save them for later use or delete them.

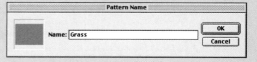

Take me to your preset
With our new pattern preset, we are ready to start removing sheep. The Pattern Stamp tool will be our tool of choice which allows you to choose pattern and brush size directly from the Options Bar.

Select the Pattern Stamp tool from the Tool palette, then select your Grass pattern from the Pattern menu in the Options Bar.

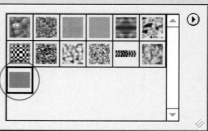

07 - Special F/X

Painting with pattern presets

Start painting
For safety, create a new transparent layer above your original image which we'll paint into to preserve the background. Here we'll start with a brush size of 100 pixels and start painting over the sheep in the foreground of our image.

Our initial selection was from the foreground, so the pattern should match the surrounding grass. We also need to pay attention to the sheep's shadows as they'll look a bit spooky if they are still there when the sheep are gone. Paint until there are no more sheep in the foreground.

Mid-level sheep
We're ready to work on the sheep in the mid-ground. To do this, we need to create a new pattern from the same area. Select the original background layer, then launch Pattern Maker (Filter > Pattern Maker). Don't worry that the sheep reappear; they'll be hidden by our painting layer. Make a selection in the mid-ground, choose Use Image Size, then click Generate. Save the pattern, from the Tile History panel and name it. Now press Cancel to exit from Pattern Maker.

More painting
With the Pattern Stamp tool active choose your newly created mid-ground pattern. Select the transparent painting layer, then paint the sheep in the mid-ground.

Background sheep

Finally we'll work on the sheep in the background. We'll need to create another pattern from the taller grass. Select the original background layer, then launch Pattern Maker (Filter > Pattern Maker).

Make a selection in the background, choose Use Image Size, then click Generate. Save the pattern, from the Tile History panel and name it. Cancel from the Pattern Maker dialogue.

Counting sheep

Now it's back to the painting layer and Pattern Stamp tool. This time select a smaller soft brush and paint out the last of the sheep. You can now survey the different areas and use the three pattern presets

to remove any remaining shadows or smooth out obvious transitions.
Next, we'll look at another technique of removing the sheep with a seamless pattern.

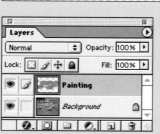

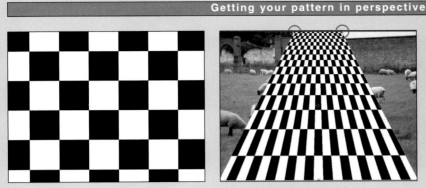

Getting your pattern in perspective

The all-in-one approach
Rather than painting your texture pattern progressively, you can create a seamless texture which will cover the whole area and use Photoshop's Free Transform tools to stretch it into shape. Here we use a checkerboard pattern to show the perspective.

Free Transform (Perspective)
Selecting the Free Transform feature (Command/Ctrl-T), we then select Perspective (Edit > Transform > Perspective) and drag the top corners of the checkerboard inwards. You can see the perspective effect quite easily.

Free Transform (Distort)
Finally, we want to bring the top of the checkerboard to meet the top of the area that we want to cover with the distorted pattern. In a few simple steps we can place a seamless texture with perspective distortion.

Preparing for perspective
To have enough pattern to cover an image, extend your canvas size (Image > Canvas Size) to three times the image width. Create a pattern with Pattern Maker which extends over the whole space and use the Free Transform tool to bring the pattern into perspective.

Cutting the grass
Use the Crop tool to reduce your image back to its original size. You can drag out rulers which will magnetically attach to the sides of the image for greater cropping accuracy.
Next we'll add some bumps to the ground for more realism.

Displacement (.PSD) file

Landscaping
We'll use the Displace and Clouds filters to add bumps. Create a new document, choose default colours (D), then select Clouds (Filter > Render > Clouds) to create a texture map.
Save the image as a Photoshop (.PSD) file, then return to your main image and select the distorted pattern layer. Choose the Displace filter (Filter > Distort > Displace) with offsets of 30%. You will be prompted to choose a file from the system. Select the clouds Photoshop file you saved.
The surface will now be uneven. To finish, paint the seams of the pattern layer with the Pattern Stamp tool to blend in.

| Difficulty: Intermediate | Colin Wood |

Special effects

Sometimes you need a special effect to enhance or to draw attention to an image. Here are some quick and effective special effects that will add variety to your layouts. Don't be afraid to extend them or try out variations. It's fun to experiment, but don't forget to save them with new names!

Here is the picture that we will use to demonstrate some cool special effects that can be achieved in very little time.

Special effect #1

Watercolour and line
First we will simulate a watercolour and forced line combination.
Our main tool will be the Threshold adjustment.

Duplicate background
First, duplicate the Background layer and make the new layer active. We will need the two layers to interact later on.

Threshold
Bring up the Threshold dialogue box using Image > Adjustments > Threshold.
This can be an interesting effect in itself, but for this tip it will be a little too dark. We can lighten it from inside the Threshold dialogue box.

Fade command caution

Note that once you have done something else, the Fade command is not available (even in the History palette) so it must be the very next thing you do. Even saving the file makes Fade unavailable.

Adjust Threshold

The Threshold dialogue has only one control (plus a preview option). When you first open the dialogue box the setting will be 128. This marks the shade half-way between 0 (black) and 256 (white).
The Threshold adjustment turns all pixels into either black or white.
Everything below 128 will be black, everything above will be white.
We wish to 'open up' the image so we will reduce the break point to 111, giving us more white pixels.

It still looks the same!

When you have used the Threshold adjustment your image will still look black and white.
Now—before you do anything else (seriously, nothing!), use Edit > Fade Threshold.
Bring the opacity down (here we have used an opacity of 35%) to allow the colours to show through.
Experiment with the blending modes such as Soft Light to vary the interaction of the two layers.

That's all there is to it. Now let's look at some other effects.

Special effect #2

Etching

We will use the same original image to simulate a photographic etching.

Although this image will be suitable for high quality printing, we will use Photoshop's Save for Web function on an image at 300dpi.

Save for Web

Use File > Save for Web to bring up the dialogue box. Select GIF compression, then reduce the number of colours to 2.
In this case Photoshop has averaged the main image to a drab green because of the amount of grass in the picture. The sky (and probably the building) has provided the other colour: white.

Settings for this picture:

Tip

You will need some white in the image to get a two-colour palette that includes white.

If there had been no white in the image (as seen here with a red sky), there would be no white in the final image.

To trick Photoshop into including white, enlarge the image to include a sizeable area of flat white.

In this case, the two flat colours (red and white) are the only colours to appear in the final image.

Colour reduction algorithms

Photoshop uses four colour reduction algorithms in its 'Save for Web' settings. These include:

Perceptual

Creates a custom palette by giving priority to colours for which the human eye has greater sensitivity.

Selective

Creates a colour table similar to the Perceptual colour table, but favouring broad areas of colour and the preservation of Web colours. This option usually produces images with the greatest colour integrity.

Adaptive

Creates a palette by sampling the colours from the spectrum appearing most commonly in the image. For example, an RGB image with only the colours green and blue produces a palette made primarily of greens and blues.

Most images concentrate colours in particular areas of the spectrum. To control a palette more precisely, first select a part of the image containing the colours you want to emphasise. Photoshop weights the conversion toward these colours.

Web

Uses the 216-colour palette that Web browsers, regardless of platform, use to display images on a monitor limited to 256 colours. This palette is a subset of the Mac OS 8-bit palette. Use this option to avoid browser dither when viewing images on a monitor display limited to 256 colours.

Still in Save for Web

You should still be in the 'Save for Web' dialog box. It will be in Indexed Color mode (Image > Mode > Indexed Color) so you will need to change the mode to RGB (or CMYK). Examine the file and you will find that it is now made up from just two colours. Amazing!

You can add an extra layer to this two-colour file and fill it with the colour of your choice. (Change the blend mode of this layer to Color and use Levels on your background layer to adjust the the tonal values for effect).

Black without Levels

Black with Levels

Special effect #3

Changing colours

This time we start with the black and white version we have have just made.

We will change both the white and the black into two other colours using a Gradient Map adjustment layer.

Bring up the Gradient Map dialogue box using Layer > New Adjustment Layer > Gradient Map.

Click in the gradient ramp to bring up the Gradient Editor dialogue box.

Photoshop will show a preview of the final result as you adjust the sliders and add/subtract colours.

Here we have used just two colours (because there are only two colours).

Tip

It is best to make your Gradient Map adjustments at 1:1 ratio as the monitor can lie!

Special effect #4

Curves with style
This is one of the quickest ways to get a special effect, and the settings can be saved and used over and over again in seconds.

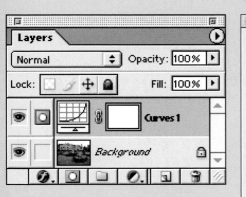

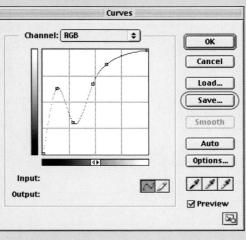

To preserve your original image, make your adjustments in an adjustment layer. That way you can always go back and make changes.

If you are sure you won't want to make changes, you can commit by simply using a Curves adjustment. Call up the Curves dialogue box for an adjustment layer using Image > Adjustments > Curves.
Click on the line and move the points until you like the effect. In either case you can save the settings for future use.

THE
BEST TIP
IN THIS BOOK

All of the tips in this book are updated versions of those that have appeared in the pages of Design Graphics magazine.
Every month there are new tips to make you more productive in Adobe Photoshop. Don't miss an issue.